Darwin's
Wager

Darwin's
Wager

Cannibal Genes, the Human Ape,
and Evolution's Final Battle

JAMES B. MILES

Matador
9 Priory Business Park,
Wistow Road, Kibworth Beauchamp,
Leicestershire. LE8 0RX
Tel: 0116 279 2299
Email: books@troubador.co.uk
Web: www.troubador.co.uk/matador
Twitter: @matadorbooks

ISBN 978 1800461 666

British Library Cataloguing in Publication Data.
A catalogue record for this book is available from the British Library.

Printed and bound in the UK by TJ Books Limited, Padstow, Cornwall
Typeset in 11pt Adobe Garamond Pro by Troubador Publishing Ltd, Leicester, UK

Matador is an imprint of Troubador Publishing Ltd

DARWIN'S WAGER

noun [Dar·win's wa·ger] [dahr-winz wey-jer]

1. the mathematical insight, attributed to Charles Robert Darwin, that it is our cultures, and the behaviours they have fashioned, that stop us eating one another

CONTENTS

ACKNOWLEDGEMENTS

When one of London's most respected literary agencies, Sheil Land Associates, said that any publisher of serious non-fiction should want this manuscript "in a heartbeat" I was over the moon, but remained nervous. Because I will never forget that in February 2003 the world's largest university press, Oxford, would tell the father of gene-centric evolutionary biology that Darwin's own understanding of human evolution was just too radical to put in front of the reading public.

So at this 150th anniversary, this sesquicentenary, of Darwin's 1871 wager I would like to acknowledge the people who have helped get us here. First and foremost the late George C. Williams, my friend and mentor, and the father of modern evolutionary biology. I would also like to thank the handful of philosophers who have spent their careers battling for Darwin's wager, sometimes without even knowing it. In particular, thanks to the philosophers Richard Double, Bruce Waller, and Derk Pereboom. I would like to thank Richard Oerton for his continuing efforts. Thanks to my brother, Dr Chris Miles, for his always excellent advice. Thanks to

Rod Mackenzie and Dr Yorick Rahman for their ideas on both the text and the cover, and for their endless good humour. There are other friends and family members that I would love to mention, but as the subject matter of this book may enrage I am leaving them unacknowledged. This was Darwin's battle, George's battle, my battle; it should not have to be their battle.

I was fortunate to have had one of the few London literary agents steeped in non-fiction publishing, as my agent at Sheil Land, Ian Drury, was formerly publishing director for non-fiction at Weidenfeld & Nicolson. So thank you, Ian. Thanks to all at Matador, and to Ben Cameron at Cameron Publicity & Marketing.

Darwin's wager has been buried for a century and a half. Darwin couldn't get the idea out, and the giants of contemporary evolutionary biology – not just George Williams, but extending to John Maynard Smith, Bill Hamilton, and George Price – couldn't get the idea out. Whether Darwin's understanding of human evolution is finally acknowledged will probably depend as much on readers as it does on these theorists. The first chapter, the précis chapter, has been made freely available for download (DarwinsWager.com), so please deliberate and confabulate, and with the author's gratitude.

1

DARWIN'S "OTHER SOLUTION"

"How did we evolve from being merely social to being moral?
... But when Darwin turns to his other solution, he lets us down."
— **Helena Cronin**, *The Ant and the Peacock:*
Altruism and Sexual Selection from Darwin to Today, pp.326–7.

Darwin knew that for very good reasons his theory of evolution by natural selection could not account for morality. Darwin understood the struggle for existence, and his theory explained aggression, but also sociality and co-operation. Yet, mathematically, co-operation had to be severely limited in mammals, restricted to the "merely social". Darwin was aware of the competition and the bloodletting, where a newly dominant young male gorilla "killing and driving out the others, establishes himself", as he wrote in *Descent of Man*. He knew about baboons using weapons to attack other baboons, where they would roll down great stones, and about orang-utans using sticks and fruit as missiles, although he also appreciated that primates could collaborate in warfare. But natural selection could not explain the evolution of human sentiments like justice, fair play and virtue. The numbers simply wouldn't work for Darwin. To explain human morality he needed another answer outside of biological adaptation. To explain morality he needed what has disparagingly been called his "other solution": *his odds-on wager that humankind is born just another brutal and amoral ape, and that it falls on culture, not biology, to civilise us.*

It is not Darwin who "lets us down". The evidence today is that it is only Darwin's wager – when allied to recent breakthroughs in philosophy – that seems to explain the human condition, from the kindness to the cruelty, the wonder to the heartbreak. Because it has been my privilege to spend the last twenty years working alongside some of the world's foremost scientists and philosophers investigating what are often described as the two great paradoxes of human self-understanding: the potential contribution of evolution to human morality, and the role played by free choice and reason in the human moral sense. As we try to make sense of an increasingly unstable world, we have been searching for our answers in the wrong places. Thanks to Darwin's wager we have the ammunition we need to fight back against the darkness and the division, although we have come close to leaving it too late.

Darwin believed natural selection operated at the level of the individual. Following his own theory to its logical conclusion he saw no good way for biological evolution at the level of the individual to have produced morality. For Darwin culture must actively combat biology. As a biologist Darwin did not wish to reach this conclusion, but he ultimately resolved to apply his own theory to humankind without fear or favour. In the mid 1960s George C. Williams, my friend and mentor, revolutionised Darwin's work when he moved selection from the level of the individual to the level of the gene, what Williams referred to as the theory of genic selection, and what later became popularly known as selfish gene theory. Though in so doing Williams realised that what had been Darwin's better-than-evens wager had now become a mathematical near-certainty. Meanwhile, detailed field observations were showing the other apes to be even more brutal and amoral than Darwin had realised, and George himself accurately predicted species-wide cannibalism within our nearest ape kin decades before it was finally recorded.

Yet because all the other leading figures in the development of modern gene-centred evolutionary biology, including names like John Maynard Smith and Bill Hamilton, were also coming to the same conclusion as Williams and Darwin, a backlash was perhaps inevitable from certain more intellectually conservative circles. This reaction against Darwin's wager argues that humankind had out-evolved the rest of nature; proposes that our species had broken from the four-billion-year pattern of natural selection to be moral *at the genetic level.* This backlash was originally known as human sociobiology, and sociobiology named us as, biologically and uniquely, "the decent animal" (E.O. Wilson, 1975a). Today the backlash is called evolutionary psychology, and evolutionary psychology names us as, biologically and uniquely, "the moral animal" (Wright, 1994). It is largely, although not exclusively, thanks to evolutionary psychology that Darwin's own understanding of human evolution has all but been written out of the records.

I first got to know George Williams in the late 1990s after I wrote a paper on the paradox of human morality for the journal *Philosophy.* Williams' groundbreaking 1966 *Adaptation and Natural Selection* is argued by Harvard's Steven Pinker to be "the founding document of evolutionary psychology" (1997a, p.56) because, as George's *Nature* obituary put it, "his major contribution, the theory of gene-level natural selection, left a profound and enduring stamp on fields from sociobiology and evolutionary psychology to behavioural ecology" (Meyer 2010, p.790). Yet Williams, like Darwin before him, is said to have let us down because he insisted on following Darwinian selection to its logical and mathematical conclusion. George and I wrote back and forth for the best part of a decade, and even when he became ill, finally passing away in late 2010. And partly because of his ill health, Williams increasingly had to look to others to champion Darwin's legacy. George invited me to come and stay with him, contacted leading journals about my work, wrote to New York publishers on my behalf, and even penned the foreword to an earlier book of mine, when writing forewords is something I think he did only twice in his forty years at the top of the Darwinian tree.

However, for the last ten years I would separately get caught up investigating the role played by reason and free choice in the human moral sense, where I got to work alongside a group of philosophical mavericks – notably Derk Pereboom, Bruce Waller and Richard Double – who felt driven to show the logical errors that parts of philosophy, and the wider social sciences, are today riddled with. The work of these mavericks, undertaken at great peril to their careers, is now starting to enter the intellectual mainstream, although it continues to be bitterly resisted from so many quarters. You may well never have heard of Derk, Bruce or Richard, but the *only* reason that the publishing sensation Yuval Noah Harari can assert as self-evident that "humans have no free will" (2018, p.300), and that this is "such a radical message" with "sinister implications" (p.251), is because of their earlier analysis. The myth of free will is dangerous, writes Harari as this radical message moves to the publishing mainstream, because it blinds us to the fact that humans are "hackable" animals subject to manipulation, including through social media.

Now free will can, at a stretch, be defined in many ways, but what *matters* about the free will debates is when free will is understood as freedom of choice. So when Harari writes "humans have no free will", he means that humans have no freedom of choice, and thus no ability to have chosen otherwise in any specific situation, no ability to have acted differently. When the American philosopher Dan Dennett writes "when we consider whether free will is an illusion or reality, we are looking into an abyss" (2008, p.249) he also signals that freedom of choice is the illusion, not the reality. And Dennett simultaneously believes that openly admitting freedom of choice to be an illusion would change forever our political, social and economic landscape, yet this potential for change frightens him, and he has worked tirelessly to close down discussion on this subject. So something extraordinary was happening within philosophy during the last couple of decades. The free will debates had always been jealously protected by philosophers, even though scientists from Darwin to Einstein regarded them as legitimate for scientific discussion. Philosophers like Dennett had managed to keep the debates monochromatic for hundreds of years, but the endless repetition was about to change. Because when free will is defined as freedom of choice, then it can easily be seen that what lies at the heart of the free will debates is the issue of undeserved dumb luck and complete lack of opportunity for some, and philosophers were reluctantly having to recognise this. In a world without freedom of choice "luck swallows everything", as one philosopher puts it. And alongside this was the realisation that a 3,000-year failure to recognise that luck swallows everything seems to have made morality impossible, thus chiming with Darwin's wager. Albeit those of us who have sought to highlight the logical flaws within free will theory tend to be subject to intense hostility. I myself have been accused of subterfuge, falsehoods, ire, mistakes, misconstrual, grand overstatement, misrepresentation, serious misrepresentation, irresponsibility, and inflammatory rhetoric.

When the editors at one major journal told me their lawyers were concerned I might be being libelled I could only shrug, but it highlights the level of vicious animosity within the field of metaphysics when a researcher bucks the trend. No one is allowed to pull back the curtain and meet the wizard, because "spin" is everything in the free will debates. As one leading free will apologist philosopher puts it, life is "a masquerade in which maintaining human dignity depends on ... degrading fellow people" (Smilansky 2000, p.278). Or as Dan Dennett likes to say, "sometimes a spin doctor is right" (2012b). When the biologist Richard Dawkins tried to raise the subject of misrepresentation within the free will debates, Dennett told him that scientists should shut up about the injustices of the free will fraud until they are willing "to engage with the best thought on the topic" (2014). By *best thought* Dennett of course meant his own, and those others who understand the importance of spin and masquerade within intellectual discourse. Dawkins has never since opened his mouth on the topic.

Darwin wagered 150 years ago that humans are born just another immoral, or at least amoral, ape, and that it is culture that must make us fair and just. So could Darwin have been right after all? Because philosophy was now concluding – or at least the mavericks within philosophy – that at least ninety per cent of the humans who have ever lived have *not* been moral beings. Evolutionary psychology breaks from the pattern of nature when it tries to name us "the moral animal", but around ninety per cent of humankind has been wilfully blind to, indifferent to, or apologists for, the problems of the least fortunate. Yet if Darwin was correct that we are not born biologically coded for morality, was he also right that we are born coded for gross amorality? Maybe even that we are born coded for the species-wide cannibalism that we now know is programmed into the other great apes?

It is difficult to imagine two vanities more perfectly suited to keeping opportunity out of the hands of vast sections of the population, and this even looks a lot like a middle-class con trick, a suburban shell game. Under the template of natural selection morality cannot be biological, so surely this should scream the importance of culture and a good start in life? Oh yes, says evolutionary psychology, but the public won't have to consider this if we just suggest that human evolution broke from the billion-year pattern of natural selection. OK, but logic also tells us that everything in human life comes down to undeserved dumb luck, so surely many get not less opportunity but zero opportunity? Oh yes, says philosophy, but the public won't have to consider this if academics plumb refuse to discuss it.

*

But why is it so urgent that we finish what Darwin and Alfred Russel Wallace started 150 years ago? Even before the 2020 global pandemic revealed debilitating fractures in key Western democracies we were in danger of losing forever the one capacity that makes us unique on this planet, of losing the one quality that truly raises us above the other animals. But just as the pandemic exposed scapegoating and short-termism – though alongside some wonderful selflessness from the often less valued parts of society – it highlighted that we can no longer afford to turn our backs on humankind's smartest thinkers.

To be clear, it is beyond surprising that the huge majority of philosophers have suppressed the understanding that there is no such thing as freedom of choice, because this knowledge turns out to be the Holy Grail of ethical thought. For 3,000 years the most sought-after principle in ethics has been the possibility of an objective base to knowledge. The absence of free choice – because it is that extraordinarily rare thing, a question that can be reduced to pure logic – is probably the only ethical absolute that humankind can ever have access to.

"Luck swallows everything" becomes the single foundation block our species must look to if we wish to build an objective moral code. By turning a blind eye to this the great proportion of philosophers have purposely left us afloat upon a sea of moral relativism, where codes of conduct have no provable truth value and provide no good way to evaluate beliefs or promote virtue. Deliberately concealing from the public the only objective moral fact that our species can ever know may one day be seen as the greatest of intellectual betrayals, the most egregious *trahison des clercs*, but to this knavery we must then add the blindness to Darwin's "other solution".

Darwin's wager tells us that morality and fair play are not the result of biology, and are not the result of reason, or at least not imperfect human reason. Morality, justice and fair play are a cultural inheritance. But, crucially, they are a *contingent* cultural legacy; one that began in myth not reason, but that can only be completed in reason not myth. It was Judeo-Christianity, and not the apologists for slavery, misogyny and aristocracy within Greek philosophical ethics, that first set us on the road towards a just and moral future. Yet completing that journey now requires a total reversal; requires rigorously tested academic knowledge over myth and ritual. But it is the fact that morality, justice and fair play are a contingent cultural legacy that means that we cannot count on morality or fairness existing anywhere else in the universe, even if the universe contains other intelligent life. And this is what makes us unique and valuable to the universe; we may be the only species with the vanishingly unlikely chance interplays of myth, dispersion and imperfect reason that gave us the opportunity to build a moral future. For example, it was not the earliest texts of Judaism that gave us the concept of justice; as Darwin realised that was a legacy of the Diaspora of the Jews. Without the Diaspora, Judaism would never have formulated an ethic of justice, produced the Essenes, or led on to Christianity, and without Christianity there would have been no Renaissance, no Reformation, and no Enlightenment as we know it.

But only reason can now complete the journey, and the evidence is that taking self-knowledge forward in this final key stage requires bipartisan, open, liberal, democratic institutions. Everything that makes us unique, everything that makes us important on a galactic scale, is bound up in finishing the journey, or at the very least in being able one day to finish that journey. But open, questioning, liberal democracy is under threat as never before. One threat is posed by what NATO's second-highest ranking officer has described as an "information warfare blitzkrieg", and what UN experts have termed the undermining of verifiable facts. The existential threat to even the idea of objective knowledge, from technologically assisted demagogues and the cynical billionaires who helped create the modern alt-right, imperils the one thing that makes our species important, jeopardises the very thing that makes us unique. But another threat, although one perhaps a little simpler to combat, is that inquisitive liberal democratic institutions appear to have run out of steam. The vast majority of philosophers, and a worryingly large number of scientists and social scientists, now have too much invested in the *status quo* to want us to finish the journey.

Frans de Waal, the celebrated primatologist, says Darwin's wager is "enough to give goose bumps" (1996, p.2), and a couple of decades ago I went to the London School of Economics as a postgraduate to give me the time and resources to investigate Darwin's odds-on wager. I went to the LSE convinced that something might be going gravely wrong in human evolutionary theory, only to discover something seriously wrong within metaphysics. I still remember sitting in a political philosophy seminar hosted by a panel of professors and being told by one of them that he "couldn't do" political thought if he didn't have faith in the existence of freedom of choice. I'd gone to LSE worried about evolutionary theory driven by goosebumps, only to encounter metaphysics driven by faith, spin, and masquerade.

Academia is not supposed to work like this. I began as a finance undergraduate for goodness' sake; I am wholly self-taught in evolutionary biology and almost entirely self-taught in metaphysics. And yet probably the most important evolutionary biologist of the last half century was expecting me to complete his life's work, complete something he had been unable to do himself despite multiple attempts. And at the same time I was peer-reviewing on philosophy in top journals, and corresponding with the biggest names in the field, while my thoughts on metaphysics were being commissioned and paid for by universities of the standing of MIT. Academia does not work this way ninety-five per cent of the time. It only needs to work this way when goosebumps, faith, and spin are driving the conversation.

*

THE SCIENTIFIC APE

While we have all heard of Charles Darwin, too few of us have heard of Alfred Russel Wallace. Wallace is the great footnote in Darwinian history; the shy, asthmatic, often penniless surveyor-turned-naturalist who independently developed a remarkably similar theory of evolution by natural selection at a time when Darwin was still conducting his investigations. Darwin had sat on his own theory for twenty years, continually refining it, and was only finally pushed to publish when Wallace, suffering from crippling bouts of malaria in South East Asia, sent him his own essay. Wallace and Darwin's unpublished works were then presented together at the Linnean Society in July 1858. It was Wallace who ended up firing the starting gun on the most controversial and far-reaching mainstream scientific theory of all time.

Wallace, like Darwin, refused to compromise when it came to humans. Wallace, "the most Darwinian of Darwinians" (Cronin 1991, p.353), was the ultimate scientist who applied his theory of natural selection without fear or favour. And, as with Darwin, he concluded that biological evolution could not explain our moral sense. While we will turn subsequently to the detail of why they and later biologists concluded as they did, for now the take-away message is that Darwin and Wallace were examples of the very best of British science. Whether they were right or wrong, they would not compromise or twist their theory in its application to humankind. They refused to distort the science to make it more acceptable to popular nineteenth-century prejudice.

This exemplary attitude within British science extended to the third great name associated with nineteenth-century Darwinism, T.H. Huxley, the mouthpiece and propagandist for Darwin's work. Thomas Huxley was the brilliant zoologist one hundred years ahead of his time when he alone worked out that birds had evolved from dinosaurs, but Huxley too realised that evolution by natural selection, what Huxley termed "the cosmic process", could not explain a sense of fair play. As Huxley put it, "the history of civilization details the steps by which men have succeeded in building up an artificial world within the cosmos" (1894, p.141). Almost eighty years later Bill Hamilton, father of the theory of "kin selection" that would be crucial to cementing selection at the level of the gene, would unconsciously echo Huxley with the words: "natural selection ... implies concurrently a complete disregard for any values, either of individuals or of groups, which do not serve competitive breeding. This being so, the animal in our nature cannot be regarded as a fit custodian for the values of civilized man" (1971, p.83).

But before we move to modern biology is it fair to call evolution by natural selection the most controversial and far-reaching mainstream scientific theory in history? There have certainly been many other controversial scientific theories, such as Copernican heliocentrism, Harvey's ideas on blood circulation, Koch and Pasteur's germ theory of disease, and Wegener on continental drift. Yet it is only Darwin and Wallace's work that took until 1996 before the Vatican accepted it as "more than just a theory". And it is the teaching in science classes of Darwin and Wallace's work, and neither Harvey nor Wegener's work, that is still resisted in parts of the Southern United States. Because part of the exhilaration is the "what if?" thinking that Darwinism still offers. What if Darwin's "other solution" is the correct one, and we humans are actually born coded for the species-wide cannibalism that is programmed into the other great apes? Darwin's final battle would still be ahead of us; a mind-boggling possibility offering a fundamental revolution in human self-knowledge.

I first became aware of the American biologist George C. Williams thanks to a 1995 book, *The Third Culture*, edited by John Brockman. Brockman is a New York literary agent who has represented the most influential and outspoken scientists on the planet. Brockman has auctioned most of Richard Dawkins' books, is Steven Pinker's agent, obtained a $0.5 million advance for the Nobel Prize winner Murray Gell-Mann (which had to be given back, but that's not part of this story), and managed to get the theoretical physicist Brian Greene a $2 million payday back in 1999 when $2 million was considered a lot of money by any self-respecting media don.

The Third Culture assembled the world's most renowned evolutionary biologists at that time, from Dawkins and UCL's Steve Jones – subsequently paid to "update" Darwin's *Origin of Species* – to Niles Eldredge and the late Stephen Jay Gould, but it was Brockman's comments on George Williams that drew my attention. "Among the evolutionary biologists, George C. Williams is the senior figure in the book. ... Few laypeople have heard of Williams. Yet nearly all evolutionary biologists, even those who do not agree with him, admire him" (1995, p.34). Or as the philosopher of science Dan Dennett wrote in the same volume: "Again and again, Williams issues his pithy little correctives to otherwise superficially good ideas and just calmly, firmly, wipes them out. Then you realize that this is a harder game to play than any of us realize, and George plays it better than anybody else in the world" (p.50).

Williams held the biologists' equivalent of the Nobel Prize, the Crafoord, also given out by the Royal Swedish Academy of Sciences but for scientific fields not covered by the Nobel, and for a world-class scientist to write back at length to an unconnected political philosophy postgrad was unheard of. George had always been known as one of the nicest guys in biology, and *Nature*'s obituary – which called him "one of the most incisive thinkers of the twentieth century" – reminded us that he not only looked remarkably like Abraham Lincoln but shared his quiet reserve too. Richard Dawkins' obituary in *Science* also mentioned Williams' Lincoln-like appearance and character, but there was more to George reaching out to me than his simple good manners. What had piqued his interest – and that of John Maynard Smith, co-developer of gene-centred evolutionary biology, and therefore co-recipient with Williams of the Crafoord Prize – was that I was investigating a logical and mathematical problem in biology that no one in philosophy had even noticed, yet that far too many modern evolutionists seemed to have a motive to sweep under the carpet.

The mathematical problem that Williams, Maynard Smith and Hamilton had uncovered, and that Richard Dawkins would also quietly highlight in the late 1970s, was that – irrespective of whether natural selection operates at the level of the individual as Darwin believed, or largely at the level of the gene as Williams and Maynard Smith had shown – biological evolution could not explain a well-developed moral sense or capacity for fair play, and for key evolutionary reasons. We are so used to modern academics (admittedly, partly driven by intense funding and marketing pressures) trying to claim everything under the sun for their work, that encountering the willingness to deny your work can be endlessly applied is sobering.

Gene-centred natural selection has swept across biology as the orthodox modern interpretation of how evolution overwhelmingly acts. But gene-centred evolution has to obey certain rules. At least within biology gene-centred evolution has largely knocked aside earlier interpretations such as the idea of selection acting with major effects at the level of the group or species ("group-selectionism"), which is prone to problems like subversion from within, somewhat similar to what is known in economics as the free rider problem. And we are using the term group-selectionism as shorthand to encompass schools like MLS, or multilevel selection, as MLS incorporates selection at the level of the group, which is what makes it controversial.

Group selection would explain human morality and fair play *if* it were a coherent and influential force in biological evolution. Unfortunately, the theoretical and physical evidence is that it is not a meaningful force. Williams himself was not averse to considering effects from group selection but while not denying that group selection could occur it was "usually too weak to produce noteworthy effects" (letter, 3 December 1998). "Actually I think group selection needs much more attention, but not with the stupidities published by people like Steve Gould and others who discuss 'species selection'. Surely any separate clades, subject to extinction, can be subject to selection. ... My personal friend and theological enemy David Sloan Wilson ... champions a locally benign form of group selection that enhances the collective fitness of large groups of organisms. I think this kind of selection unimportant" (letter, 2 September 2003). Group-selectionism's attempt to claim, or at least imply, what can be called "morality as a biological adaptation", even if an adaptation at the level of the group, is deeply problematic. We do not see morality or a sense of fair play in the rest of the natural world for very good individual selection and gene selection reasons.

> "The dominant male, Humphrey, held a struggling infant about 1.5 yr old, which I did not recognize. Its nose was bleeding, as though from a blow, and Humphrey, holding the infant's legs, intermittently beat its head against a branch. After 3 min, he began to eat flesh from the thighs of the infant, which then stopped struggling and calling."
>
> **– David Bygott,**
> "Cannibalism among wild chimpanzees",
> *Nature* (1972, p.410)

Above is Darwin's dark secret. All the models tell us that we never out-evolved – could never have out-evolved – Humphrey's billion-year genetic pattern. The models suggest that morality, fair play, justice, and large-scale settled existence, are only possible to the extent we have resisted this natural world heart of darkness; have built up an artificial world within the cosmos, as Huxley put it. Because the alternative argument here, morality as a biological adaptation at the level of the individual or gene, is equally flawed not just as it too looks to situate humans outside the rest of the natural world, outside the rest of the billions of years of evolution on this planet, but fundamentally because it breaks the rules of gene- and individual-level selection. When it comes to a discussion of morality, human sociobiology and evolutionary psychology turn out to be as much based on incoherent group-selectionism as are the more traditional schools of multilevel selection.

		Requires a change to the template of evolution?	Fails the parsimony test?
Option 1	Multilevel-selectionism / Group-selectionism	YES	YES
Option 2	Sociobiology / Evolutionary psychology ("implicitly group-selectionist" – Dawkins)	YES	YES
Option 3	Darwin's "other solution" / Individual- or Gene-selectionism	NO	NO

Sociobiology, originating in the mid 1970s with the Harvard biologist Edward O. Wilson, was defined as the scientific study of the biological basis of all forms of social behaviour in all kinds of organisms, including man. This field of study extended to humans should have been non-controversial – there logically *is* a biological basis to study, be the answer 100%, 0%, or a shifting component somewhere in between – except that central to human sociobiology from day one was the claim for morality as a biological adaptation. Yet sociobiology fell into disfavour by the mid 1980s and largely for the wrong, and partly unfair, reasons. All sociobiology, at least when explaining human morality, was a form of distorted and confused group-selectionism while claiming to be built on the gene-selectionist work of Williams and Maynard Smith. While this should have been obvious to anybody who read the initial papers and books, it should have become obvious to everybody when Ed Wilson simply upped sticks and decamped to the MLS – overtly group-selectionist – tradition in 2010.

As one evolutionary psychologist, Robert Wright, puts it, the sociobiology brand had become toxic (he uses the term "tainted") by the mid 1980s. Sociobiology "went underground", Wright says, and emerged as evolutionary psychology in the early 1990s. But the problem was that evolutionary psychology inherited the core conceit of human sociobiology, the same distorted and confused group-selectionism. Morality was still argued as being a biological adaptation, albeit often a unique adaptational by-product. Even as Stephen Jay Gould and David Sloan Wilson were openly invoking group-selectionism to explain human morality, Steven Pinker, for example, was relying on what Dawkins terms "implicitly group-selectionist" theorising (1989, p.191) for his equally incoherent claim that adaptation caused humans to come to view non-kin as kin ("fictive kin") and thus create what Pinker terms vast "faux-families" (2012) of complete strangers.

In science the principle of parsimony, sometimes called Occam's razor, is that simpler solutions are more likely to be correct, because they introduce fewer steps and less opportunity for mistakes, wishful thinking, and bias. So there are three options for explaining the human animal. In explaining human behaviour Option 1 throws away the pattern of natural selection that works perfectly well for explaining all other life, including Humphrey and his conspecifics. Option 1 adds extra steps, and requires a rewriting of evolutionary principles. In explaining human behaviour Option 2 promises to use that pattern of natural selection that Option 1 throws away, Humphrey's pattern, but then posits the evolution of new methods of operation never before needed, the unexplained rewriting of an ancestral six million year background code, and resorts to "implicitly group-selectionist" theorising. Option 2 adds extra steps, and requires a rewriting of evolutionary principles.

Only Option 3 does not change the model of natural selection that adequately explains all other life on Earth. Only Option 3 does not add extra steps. It is beyond unreal that for forty years now only Options 1 and 2 have been debated; in countless books, in untold newspaper articles written by people from every conceivable intellectual background, and on every campus. The *only* option that does not attempt to rewrite the rules of natural selection, and the *only* option that leaves us as biologically just another animal, is the *only* option that we have never been allowed to consider. Sorry, that's not quite true. Because Darwin considered Option 3. And Darwin chose Option 3.

Darwinism is essentially about Option 3. Many think Darwinism is about the might of science set against Creationism, Intelligent Design, and the forces of anti-science, but the truth is more prosaic than that. Creationism is just a subset of a wider debate that has been going on in biology for 150 years. Darwinism has always been a struggle between two very different views of our species. On the one side there are those, including Darwin, Huxley, Williams and Hamilton, who wished to place humankind within the natural world. To the other side are those, including great nineteenth-century scientists like Richard Owen and Sir John Herschel, and in the modern period E.O. Wilson, Helena Cronin and Steven Pinker, who wish to set humankind biologically apart from the rest of nature.

Darwinism is about Option 3. Darwinism has always been all about Option 3.

*

THE UNNATURAL APE

There is a delicious irony that Darwin and Wallace – one an illness-prone gentleman-amateur working quietly in his garden, the other an almost painfully shy former surveyor suffering from crippling malaria, both the gentlest of men, and both operating outside and largely in opposition to mainstream academia – may have had a more realistic appreciation of the logical paradoxes of their theory than overexposed media dons working at billion-dollar colleges like Harvard and MIT a century and a half later. Yet there is also a real sense that many of the mistakes of the last few decades – across evolution, but separately in the philosophical work we shall come on to – have been made worse by the academic process itself, and by the financial, cultural and ideological pressures within contemporary academia.

For example, there is a sense that political pressures within American academia have been allowed too much influence. Although group-selectionism may have been strongly championed up to the early 1960s within British naturalism, led by the writings of the English zoologist V.C. Wynne-Edwards, this changed significantly after the work of Williams and Maynard Smith. Yet not in America. As Richard Dawkins put it in the 1989 second edition of *The Selfish Gene*, while group selection was out of favour with British naturalists from the early 1970s this was most certainly not the case with large parts of American naturalism. "Group selection ... is even more out of favour among biologists than it was when my first edition was published. You could be forgiven for thinking the opposite: a generation has grown up, especially in America, that scatters the name 'group selection' around like confetti. It is littered over all kinds of cases that used to be (and by the rest of us still are) clearly and straightforwardly understood as something else, say [Hamilton's] kin selection ... and it is irritating to find that we are now two generations, as well as two nations, divided only by a common language" (p.297).

There have always been suspicions that American advocacy of group selection is at least partly political, and these only became stronger after sociobiology came on the scene in the mid 1970s, only a handful of years after genic selection had begun sweeping across biology. We shall return to this point in a moment, but let us start by noting that Edward Wilson's human sociobiology was also somewhat ideological in outlook and flavour, and many British biologists, such as Maynard Smith, Hamilton and Dawkins, viewed the new discipline of sociobiology with scepticism. Sir Peter Medawar, the Nobel-Prize winning biologist – he won the 1960 Nobel Prize for medicine; as noted previously Nobels are not given for biology – was typical of the disbelief. As the historian of science Ullica Segerstrale puts it: "What united IQ research and sociobiology in Medawar's mind was that for him they were both examples of 'unnatural science'. ... According to the author, unnatural sciences typically use mathematics or statistical models in order to lend themselves an aura of respectability" (2000, p.281).

Around the same time American naturalists, such as Stephen Jay Gould and the geneticist Richard Lewontin, were also opposing sociobiology, though often seemingly for the wrong reasons. Gould and Lewontin famously noted – and quite correctly – that sociobiology was usually telling unfalsifiable "Just So" stories that were unprovable narratives and thus by default anti-scientific. However, suspicions remained that Gould and Lewontin, and many in their group-selectionist circle, were often driven as much by left-wing ideology. Gould and Lewontin were key members of what was called the Sociobiology Study Group, an academic organisation formed to counter sociobiological explanations of human behaviour, and which later associated itself with the Boston arm of Science for the People, thereby becoming the larger Sociobiology Study Group of Science for the People. Science for the People was however an avowedly left-wing organisation that had grown out of protests against the Vietnam War. But what the Sociobiology Study Group did not do was criticise either Wilson or human sociobiology for its most obvious failing: its confused models due to its implicitly group-selectionist leanings. Leanings made obvious to all when E.O. Wilson was able a few decades on to move his allegiance from nominal gene-selectionism to overt group-selectionism without believing it undermined the integrity of human sociobiology in any way.

Evolutionary psychology, sometimes "EP", is a broader church, and has tried to distance itself from human sociobiology, including from many of the right-leaning associations of the early sociobiologists. And yet in many ways evolutionary psychology is more typically brash and ideological than either traditional group-selectionism or sociobiology. Though, as a broader church, evolutionary psychology retains many members who are unrepentant sociobiologists, and even race scientists. Indeed, a leading EP conclave, which is found online at *Psychology Today*, formally labels itself a forum for "Evolutionary Psychology (Sociobiology)". *Scientific American*'s John Horgan interviewed the foremost figures in the development of EP in the mid 1990s, and attended one of their major conferences, a meeting of HBES, the Human Behavior and Evolution Society. "But serious disagreements lurk beneath the seeming unity of the gathering. … To what degree do the differences between individuals and ethnic groups reflect genetic rather than cultural influences?" (1995, p.152). So although in its literature EP professes that our similarities are genetic and our differences cultural, it still shelters many who wish to put individual differences – and even ethnic behavioural and intellectual differences – down to biology.

Yet the cultural component remains, and whereas traditional group-selectionism and human sociobiology were being driven largely from America, evolutionary psychology was dominated by both Americans and Canadians (interestingly, Canadian academia also disproportionately dominates in the link we shall see later between free will apologism and social psychology). While early EP was boosted by American psychologists and anthropologists like John Tooby, Leda Cosmides and Donald Symons, it was also simultaneously or soon after boosted by the Canadian psychologists and anthropologists Jerome Barkow, Martin Daly, Margo Wilson and Steven Pinker. "The HBES conference demonstrates, if nothing else, the astonishing ambition of the new social Darwinists. …

The meeting sounds at times like a pep rally. There is much gleeful bashing of those deluded souls who think culture – whatever that is – determines human behavior" (Horgan 1995, p.152). Social science advancing by pep rally? Gleeful bashing of academic opponents? All this is so very much not the British or Continental way of advancing scholarly knowledge. And EP, and the funding it offers groups not previously capable of accessing such resources, has certainly changed the smell of evolutionary debate. As Horgan noted: "In the seven years since the HBES was founded, it has attracted a growing number of psychologists, anthropologists, economists, historians and others seeking to understand human affairs" (p.151). Psychologists, anthropologists, economists, and historians? So not so much biologists then?

Sociobiology and, particularly, evolutionary psychology came to have undue influence because they were at first used by biologists, who then lost control of them. During the final quarter of the twentieth century there was an open war taking place within biology. Much of the emotion was over levels of selection, and was partly a reaction to the runaway success of Williams' and Maynard Smith's genic selection theory, but there were other differences too. For instance, Darwinian evolutionary gradualism seemed to be under attack from Gould and Eldredge's theory of punctuated equilibrium, which invoked long periods of stasis broken up by rapid and only occasional change. At least in the popular press the war was regularly presented as "Dawkins versus Gould", although even the ever-thoughtful John Maynard Smith and the gentle George Williams would end up saying some unwise and unnecessary things. But the worst mistake gene-selectionism made was that it started a proxy war. It allowed the sociobiologists and evolutionary psychologists to wade in on its behalf, and speak in its name. It did this as it hoped to free up the considerable time it was wasting fighting distracting battles but also because, frankly, it took too much pleasure from seeing Gould, Eldredge and Lewontin savaged.

The journalist Andrew Brown catalogued "the Darwin wars" in the 1990s, and he gives us his view of the character of the evolutionary psychologists. Gould was particularly loathed by them, Brown wrote, reporting that Leda Cosmides and John Tooby's attack on Gould was "so blistering" that the *New York Review of Books* "refused to print it" (1999, p.150). Brown's position was that their attack was "extraordinarily ... unjustified" against "a man who has won just about every prize going for science writing" (p.151). Gould could certainly be distracting, but he probably did more to promote the teaching of evolution in the schools of the United States than any other scientist. And far more, it goes without saying, than any psychologist or anthropologist. Gene-selectionism had kept EP around to fight its battles for it, but in doing so made a critical error. Because sociobiology had been relabelled as a form of psychology – psychology is a soft or social science, not a hard science like the natural and the physical sciences – it could now only be performed by social scientists; by psychologists, anthropologists and economists. Rightly or wrongly there is seen to be a scientific pecking order of hard to soft driven by capacity for objective observation and experimentation, something often impossible in the social sciences. A biologist will not write within a field that incorporates the word "psychology", in part because of inherent weaknesses within the discipline, including problems with its methodological competence and statistical understanding. As a *Nature* headline put it in August 2015, "Over Half of Psychology Studies Fail Reproducibility Test", while the article itself went on to say "don't trust everything you read in the psychology literature. In fact, two thirds of it should probably be distrusted".

So biologists had let themselves be frozen out from investigating what Darwin himself termed "the highest & most interesting problem for the naturalist" (Raby 2001, p.134), and future investigation was unfortunately now in the hands of the evolutionary psychologists. Not, though, that there is anything fundamentally wrong with the basic concept of EP – as above, the field of study should have been as non-controversial as the field of study of human sociobiology should have been – but because of the discipline's performance to date. The poor performance lies in the lack of theoretical, or even historical, evolutionary knowledge, in the near absence of statistical aptitude, in the "implicit" group-selectionism, in the brashness, ideology and pep rallies – including an almost bro-culture enthusiasm for highlighting the evolutionary imperative of male aggression, male promiscuity and gender stereotypes – and in the illogical or questionable celebration of anti-Darwinian free choice by so many EP theorists. Evolutionary psychology could have been so much more intellectually impressive than it has been.

For instance, are you aware of just how commonplace bisexuality is in nature, and how common it is in our closest living ape kin, where it is species-wide? No? With foreign correspondents saying that in Putin's Russia homosexuals now occupy the scapegoating role once reserved for Russia's Jews, and almost half of UK fourteen-year-old girls who feel drawn to other girls self-harming, the time must be ripe for an informed re-evaluation of the biological normalcy of bisexuality. Because there are good evolutionary reasons for widespread bisexuality, and even homosexuality. If Steven Pinker and Harvard's evolutionary psychology department had promoted this knowledge it would have provided an important and difficult-to-miss corrective to the know-nothings who claim homosexuality and bisexuality to be against nature. It was only in 1973 that the American Psychiatric Association removed homosexuality from its list of "mental disorders", though maintaining it as a "sexual orientation disturbance" until 1987, but our closest living relative is a species of rampantly ambisexual great ape. Dawkins writes that "they seem to copulate in all possible combinations at every conceivable opportunity" (1998, p.211). So the fascinating inversion here is that homosexuality has never been a deviation from human "nature"; instead it appears to be homophobic internet trolls who are the "deviants" against human nature. In point of fact, not only are we genetically programmed to find bisexuality no big deal, there is an intriguing outside chance that evolution coded every last one of us to be bisexual.

Oh, and Darwin's wager would seem to kill stone dead the intellectual justification for a resurgent race science, or what the alt-right wants to call "human biodiversity", or "HBD". Plus with even the *Guardian* appearing to surrender – in an article entitled "So It Is Nature Not Nurture After All?" – to the opinion that biology tells us that "we cannot do much about" those at the bottom of society, and where certain children should be brought up to only "minimal levels of literacy and numeracy" (Anthony, 2018), it is long past time for a final reckoning with the continuing ignorance of so much of behavioural genetics. And despite the grand title, behavioural genetics is just a sub-branch of psychology, with all that that should now imply. Because although philosophers do not want us to pull back the curtain and meet the wizard, they have at least worked out where the wizard is. The huge majority of behavioural geneticists haven't so much as noticed the curtain. Which strongly suggests that behavioural genetics is not competent to investigate either morality or social position, and possibly not intelligence. *Guardian* science editors may now be considering the contention that poor children, argued by some to be destined by biology to sink to the bottom, should be brought up to only "minimal levels of literacy and numeracy", but it is behavioural geneticists who often appear to have wasted vast educational opportunities.

For all the above reasons, evolutionary psychology could have been so much more impressive. But instead, the concerns of EP have been so predictably heterosexual, so predictably white, and so predictably North American upper middle class.

*

THE PHILOSOPHICAL APE

For Darwin and Wallace, humans were "the highest & most interesting problem for the naturalist" for negative reasons, because our species did not behave like the rest of nature. Darwin and Wallace's biological models said that we should have behaved like a chimpanzee; living in fission–fusion societies of not much more than one hundred, and incapable of compassion and kindness. For Darwin and Wallace the most interesting things about humans cannot be explained biologically, so it is arguably not the biologists' job to explain what is interesting about the human animal. "Human societies change far too rapidly for the differences between them to be accounted for by genetic differences between their members", as John Maynard Smith put it. And "as differences are what we are primarily interested in, there is little an evolutionary biologist can say" (1992, p.82).

So if far and away the predominant evolutionary understandings of both Darwin's time and our time tell us that we cannot place morality within our DNA, we are forced to look next at the non-biological answers. If not coded for at the genetic level, can morality perhaps be down to a unique human rationality? Or what about our much vaunted "free will" that might take us outside biology, environment, and even reason? But the first problem is that more than eighty-six per cent of 2,000 top philosophers surveyed now understand that free will – defined as freedom of choice remember; the ability for an individual ever to have chosen otherwise – is a logical impossibility. The other 13.7% do still believe in the possibility of free choice (7.7% fully accepting, 6.0% "leaning toward"), but they are increasingly seen as part of an anti-evidence and spiritualistic camp within philosophy. This 13.7%, "dominated by theism, a rejection of naturalism, libertarianism about free will, and non-physicalism about the mind, seems to reflect a rejection of a naturalistic world view" (Bourget & Chalmers 2014, p.489).

And yet most of the 86% who recognise that, logically, there can be no such thing as free choice also think that the public is too "weak" and too "ignorant" to handle this knowledge. According to one major free will philosopher, Saul Smilansky, non-philosophers are "fragile plants" who "need to be defended from the chill of the ultimate perspective in the hothouse of illusion" (2011, p.436). Unfortunately this suppression of knowledge has significant political and economic consequences. In a world without free will "luck swallows everything", as the Oxford philosopher Galen Strawson put it (1998), and all of life reduces to the pure lottery of biological and environmental luck. There are no self-made men and women, there is no opportunity for all, no liberty for all, and all success is down to undeserved dumb luck, and predominantly undeserved environmental luck. Similarly, no one chooses to be a failure, but is forced to play the hand he or she is first born to and then raised with.

Luck swallows everything, but luck also ramifies, and the born lucky tend to get even luckier over time, while the born unlucky tend to get even more unlucky over time. And the rules of course get written by the lucky; life reduces to winners' justice, which means no justice, at least in states such as Britain and America where intellectuals like Smilansky and Dan Dennett sanctify the deceit of free will. There "is a deep *cultural* connection", writes my colleague the philosopher Bruce Waller, between strong belief in self-creation and free choice, and extremes of poverty and wealth. The greater the commitment to these conceits, the more the "absence of genuine opportunity for large segments of the culture", the greater the disparity between rich and poor, the weaker the commitment to equal opportunity, and the more meagre the "support system for the least fortunate" (2015, p.208).

Dennett – someone who Richard Dawkins regularly describes as "sort of an intellectual elder brother" – tries to counter the *luck swallows everything* moral chasm by arguing that there is

27

no such thing as luck in human life because, he says, 99% of poor black Americans get exactly the same opportunities as 99% of rich white Americans. And besides, Dennett continues, even if this isn't actually true those who don't get such good luck are irrelevant. Those treated unfairly can be discounted when evaluating fair treatment, he has written, because life doesn't need to be fair, it just needs to be what he terms "fair enough". As Waller notes, "Dennett seems comfortable with 'fair enough', and he can champion such a system and not blink" (2012). Yet Dennett's views are not even rare amongst philosophers; they are mainstream. Another tradition of liberal – and largely North American – free will apologist philosophy, termed essentialism, goes further in trying to claim that the least fortunate are, biologically, often not our equals, and are thus deserving of lesser consideration and lesser rights.

So not only can free will not save morality for humankind, it appears human reason cannot either, given that the vast majority of the most highly trained logical thinkers on the planet have behaved in appallingly unfair and unjust ways. "Is it fair…? Life isn't fair", shrugs Dennett (2012). Around ninety per cent of philosophers are wilfully blind to, indifferent to, or apologists for, the problems of the least fortunate. And if you wish to understand why the absence of free will is so important for humankind to internalise, outside of the possibility for moral absolutes this gives us, it is the fact that as biology cannot give us morality, and as imperfect human reason cannot give us morality, then without free will morality becomes wholly the preserve of culture. Morality, fair play and justice will only exist if cultures, meaning now the *best* cultures, fight tooth and nail. Civilised human behaviour, as Huxley and Hamilton pointed out, requires strong, confident cultures that are fully aware of the risks they face. The best cultures can and must be open to criticism but, self-evidently, they cannot in any way, shape or form tolerate the undermining of verifiable fact, information warfare blitzkriegs, the existential threat to even the idea of objective knowledge, or attacks upon robust, questioning, intellectual debate.

Yet philosophers have also sought to silence and suborn the handful of scientists who have tried to speak out regarding the free will frauds. A few years ago *Edge.org*, John Brockman's invite-only web forum for "scientific intellectuals", asked its members for proposals for their most dangerous idea. Richard Dawkins wrote that his most dangerous idea was that the world would "eventually grow out of" and "even learn to laugh at" the free will conceit, with all the social upheaval that would follow should the public wake up to this knowledge. According to Dennett (2008, p.253), Dawkins "later regretted sending and tried unsuccessfully to retract" his writing. Dawkins' regret and attempted self-censorship may have had something to do with the icy reception he received from his friend and intellectual elder brother, who has written that Dawkins, "when he's not thinking carefully", is among that foolish group of scientists – which Dennett admits includes Einstein and the late Stephen Hawking – who see the free will myth as "a major obstacle to social reform" (2014). The damage the free will myth does to life's least fortunate is now well recorded, and in June 2009 the Joseph Rowntree Foundation published research showing that 83% of Britons think that "virtually everyone" remains in poverty in Britain not as the result of social misfortune or biological handicap but purely through free choice.

We will be examining philosophers' motivation for maintaining what Smilansky calls a necessary "masquerade", what Dennett calls "spin", but one factor that should not be underestimated is that philosophy is a non-vocational subject. Why does this matter? It matters because, particularly in countries with huge student debts like America and increasingly Britain, only the cosseted and independently wealthy can afford the gamble of studying for perhaps seven to ten years a subject that has no guaranteed utility in the workforce. Hence the great majority of senior philosophers in the Anglo-American world – being the world that dominates the free will debates – come from backgrounds of deep social and economic privilege, and do seem to find it difficult to empathise with life's less fortunate.

*

THE HUMAN APE

Billions of years of evolution, 150 years of orthodox evolutionary theory, plus philosophical logic, tell us that we did not evolve to be moral. Darwin seems to have been right that we are not born moral, he may have been right that we are actually born amoral or immoral, and it might further be true that we carry the same biological code for cannibalism as the rest of the great apes. So. Troubling? Distressing? Perhaps not. Is there a reason, in fact, why we should be profoundly grateful that we are not "the moral animal" at the genetic level?

	Segregation (existence of)	Smallpox (eradication of)
Biology benign, culture malign	Evolutionary psychology	[Evolutionary psychology]
Biology benign, culture benign	N/a (paradox)	Evolutionary psychology
Biology malign, culture malign	Darwin's wager	N/a (paradox)
Biology malign, culture benign	[Darwin's wager]	Darwin's wager

To quote Cosmides, Tooby and Barkow's seminal work: "The central premise of *The Adapted Mind* is that there is a universal human nature, but that this universality exists primarily at the level of evolved psychological mechanisms, not of expressed cultural behaviors. On this view, cultural variability is not a challenge to claims of universality, but rather data that can give one insight into the structure of the psychological mechanisms that helped generate it" (1992, p.5). Evolutionary psychology holds that our similarities are genetic, but our differences are cultural, and John Horgan cites their literature. "'Evolutionary psychology is, in general, about universal features of the mind,' they have written. 'Insofar as individual differences exist, the default assumption is that they are expressions of the same universal human nature as it encounters different environments'" (1995, p.153). Why the table, then?

Smallpox was one of the most devastating diseases known to humans, highly contagious through close contact and with a mortality rate of around 30% but higher for babies. It has now been eradicated. Segregation is something a little different. It is still with us. It is still all around us. It is the separation of people, often along racial or ethnic lines, using law, ritual, or social norms. Segregation is far more common within human populations than is co-operation to eradicate poverty or disease. Throughout human history our similarities have tended to reflect widespread viciousness and immorality, while our differences have usually been the instances of warmth and morality. Which means that evolutionary psychology *would have to put a tendency towards slavery and segregation within basic human nature, and fairness and morality as cultural.* Whereas Darwin's wager also puts fairness and morality as cultural, but could end up putting a tendency toward slavery and segregation as either biological or as, probably more likely, cultural too. If you don't want to have an attachment to slavery and segregation sitting within universal human nature, your *only* hope is Darwin's wager.

A little more background though. The eradication of smallpox is one of the greatest medical achievements of all time. It was declared eliminated in 1980 after significant transnational co-ordination and a global immunisation campaign spearheaded and partly funded by the World Health Organization. Initial donations of the vaccine came from the Soviet Union and the United States. The last European outbreak was in Yugoslavia in 1972, and final eradication in the mid 1970s in the Horn of Africa was complicated by a lack of infrastructure, civil war, famine and the resultant refugees, but through quarantine and re-vaccination the last known case was in 1977. From start to finish the final programme took around ten years to complete.

Segregation in the Southern US is well remembered, but what is less discussed is that formal segregation also existed in many parts of the Northern US. Black Americans were restricted to certain neighbourhoods, and Martin Luther King marched in Chicago to protest race-based housing there. Some Northern schools, including in Pennsylvania and New Jersey, enforced segregation even when it was illegal. And laws prohibiting interracial marriage and interracial sex were on the statutes in a number of Northern states. Between 1913 and 1948 sixty per cent of all US States maintained anti-miscegenation laws.

Segregation was ended in the US two generations ago, though the shadow of slavery followed by segregation remains very long. So this ending attests to rarity? Not a chance. Racism and segregation are all around us today, even within democracies. India is the world's largest democracy, home to over 1.3 billion people, but in India's caste system status is defined solely by birth. The system may have existed for over 3,000 years and is not restricted to Hinduism, as it was taken up by Muslims, Christians, Sikhs and Jains. Since 1950 overt caste discrimination has officially been banned and quotas imposed, but financial, educational, and social discrimination continues largely unchecked, as does horrific violence against those low down the scale. The outcastes, the Dalits, the "untouchables", are India's lowest of the low, lower even than the Shudra or "servant" caste, with the BBC reporting ("Caste Hatred in India") that in 2016 alone more than 40,000 crimes against low castes were recorded, although such crimes are believed to be vastly under-reported. "Untouchables" account for around 25% of India's population, and are often of darker skin than high castes. Or what about Israel, another democracy, where Palestinian Israelis account for a fifth of the population but have worse access to education and healthcare, a much harder time leasing land from the State, and where Israel has now given Jews an exclusive right to national self-determination?

This vanity that we are, biologically, "the moral animal" explains nothing. It doesn't explain why half of America had to be forced at gunpoint to renounce first slavery, and then segregation, and today it doesn't explain at least two-thirds of Americans, or two-thirds of Britons. It doesn't explain a billion high or higher caste Indians, or three quarters of religion. It doesn't explain Netanyahu's Israel or, to be blunt, the whole of the Middle East and most of Asia. It doesn't explain China's brutal internment of perhaps a million Muslim Uighurs and Kazakhs in its vast re-education camps. It doesn't explain Putin's Russia. And it doesn't explain 90% of humanist philosophers; it doesn't explain nine-tenths of the most rational thinkers on the planet. Whereas Darwin's wager – this mathematical realisation that it is culture, in all its forms, that makes us human – may explain everything; both the kindness and the moral duplicity we see all around us, the wonder and the heartbreak, the rationality and the irrationality. So, no, we really don't want to be the moral animal of the evolutionary psychologists, and it is not Darwin who "lets us down".

*

Darwin never got to fight for his wager. Darwin could not fight for what Huxley termed "man's place in nature" because Darwin was too busy fighting to save his entire theory. When Darwin died in 1882 evolution by natural selection seemed to rest on some very shaky foundations. "You will think me very conceited when I say I feel quite easy about the ultimate success of my views, (with much error, as yet unseen by me, to be no doubt eliminated)", Darwin presciently wrote in 1861 to Sir John Herschel, the celebrated astronomer (Warner 2009, p.438). Herschel had once been a friend and mentor to the peripatetic younger Darwin, but was now an implacable opponent of his and Wallace's theory. Herschel had upset Darwin by calling natural selection "the law of higgledy-piggledy", and likening it to the Laputan method of making books, in *Gulliver's Travels*, by the random mechanical combination of words.

According to the best science available at that time, the Earth was simply not old enough for long geological periods and the gradual saving of slight improvements that would, over very many generations, allow a blind, physical process of accumulating small beneficial mutations to create wonders like the eye and the hand. Up to the time of his death Darwin's scientific opponents had badly miscalculated the Earth's relative rate of heat loss, and thus age, because radioactivity and nuclear processes were yet to be discovered. Furthermore, Darwin never had a theory of particulate inheritance, and without it beneficial variations would have blended away, not carried forward. The period from the 1880s up until the 1920s has been called "the eclipse of Darwinism", and where evolution by natural selection was seen by biologists as just one theory among many, and not a particularly good candidate at that. It was not until Darwin's work was combined with the discrete inheritance mechanism offered by Gregor Mendel that Darwinism would sweep away the competition.

Darwin's wager was lost to science for almost a century. For the first half of this period Darwinism itself was largely being ignored, while for much of the second half the wager was hidden by the strong influence of an ascendant group-selectionism. It was only when Darwinism was firmly put back at the level of the individual, and then at the level of the gene, from the 1960s, both theoretically and observationally, that Darwin's wager re-presented itself to science. But something extraordinary then happened. Darwin's wager is ultimately a mathematical conclusion. In fact it involves highly complex mathematics, a merging of population genetics, game theory, and cutting-edge equations and modelling. John Maynard Smith admitted that he once spent "several months trying to understand the maths" (1992, p.52) behind Ed Wilson's early 1980s collaboration with the mathematician Charles Lumsden, before concluding that their mathematical models "fail to demonstrate any synergistic effect". But at just the stage when evolution required the input of the best mathematical biologists if we were ever to understand the biology behind the human condition, humankind was being handed over to a cabal of North American social scientists; "psychologists, anthropologists, economists, historians and others". Yet through its very conceptualisation, evolutionary psychology was incapable of comprehending the necessary mathematical theories. Recall the 2015 *Nature* exposé: two-thirds of what you read in the psychology literature "should probably be distrusted". Psychology is today largely synonymous with the misunderstanding of even basic mathematics, such as p-values and simple statistical relevance, and indeed is currently going through an internal crisis of confidence because of this. Darwin's wager, our biological understanding of the human animal, requires knowledge of complex mathematics, but evolutionary psychology often can't even offer us knowledge of simple mathematics. Human Darwinian theorising can now only be resolved through mathematical biology, but it has been handed over to the non-mathematicians and the non-biologists. No one from "EP" – no psychologist, no anthropologist, no economist, no historian – has the required skills to resolve Darwin's wager. And there is an irony here. Evolutionary psychology's founding belief that Darwin and Hamilton were wrong about the human animal thus makes EP entirely a *faith-based* discipline. Where once Darwinism was seen as the vanguard of scientific scepticism, and Huxley coined the very term "agnosticism", today a large part of human Darwinism has become its own sham-rational cult.

Though there is an associated problem which would exist independent of the involvement of EP. The necessary mathematics has grown so complex and opaque to all but a few, taking "several months" to corroborate or even understand, that it is at the level where any amount of nonsense might be successfully hidden away in the maths. And this mirrors what may be a worrying pattern in modern physics. Large parts of theoretical physics, including string theory, have been called "math fiction", its models "contrived", and the whole discipline "not even wrong"; the last a specific term of abuse started by Wolfgang Pauli and meaning physics that is so poor it is little more than non-scientific storytelling. But string theory is now so embedded in the very funding of academic physics that no one is encouraged to ask the question of whether the whole enterprise was a serious mistake from the start, while the paranoia of the string theory community is palpable. According to the theoretical physicist Peter Woit one Harvard physicist has suggested, in all apparent seriousness, that academics who criticised the funding of superstring theory were "terrorists who deserved to be eliminated by the United States military" (2006, p.227).

So when it comes to Darwin's wager, even though we should listen much more closely to the best mathematical biologists – and John Maynard Smith, generally seen as the father of evolutionary game theory, was perhaps the finest mathematical biologist operating in the latter half of the twentieth century – and much less closely to the non-mathematicians and the poorer mathematicians, we *cannot* now leave it up to the maths. And this is one of the reasons for this book. If we are ever to know if Darwin was right about the lack of innate morality within the human ape we must go deeper. We should take account of the mathematical models, but we must also look at the very principles and processes behind evolution by natural selection, and we must look at the probabilities. We can use recent philosophical breakthroughs to test whether Darwin was correct after all. We can investigate the historical experience of the human ape, and both humankind's rationalism and anti-rationalism. And as part of the journey we shall, for instance, see the fundamental ignorance of the economic one per cent, and how they cannot help but give succour to extremists, conspiracists and scapegoaters. And we shall be forced to ask whether even democracies – from India to Israel, and Britain to the United States – can be moral, fair or just.

Taken together, Darwin's "other solution", the absence of free choice, and the "masquerade" and indifference to unfairness of nine-tenths of our most logical thinkers, perfectly explains why for the great majority of human history immorality has trumped morality. And, yet, after 3,000 years of largely flawed ethical inquiry our species is finally within touching distance of objective morality, a truly stunning and unmatched human intellectual achievement, so there is everything still to play for.

Our capacity for morality is unique on this planet, but it may well be unparalleled in the universe, making us important on a galactic scale. Darwin died before he got the chance to defend his wager. It is time to fight his final battle for him.

2

A DEEPLY UNPLEASANT TASK

"Maynard Smith, Williams, Hamilton, and Dawkins ... have largely
eschewed the deeply unpleasant task of pointing out more egregious sins
in the work of those who enthusiastically misuse their own good work."

– **Daniel Dennett**, *Darwin's Dangerous Idea* (p.485)

On 22 December 1857 Darwin wrote to Alfred Wallace, the co-
developer of the theory of evolution by natural selection. "You
ask whether I shall discuss 'man'; I think I shall avoid the whole
subject, as so surrounded with prejudices, though I fully admit
that it is the highest & most interesting problem for the naturalist"
(Raby 2001, p.134). It is well understood that both Darwin and
Wallace had explanations for non-human behaviour, including
animal altruism, explanations that have largely stood the test
of time. What is much less widely understood, however, is that
both Darwin and Wallace, while fully able to explain small-scale
non-human altruism, the care of offspring and the exchanging
of favours, felt unable to give a biological explanation to human
morality, kindness, justice, or our sense of fair play.

It is rare for senior thinkers to admit to holes in their theories, and unusual for theorists to admit to fascination with behaviour that cannot be explained by their work. Indeed to admit to being fascinated ("most interesting problem for the naturalist") by behaviour *because* it cannot be explained by their work. But rather than being the focus of admiration for admitting to the limits of biological evolutionary explanation, Darwin and Wallace are today excoriated by social scientists – from psychologists and anthropologists to linguists and sociologists – who feel they should not have highlighted their reservations and the gaps in their theory. Wallace has largely been written out of evolutionary history partly because of his refusal to use his and Darwin's work to explain that which it could not explain, while it is argued that even Darwin "lets us down". Darwin is accused of being "misguided" (Wright 1994, p.183), and of making "his big mistake", when he refused to hide glaring abstractive concerns over the possible adaptationist logic of human moral behaviour.

But what if Darwin and Wallace did not let us down? What if, alongside major theoretical advances in philosophical logic, we now have to re-evaluate everything we thought we understood about the evolution of human social and moral behaviour?

*

NATURAL SELECTION, AND THE LEVELS AT WHICH SELECTION CAN, AND CANNOT, ACT

Evolution, the understanding that species change with time to form entirely new species because of the inheritance of different characteristics, was not new when Charles Darwin produced his work. Transmutation, as it was then called, was already in the air when Darwin published *Origin of Species*. Charles' grandfather, Erasmus Darwin, was among those who had produced early theories of "perpetual transformations" within nature. The Frenchman Jean-Baptiste Lamarck had proposed an even more influential, and alternative, theory of evolution that Darwin himself toyed with for many years before ultimately rejecting. And Robert Chambers' bestselling *Vestiges of the Natural History of Creation* had already prepared Victorian society for the fundamental shift in world views, as the old Biblical static ordering of separately created species would be swept away, to be replaced by a transmutationary landscape. But what Charles Darwin and his contemporary Alfred Russel Wallace were to discover was one particular and ultimately very convincing explanation for evolution, that of evolution by "natural selection".

Even during Darwin's time, though, there had been distracting, and sometimes deeply worrying, objections to natural selection, such as when the brilliant but arrogant physicist William Thomson, much later Lord Kelvin, mistakenly challenged that the Earth was simply not old enough to allow for Darwinian gradualism. Darwin and Thomson had to agree to disagree, but Kelvin, whose name would be given to the temperature scale, had miscalculated by a factor of almost fifty the Earth's age, estimated through the relative rate of heat loss, as he knew about thermal conductivity but radioactivity and nuclear processes were at that stage unknown. Darwin also did not have a theory of inheritance, and another major objection was that without a robust theory of discrete inheritance, beneficial variations would have blended away under natural selection, not carried forward. Hence real challenges remained for Darwin and Wallace's theory until it was synthesised with Gregor Mendel's rediscovered work on peas and particulate, not blended, inheritance in the early twentieth century. But from the 1920s, and after work including Thomas Hunt Morgan and his famous fruit flies with their discrete mutations, geneticists were comfortable combining Mendelism and Darwinian gradualist natural selection. Neo-Darwinism had now given over to what by the 1940s was known as the "modern synthesis" of Darwin and Mendel.

Natural selection applies to entities with the characteristics of multiplication, variation and heredity. What this means is that natural selection works on entities that can make copies of themselves. Variation means that copying, however, will never be perfect, and it is random copying errors that are essential if the process of evolution is to occur. Once the error or mutation has occurred, heredity will ensure that a mutation can reappear in all future generations. Over time evolution will tend to favour higher multiplication, longevity (the ability to survive long enough so as to be able to reproduce) and heredity. Natural selection is the process that determines that traits which are conducive to superior replication – Darwinian "fitness" – will, of mathematical necessity, tend to become increasingly common in a population over time.

Adaptation was key to Darwin's explanation of evolution by natural selection. Adaptation, or perfection of design, is explained as the gradual adjustment in form and behaviour as selection saves what is useful, and discards what is less useful, and slowly improves designs to fit an environment. Natural selection can this way often produce extremely precise, though never perfect, contrivances. Gradual saving of slight improvements will, over very many generations, allow a blind, physical process of accumulating small beneficial mutations to create the wonders of nature that the late eighteenth-century theologian William Paley had seen as proof of God's intervention; the eye or the hand. Paley's assumption of a forward-looking Creator necessary to fashion the most intricate designs in nature – natural equivalents, said Paley, of such perfect human creations as the watch – falls away. The "blind watchmaker" of natural selection becomes the main mechanism for creating the wonderful diversity of plant and animal life we see around us.

In 1859 in *On the Origin of Species* Darwin wrote that "natural selection can act only through and for the good of each being. ... Natural selection ... will adapt the structure of each individual for the benefit of the community; if each in consequence profits by the

41

selected change" (pp.133–5). Darwin was what is called an individual-selectionist; he believed that nature could select only through and for the good of the individual. Darwin here is explicitly disavowing community or "group" selection, or the idea that nature will select for the benefit of the community or group rather than its component parts. Here any benefit to a group can only be as a by-product of what is good for its individuals. The selfish gene revolution, the modern biologists' explanation of Darwinism that sees selection as predominantly operating at the level of the smallest unit, the gene, rather than at the level of the individual, is generally held to have started in 1966 with the publication of the American biologist George C. Williams' *Adaptation and Natural Selection*. Williams saw himself as continuing in a tradition first anticipated by major biologists such as R.A. Fisher, J.B.S. Haldane and Sewall Wright in work dating back to the early 1930s, but it was not until Williams' clear analysis that the incompatible traditions began to diverge.

Gene-selectionism, or as Williams put it "the formally disciplined use of the theory of genic selection for problems of adaptation" (1966, p.270), sees apparent individual selection reinterpreted as, not what is good for an individual, but as what is good for its genes. Since the fate of an individual and the fate of its genes are very closely – but not perfectly – linked, individual selection is often for practical purposes synonymous with gene selection. Unless evidence contradicted, the gene was to be recognised as the fundamental unit of selection, and Williams proposed that in evolutionary theory a gene could be regarded as any "hereditary information for which there is a favorable or unfavorable selection bias equal to several or many times its rate of endogenous change" (p.25). This concept of the gene as any unit of developmental information visible to natural selection has become the standard definition of the gene within the discipline, and the start of what is called the adaptationist programme within Darwinism. However, the terms *selfish gene* and *selfish gene-ery* did not emerge until Richard Dawkins popularised the programme a decade later in his 1976 bestseller, where he explained that "I must argue for my belief that the best way to look at evolution is in terms of selection occurring at the lowest level of all. In this belief I am heavily influenced by G.C. Williams's great book *Adaptation and Natural Selection*" (p.11).

Williams' book, subtitled *A Critique of Some Current Evolutionary Thought*, was also a criticism of theories of group selection, or the enduring idea that nature might select for the advantage of the group even at the cost to the individual. Biologists had a long track record of appealing, sometimes only implicitly, to "greater good-ism" and the idea that nature may select for the good of the group, local population or species, but in 1962 in his *Animal Dispersion in Relation to Social Behaviour* the biologist V.C. Wynne-Edwards (who coined the term group selection) had proposed that nature could and did select for the benefit of the group even at the expense of the individual. A serious attempt to resolve the group selection question was now unavoidable, and it fell to both Williams and the English biologist John Maynard Smith.

		Requires a change to the template of evolution?	Fails the parsimony test?
Option 1	Multilevel-selectionism / Group-selectionism	YES	YES
Option 2	Sociobiology / Evolutionary psychology ("implicitly group-selectionist" – Dawkins)	YES	YES
Option 3	Darwin's "other solution" / individual- or gene-selectionism	NO	NO

Williams' book-length response was a review of the range of instances cited as examples of group selection. While noting that group selection was not theoretically impossible, Williams concluded that the adaptations in question could almost invariably be explained in terms of selection at levels lower than the group. Furthermore, Williams pointed out in *Adaptation and Natural Selection* that group selection failed science's parsimony test; theorists did not need to appeal to a higher level solution when a lower level solution had already solved the problem. Williams did not argue that group selection could not happen, only that it would usually be too weak to produce noteworthy effects, and because of the much stronger and often counteracting forces operating at the lower levels. Williams freely admitted that "actually I think group selection needs much more attention" (letter, 2 September 2003), and it was his willingness to listen to alternative ideas – even ideas that he had made his reputation by undermining – maintain an open mind, and keep testing his own understanding, that left him on good terms with almost everybody in the field.[1]

Maynard Smith's analysis in the journal *Nature* in 1964 was to similarly note the difficulties with group-selectionist theories, including the damaging spread of the "'anti-social' mutations" that Wynne-Edwards was denying would propagate. "Every time a group possessing the socially desirable characteristic is 'infected' by a gene for anti-social behaviour, that gene is likely to spread through the group. ... Thus it would only be plausible to suggest that there are genetic reasons why anti-social behaviour should not increase if it were also suggested that selection had already produced an extreme degree of anti-social behaviour, and this

---

1   When I was looking to send a thank you to George for his support and assistance, it was his friend the leading multilevel-selectionist David Sloan Wilson who helpfully suggested that George and his wife Doris might enjoy a case of sherry. The *New York Times* noted that Dave Wilson had recounted in interview that as a graduate student he once strode into George's office saying "he would change the professor's mind about group selection. 'His response was to offer me a postdoctoral position on the spot'" (Wade, 2010).

is precisely what Wynne-Edwards denies. In fact, 'anti-social' mutations will occur, and any plausible model of group selection must explain why they do not spread" (pp.1145–6). George Williams would make a similar point in his 1966 work, preferring the term "poisonous" mutations to "anti-social" mutations. "Only one locus is involved. One cannot argue from this [legitimate] example that group selection would be effective in producing a complex adaptation involving closely adjusted gene frequencies at a large number of loci. Group selection in this example cannot maintain very low frequencies of the biotically deleterious gene in a population because even a single heterozygous male immigrant can rapidly 'poison' the gene pool" (1966, p.118).

Evolution is a struggle for survival and works because it is. Organisms within groups are still competing against one another, and the organisms that begin to take the benefits without paying the costs will be favoured by evolution. Those organisms that acted for the good of the group, rather than at all times being driven by what is good for themselves and their genes, would be taken advantage of and would not be the successful ones.

What gene- and individual-selectionists argue is that group selection is likely to be a very weak force in evolution because the conditions required are so onerous. A group consisting almost entirely of altruists *can* do better than a group consisting entirely of selfish individuals, because the altruism benefits the entire group. The selfish group won't have this advantage. But, as Williams and Maynard Smith independently demonstrated mathematically in the mid 1960s, the problem is explaining how a group consisting entirely of altruists could have come about in the first place. "There is one special form of group selection which is worth considering in more detail, because it can, perhaps, explain the evolution of 'self-sterilizing' behaviour. ... With an intermediate amount of gene flow between colonies, selection could both establish and maintain timid or altruistic behaviour, provided that colonies with altruistic behaviour have a large selective advantage, and that colonies are founded by very few individuals. The model is too artificial to be worth pursuing further" (Maynard Smith 1964, p.1146). "Lewontin has produced what seems to me to be the only convincing evidence for the operation of group selection. ... We must conclude that group selection has not been important" (Williams 1966, pp.117, 123). Or as Dawkins and the Oxford zoologist Mark Ridley put it, "mathematical models show that, except in very special conditions which are almost never realized in nature, group selection will lose because it is so slow" (1981, p.22). In a group consisting of both altruists and selfish individuals the altruists will be eliminated by within-group selection because of the problem of subversion from within. It is theoretically possible that a wholly altruistic group could arise if the group was small in number. In such a case, random genetic drift could hypothetically establish altruism within such a population. However, it could only be immediately maintained if there is little migration in from normal selfish groups, otherwise the new immigrants would end up driving the altruists to extinction.

For group selection to be a serious force in evolution it would require between-group selection – where the altruistic inclination can be favoured because it would favour the group in competition with other groups – to be stronger than any within-group selection against altruists. Building from his own work in the 1960s, in the 1970s William Hamilton took the theories of Williams and Maynard Smith further to show that the force for group selection would only be able to continue indefinitely if there was periodic re-assortment of the various groups such that altruists could be re-concentrated in some groups. If this didn't happen such altruists would inevitably be eliminated by within-group selection. But the problem is coming up with a process of re-assortment that allows altruists to recombine in such a way that they will not immediately be taken advantage of by non-altruists.

While the group-selectionists tend to see it differently, orthodox Darwinism, at least when it is in the hands of biologists, has since been a continuously improving attempt to explain natural selection as operating at the lowest levels, that which is of benefit to the individual or, more specifically, its genes. Major multilevel selection biologists like David Sloan Wilson like to draw attention to, for example, studies showing that the majority of evolutionary anthropologists now subscribe to multilevel selection over gene selection (Wilson 2015; "The Tide of Opinion on Group Selection has Turned"), and as evidence for the wider acceptance of multilevel selection. But this is a little coloured; anthropologists, evolutionary or otherwise, are still social scientists. Anthropologists are generally not biologically trained, and certainly not to a high enough degree, and do not appreciate the mathematical models that sit behind the arguments of Haldane, Williams, Maynard Smith and Hamilton. Saying most anthropologists subscribe to multilevel selection over gene or individual selection isn't really germane. The levels-of-selection debate is a question written into the very mathematics that underlies biological evolution, and it can only be for mathematical biologists to resolve in the first instance. Not anthropologists. Not psychologists, evolutionary or otherwise, with their less-than-perfect understanding of statistics. And not philosophers, albeit philosophical logic can at least seemingly add to the wider understanding.

*

THE PROBLEM OF ALTRUISM

Whether selection acts at the level of the gene or the individual, altruistic sacrifice would at first glance appear to cause a problem for Darwin and Wallace's theory of evolution by natural selection. But Darwin realised that there were forms of apparently altruistic and even sacrificial behaviour that could pay dividends to the individual so behaving, and in the orthodox gene-selectionist tradition represented by Williams, Maynard Smith, Hamilton and Dawkins natural world altruism has been explained through two main mechanisms known as kin selection and reciprocal altruism.

Kin selection explains the evolution of altruistic characteristics towards close relatives as a gene for altruism can spread because it enhances its own replication through its survival effects on the relatives. The understanding that animals sacrifice for immediate kin was of course central to Darwin's theory, with fitness defined in terms of simple biological success. But in 1964 kin selective altruism would become one of the building blocks of modern genic selection theory after the publication of W.D. Hamilton's work. Bill Hamilton suggested that animals seek not to maximise their own fitness, but rather their own "inclusive fitness". The understanding is that genes pass into future generations not only through direct offspring, but also through relations. In normal diploid organisms like primates, a parent shares a genetic relationship of one half with its child. But the parent also shares such a relationship with its siblings because of inheritance from their shared parents. It will statistically share a quarter relationship with the sibling's offspring, and so on. Relations, and not just offspring, carry an individual's genes into subsequent generations, and so it makes sense – from the "point of view" of an animal's genes – for a degree of sacrifice for near-relatives.

Hamilton took these relationships – which had earlier been noted by the geneticist J.B.S. Haldane in a 1955 paper where he wrote of sacrifice that "if you save a grandchild or nephew the advantage is only two and a half to one. If you only save a first cousin, the effect is very slight" (p.44) – and provided a rigorous mathematical formulation of the altruism that could, and could not, be expected under such genetic inheritance. Kin-directed altruistic behaviour can be maintained under selection pressures provided the cost of that behaviour to the altruist (in terms of reduced personal fitness) is less than the benefit of the behaviour to kin (in terms of inclusive fitness) multiplied by the coefficient of relatedness. Hamilton further extended the work to encompass the haplodiploid sex inheritance system, and provided a mathematical rationale for social insect eusociality in terms of the even closer three-quarters average genetic relationship between sisters. Darwin himself had considered issues like neuter insects, and the problem of insect sterility, in the earliest editions of *Origin*, where he wrote, "this difficulty, though appearing insuperable, is lessened, or, as I believe, disappears, when it is remembered that selection may be applied to the family, as well as to the individual, and may thus gain the desired end" (1859, p.258).

Reciprocal altruism is the exchanging of altruistic favours such that each benefits more from co-operating than it would from not co-operating, or "you scratch my back, I'll scratch yours". Darwin wrote that "social animals perform many little services for each other: horses nibble, and cows lick each other, on any spot which itches: monkeys search for each other's external parasites" (1871, pp.74–5). Animals also render more important services, he continued: pelicans fish in concert, wolves hunt in packs, and "social animals mutually defend each other". Mutually beneficial co-operation and reciprocity was strongly debated in late nineteenth-century Darwinism, especially after the Russian naturalist and anarcho-communist Peter Kropotkin published his thoughts on "mutual aid". However, Kropotkin wanted to put benevolence back into nature, where Darwin had seen competition and bloodletting, and Kropotkin was initially writing against Huxley's views on the "struggle for existence" and the Hobbesian war of each against all. "The ants and termites have renounced the 'Hobbesian war,' and they are the better for it." Animals do indulge in co-operative acts towards those that may not be closely related, not through Kropotkin's benevolent instinct – "a feeling infinitely wider than love or personal sympathy" – but because the acts are for the self-interested benefit of each party, and Williams referred to this in his earliest work. "A consistent interaction pattern between hens in a barnyard is adequately explained without postulating emotional bonds between individuals. One hen reacts to another on the basis of the social releasers that are displayed, and if individual recognition is operative, it merely adjusts the behavior towards another individual according to the immediate results of past interactions" (1966, p.95). In 1971 Robert Trivers coined the term reciprocal altruism to describe Darwin's trading of favours within the natural world. Favours can be returned immediately, or at a later time provided the animals can remember interactions and recognise parties, as hypothesised by Darwin, and now termed "delayed" reciprocal altruism. Such mutually beneficial actions therefore benefit an individual's genes, and a mutation that first promotes such behaviour can be positively selected.

Examples of reciprocal altruism in the natural world are numerous, and include the mutual grooming of primates, and even the oft-cited actions of the tiny cleaner fish. Various species of cleaner fish occupy specific locations, and offer services to larger fish by cleaning them of parasites and unwanted particles. The cleaner fish thereby obtains a reliable food supply from the visitor, as well as a degree of protection from the larger fish. The cleaned fish benefit from having dead tissue and such removed. Darwin's performance of "many little services" and mutual defence was then to be greatly developed and given a more mathematical basis through the work of John Maynard Smith, who was able to formulate algorithmic strategies of co-operation and confrontation.

Both kin selection and reciprocal altruism are sometimes referred to as "technical" altruism, to make the point that such altruism is ultimately self-serving. All altruism in the non-human world reduces to selfish genetic prudence.

*

FROM THE "MERELY SOCIAL" TO THE MORAL

> "But natural selection ... implies concurrently a complete disregard
> for any values, either of individuals or of groups, which do not serve
> competitive breeding. This being so, the animal in our nature cannot
> be regarded as a fit custodian for the values of humanity."
>
> – **W.D. Hamilton**, "Selection of selfish and altruistic
> behaviour in some extreme models" (1971a, p.219)

But as Williams, Maynard Smith, Hamilton, Dawkins and biologists not wedded to group selection realised, neither Darwin's individual-selectionism, nor Williams' and Maynard Smith's genic-selectionism, would allow for adaptations like fair play, decency, justice or morality, or for the cohesion of large groups in non-inbred diploid organisms.

"Moving on to humans, however, Darwin does recognise that here there may be real self-sacrifice; moral considerations are likely to clash with our selfish interests, even overriding our bid for self-preservation. ... How did we evolve from being merely social to being moral?" asks the evolutionary psychologist Helena Cronin (1991, p.326). So what was Darwin's answer? "Uncharacteristically, he seems quite explicitly to be offering a higher-level solution" (p.328). But Darwin knew that selection could not operate biologically at the level of the group; Darwin in other words recognised that morality and fairness could not be explained by a working model of biological adaptation. Although nature had given us certain traits which could be built upon, or twisted, something else had to be doing the building and the twisting. Darwin realised that something *more* was needed. How could truly virtuous human self-sacrifice, where, said Darwin, the bravest men "freely risked their lives for others" (1871, p.163), come about? Ultimately, Darwin said, the social virtues could only be explained as cultural, not biological. Guided by the approbation of our fellow men, ruled by deep religious feelings, confirmed by instruction and habit, "all combined, constitute our moral sense or conscience" (p.166). "A belief constantly inculcated during the early years of life, whilst the brain is impressible, appears to acquire almost the nature of an instinct" (p.100). Unlike evolutionary psychologists such as Steven Pinker and Helena Cronin, Darwin would not – for good biological reasons – try to argue that humans are born coded for decent and virtuous behaviour, or that morality is a biological adaptation. The answer for Darwin was that culture took just another biologically selfish ape capable only of "you scratch my back, I'll scratch yours" (what Darwin called the "first origin") but then twisted it into an altruistic human, through positive and negative peer pressure, myth, instruction and habit.

Now this is undoubtedly an oversimplification of *Descent of Man*. First, as Cronin notes, "it seems that there can be no definitive answer as to what Darwin really had in mind" (1991, p.306). Second, as Richards (1987) points out, Darwin left enough room in *Descent* for accusations of both Lamarckism and group-selectionism. The crucial point, though, is that Darwin recognised that individual selection could not explain human decency. He considered biological group selection, but knew it could not work mechanically, so ultimately ended up wagering on our second inheritance system, culture, overwriting our first inheritance system, biology.

Alfred Wallace, "the ever-vigilant defender of natural selection, the ultra-adaptationist, the most Darwinian of Darwinians" as Cronin calls him (1991, p.353), also pondered "the inverse problem" as he called it in his 1870 essay *The Limits of Natural Selection as Applied to Man*. "An attempt … to deduce the existence of a new power of a definite character, in order to account for facts which, according to the theory of natural selection, ought not to happen" (reprinted in 1891, p.188). Wallace is the great footnote in Darwinian history, though he never bore Darwin malice for this. Yet, as noted, an attempt to account for facts which, according to the theory of natural selection, "ought not to happen". In his endeavour to explain that "new power", Wallace, heavily influenced by a thriving nineteenth-century spiritualist movement, turned to non-material answers, and this is part of the reason that biologists have been a little embarrassed to remember him. However, the Harvard biologist Andrew Berry has made the intriguing suggestion (2000) that Wallace may have been attracted to spiritualism in part because of his deeper probing into naturalism and field studies; in other words because he was "the ultra-adaptationist" and "the most Darwinian of Darwinians". As Berry notes, of all the nineteenth-century naturalists only Wallace had first-hand knowledge of both what were then termed the "lowest" humans and the "highest" apes, so perhaps only he could have grasped how profound "the inverse problem" was, and how radical the solution needed to be. Darwin and Wallace didn't let us down, they weren't "misguided", when they legitimately refused to claim for biology that which could not be supported by the theory or evidence. They didn't make their "big mistake"; they simply recognised that humans could not have out-evolved the biological pattern that exists across the rest of nature. Genetically, we are not evolutionary psychology's moral animal; biologically, we are not sociobiology's decent ape.

And for Thomas Huxley, too, Darwin's bulldog, the brilliant zoologist and propagandist who coined the term Darwinism, natural selection – which Huxley called "the cosmic process" – could not explain human morality. "Let us understand, once for all, that the ethical progress of society depends, not on imitating the cosmic process, still less in running away from it, but in combating it" (1894, p.141). This is Darwin's wager. This is what George Williams would separately call the Huxley–Dawkins nature-as-enemy idea, and because Huxley had published his main arguments in his extended 1894 essay "Evolution and Ethics".

Williams, together with the science historian James Paradis, would end up publishing an entire 250-page book – *T.H. Huxley's Evolution and Ethics* – around nothing other than Darwin's wager.

*

EVOLUTIONARILY STABLE STRATEGIES

Some of John Maynard Smith's most valued work dates from the early 1970s when he became the first to apply game theory modelling to the natural world. Game theory is a branch of mathematics developed by Morgenstern and von Neumann in the 1920s as a way of formalising social questions and activities, based on the underlying assumption of each player in the game acting rationally. The most famous game theory scenario is called prisoner's dilemma, where co-operation will not evolve in rational self-interested players who never have to repeat the game. But co-operation can evolve when the game is continuously repeated, known as iterated prisoner's dilemma. Under these circumstances long-term expedience is best served by co-operative strategies of enlightened self-interest among players who continually have to interact. And such low-level co-operation is exactly what we observe in the natural world, and where natural selection has replaced the rationality of the player and in the form of reciprocal altruism and delayed reciprocal altruism.

Evolution is a struggle for survival, and works because it is. As Williams demonstrated in 1966, any adaptation that somehow managed to evolve for the good of the group would suffer from subversion from within. Organisms within groups are still competing against one another, and the organisms that begin to take the benefits without paying the costs will be favoured by evolution. Those organisms that acted for the good of the group, rather than at all times being driven by what is good for themselves, would be taken advantage of and would not be the successful ones. Subversion from within has consequences. Maynard Smith made a major breakthrough when he applied game theory to the natural world to develop the concept of the *evolutionarily stable strategy*, or ESS. These strategies are the possible group behaviours nature has discovered within the limits set by given genetic inheritance and reproduction systems. For example, natural selection has ensured that for non-inbred diploid organisms close co-operation is only possible in small groups; for all other apes, it is only possible in groups of around five to not much more than one hundred. An ESS is defined as a strategy which, if most members of a population adopt it, cannot be bettered by an alternative strategy. Such a strategy cannot then be bettered by an aberrant individual; the strategy becomes stable and cannot be subverted from within. No deviating individual will have a higher fitness or potential for reproduction, and the trait thus becomes fixed. It is the paradigm of game-theoretic modelling, where it is Darwinian selection playing the role of the rational policy selector. "The use of optimization is easier to justify in biology than in economics, because natural selection provides a dynamics which will, subject to constraints, cause a population to evolve towards an optimum", as Maynard Smith noted in his concluding remarks in *Evolution of Social Behaviour Patterns in Primates and Man* (1996, p.291). Groups are made up of competing individuals, and natural selection creates limits on group sizes, dependent on the level of co-operation necessary between the individuals (reciprocal altruism), and the degree of relatedness amongst them (kin selection, the sacrifice one organism makes for close relatives).

Biological theories of altruism work, in diploid/non-inbred/non-sterile caste species, for small family groups where there is a high degree of genetic relationship, and for small reciprocating groups where the parties regularly interact and can consequently recognise each other and remember the interchanges. Natural world "tit for tat" exchanges can only work under such a system. If one chimpanzee grooms another chimpanzee it is because it is looking for something in return from that other chimp. Group size is a function of many factors, including food availability and security. The type and frequency of prey may necessitate a larger group for regular successful kills, but this larger group means the disadvantage of having to share a kill amongst a larger number. Open areas require larger groups for protection of members against predators; in a wooded area smaller groups afford sufficient protection because individuals can more easily escape in the trees. Nevertheless, one crucial restraining *upper* limiting factor will be given by the degree of interaction necessary between group members. Wildebeest may sweep majestically across the plains in groups of many thousand, but wildebeest don't have to co-ordinate and share a kill and don't therefore have to work together. Behaviour that necessitates many interactions between group members requires strong group cohesion. This means individuals need to know each other well. Nature has established that for primates such cohesion cannot be left to degree of relatedness alone. Grooming is an essential part of primate behaviour because it allows members to form bonds and get into reciprocating relationships.

But group cohesion in primates is limited. Firstly, there is the need for strong reciprocating relationships that require detailed knowledge of your associates; detailed knowledge that can only be gained and maintained by forfeiting the possibility of a larger, more loosely knit structure. Secondly, grooming takes time. Primates may spend up to twenty per cent of their time grooming for cohesion. They cannot afford more because over eighty per cent of their available time must be spent hunting and working. So there are reasons for group sizes in nature. Group size is effectively kept stable by the positive and negative forces at play. Hence chimpanzees live in groups of rarely above one hundred members, and forage in much smaller groups. Even where we leave the apes and look at the less cohesive – and less closely co-operating – monkeys, we find that baboons will usually live only in groups of a couple of hundred. One species of baboon can live in groups of up to 800, though what we always find with large groups in the primates is that they will be made up of numerous smaller subgroups, with little peaceful interaction occurring between subgroups. Yet humans coexist and interact peacefully in our *millions*. The only other animals capable of such a scale of interaction are the social insects, but if we are looking for biological answers we cannot model ourselves on the social insects.

As noted, Darwin wrote to Wallace that: "You ask whether I shall discuss 'man'; I think I shall avoid the whole subject ... though I fully admit that it is the highest & most interesting problem for the naturalist". For a biologist man is just one of millions of extant animal species, and from a biologist's technical point of view not a particularly interesting species at that. But man is the "highest & most interesting problem" because we do not behave as the above principles would have predicted. I believe George Williams wrote just two forewords in his forty years at the top of the Darwinian tree. One was in relation to creatures that are truly of interest to evolutionary biologists, when he wrote the foreword to George Barlow's analysis of the cichlid fishes. Williams had referred to the cichlids in his 1966 *Adaptation and Natural Selection*. But it was in Barlow's book, *The Cichlid Fishes*, subtitled *Nature's Grand Experiment in Evolution*, that Williams explained why these species hold such fascination for so many biologists, himself included. Williams wrote that he had known and admired Barlow since they were ichthyologists together in college, but "I have known and admired cichlids for an even longer time". Cichlids are often cited in relation to the speed and extent of their development in African lakes, and the hints this gives to speciation and other steps in evolution, but there are also "an enormous list of important questions that, as yet, have no answers or, even worse, have too many answers" (2000, p.ix). And the second foreword he wrote was also for a book he deemed important, though unlike Barlow's book it was not about the illuminating application of Darwinian theory, but about the opposite: its subversive misuse.

*

A CIRCUS BEAR ON A UNICYCLE

"Civilized human behavior has about as much connection with natural selection as does the behavior of a circus bear on a unicycle."

– **Mark Ridley** and **Richard Dawkins**,
"The natural selection of altruism" (1981, p.32)

In 1975 the Harvard entomologist Edward O. Wilson, a recognised expert on insect behaviour, was to coin a new term, *sociobiology*. Sociobiology was defined as the scientific study of the biological basis of all forms of social behaviour in all kinds of organisms, including man. As noted previously, this field of study extended to humankind could have been non-controversial. There logically *is* a biological basis to study, be it that the final answer is 100%, 0%, or a shifting range somewhere in between. Richard Dawkins made the same point in his essay "Sociobiology: The New Storm in a Teacup": it is a field of study, not a point of view, Dawkins explained (1986).

In many ways the groundwork for what was to come in the form of human sociobiology had been laid in the late 1950s by the Nobel Prize-winning linguist Noam Chomsky. Chomsky had shown that the capacity for language acquisition is an innate, inborn capacity within the human animal; that we have a natural language "organ". Many cognitive theorists since then have tried to argue that the demonstrable genetic capacity for language acquisition is evolutionarily equivalent to the suggestion that our behaviours have a strong genetic component. The inevitable result was what would become known as "human sociobiology". Chomsky himself was to strongly refute such suggestions, but as the science writer John Horgan put it in *The End of Science*: "Edward Wilson and other scientists who attempt to explain human nature in genetic terms are all, in a sense, indebted to Chomsky" (1996, p.151).

The problem though was never the field of study; the problem was that central to sociobiology from day one was the claim for "morality as a biological adaptation". In his 700-page magnum opus *Sociobiology* Wilson summarised the previous five decades of research into animal social behaviour by biologists all over the world. But in the final chapter Wilson turned to humankind, and provided his own rather more unique interpretation; as Maynard Smith put it: "the last chapter – it seemed to me half-baked, silly" (in interview with Segerstrale 2000, p.241). It was half-baked for Maynard Smith because not only did Wilson wish to put cultural behavioural differences down to biology, and thus develop a new discipline of "anthropological genetics" focusing on cultural behaviours, but because Wilson admitted that demonstrating "the *genetic evolution of ethics*" (emphasis in the original) was a "missing" but "important piece" of the sociobiology project. And notwithstanding the problem that "to the extent that unilaterally altruistic genes have been established in the population by group selection, they will be opposed by allelomorphs favored by individual selection" (1975, p.563).

While not offering any evidence for "the *genetic evolution of ethics*" in 1975, this didn't stop Wilson suggesting to the *New York Times Magazine* that year that "Human Decency is Animal" (1975a). And three years later he would publish a book solely about human sociobiology, *On Human Nature*, where he would explicitly claim that "morality evolved as instinct" (1978, p.5).

Or as another early sociobiologist, Michael Ruse, puts it: "The position of the modern evolutionist, therefore, is that humans have an awareness of morality – a sense of right and wrong and a feeling of obligation to be thus governed – because such an awareness is of biological worth. Morality is a biological adaptation. ... Perhaps we really ought to hate our neighbours, but we, poor fools, think otherwise!" (reprinted in 1989, pp.262, 271). And Richard Dawkins and his zoological colleague at Oxford, Mark Ridley, would come to coin the term "evangelistic" sociobiology (1981, p.36) to refer to both Wilson's writing and the many other sociobiological hypotheses then around that were claiming far more for biology and evolution than Darwin's understanding, or modern orthodoxy, actually allowed.

3

THE DARWIN WARS

"As an enthusiastic Darwinian, I have been dissatisfied with explanations that my fellow-enthusiasts have offered for human behaviour. They have tried to look for 'biological advantages' in various attributes of human civilization. ... Frequently the evolutionary preconception in terms of which such theories are framed is implicitly group-selectionist."

– **Richard Dawkins**, *The Selfish Gene*
(1989 edition, pp.190–1)

Following on from the previous chapter, then, by doing what he was doing Darwin was trying to keep humankind within the four-billion-year[2] template of life on Earth. But what would it really mean to step outside that template? While the multilevel-selectionists are, indeed have to be, open and above board in their group-selectionism, which can then be quickly assessed against all

---

2   Current thinking is that life on Earth is at least 3.5 billion years old, likely to be 3.7 billion years old, and may even be up to 4.3 billion years old. It all depends on how "hell-like" the period known as the Hadean (after the god of the underworld) was, and recent evidence suggests that it may have been less inimical to life than previously thought.

the problems with group selection mentioned in the last chapter, a much more opaque situation is presented in the "implicit", or hidden, group-selectionism of those who at the same time profess to be good gene- and individual-selectionists: the sociobiologists and evolutionary psychologists.

> "Although the genes have given away most of their sovereignty, they maintain a certain amount of influence in at least the behavioral qualities that underlie variations between cultures. ... Even a small portion of this variance invested in population differences might predispose societies toward cultural differences. ... In short, there is a need for a discipline of anthropological genetics."
>
> – **E.O. Wilson**, *Sociobiology: The New Synthesis* (p.550)

Sociobiology's founder, Edward O. Wilson, wrote in 1978 that "it is only in the lower animals, and in the social insects particularly, that we encounter altruistic suicide comparable to man's" (p.151). Which is certainly correct as far as it goes. But when trying to explain this observation Wilson was to write that where such genuinely altruistic "behavior exists, it is likely to have evolved through kin selection or natural selection operating on entire, competing family or tribal units" (p.155), and that "the genetic capacity for blind conformity spreads" (p.187). The problem with the above is that the former claim is explicitly group-selectionist when claiming selection at the level of the competing (non-familial) tribal unit, while the latter claim is implicitly group-selectionist as individuals without the putative trait of blind conformity would be taken advantage of and out-competed by their less helpful conspecifics. The sociobiologist Michael Ruse did point out quite early on that Ed Wilson had an obvious weakness for explicitly group-selectionist argument – "curiously, the one human sociobiologist who is prepared to take seriously non-individualistic mechanisms of change is Wilson" (reprinted in

1989, p.163) – though Ruse failed to point out the only slightly less obvious implicit group-selectionism in his (see below) and others' work. And it was this implicit group-selectionism that was evident in the writing of all the influential sociobiologists, and that would later transfer to every single evolutionary psychologist up to and including Helena Cronin, Donald Symons and Steven Pinker.

		Requires a change to the template of evolution?	Fails the parsimony test?
Option 1	Multilevel-selectionism / Group-selectionism	YES	YES
Option 2	Sociobiology / Evolutionary psychology ("implicitly group-selectionist" – Dawkins)	YES	YES
Option 3	Darwin's "other solution" / individual- or gene-selectionism	NO	NO

Turning from E.O. Wilson to Richard Alexander, a zoologist and early fan of sociobiology, we hear that "population-wide indiscriminate beneficence might also evolve when small 'populations' are regularly composed of relatives related to a similar degree" (1987, p.100), and that this can thus be the basis for explaining human large-scale generosity. But such a claim flies directly in the face of the mathematical models of Williams, Maynard Smith and Hamilton built into the last chapter. Sociobiologists even invented completely new mechanisms to explain their ideas, such as indirect or third-party reciprocal altruism, where returns may eventually come back from society at large. Hence Alexander: "Moral systems are systems of indirect reciprocity" (p.77). But such hypothetical moral systems can be subverted from within, and are not evolutionarily stable. Or there is Robert L. Trivers, a respected biologist but one who shares with Wilson the driving need to put human morality as a biological adaptation. "We routinely share food, we help the sick, the wounded and the very young", Trivers wrote under a section headed "Reciprocal Altruism in Human Evolution" (1985, p.386). As early as 1971 the august *Quarterly Review of Biology* was allowing Trivers to claim that "selection may favor a multiparty altruistic system in which altruistic acts are dispensed freely among more than two individuals" (p.52), and where we are "acting altruistically toward a third individual uninvolved in the initial interaction" (p.53). All of which would be subject to subversion from within, all of which "will be opposed by allelomorphs favored by individual selection" as even Ed Wilson himself put it, and all of which sits outside the models of Darwin, Williams, Maynard Smith and Hamilton.

Beyond Wilson, Alexander and Trivers it is difficult to find a sociobiologist who was a trained biologist, but when we turn to some other big names in early sociobiology such as the philosopher Michael Ruse we should recall that we have already met his claim that: "our sense of morality is an adaptation" (1989, p.231). Indeed, according to Ruse, and flying directly in the face of four billion years of evolution, "one will probably function most efficiently when one has no hope of return at all" (p.231). Yet this would be wide open to subversion from within, which is why such a system never evolved in the millions of other species that currently inhabit this planet, nor is believed to have evolved in the billions of species that have ever lived on this planet. But this doesn't stop Ruse celebrating the good fortune that "we humans should just so have happened to have evolved to that very morality which is endorsed by God" (p.272). Chimpanzees live in "a world without compassion" (de Waal 1996, p.83), and they live in such a world for very good, and very efficient, gene-selectionist reasons. And yet for Ruse, Wilson and Trivers human DNA apparently evolved to be the polar opposite of that chimpanzee world without compassion; we evolved Christian compassion, "that very morality which is endorsed by God". This is such a different view of evolution from that held by Darwin and Huxley, and is in fact much closer to the view of evolution held by the Russian naturalist and anarcho-communist Peter Kropotkin that we saw in the last chapter.

Or there is the psychologist David Barash, who proposes that "unilineal descent permits extraordinarily large numbers of individuals, from dozens to millions, to unite under the aegis of common ancestry" (1982, p.133). So while other apes must live by the rules of natural selection that limit their groupings to around five to one hundred, the human ape evolved a biological mechanism that allows us to form groupings of millions. "With the elaboration of enough social complexity, 'indirect reciprocity' may have followed … in which the return is from society at large, rather than specific, benefited individuals", says Barash (p.137). Barash at least restricts himself to the claim "may have followed", but it cannot have followed, as it would have been subverted from within; such indirect reciprocity would not have been evolutionarily stable. And while conscious (rather than manipulated – think cuckoos) adoption of unrelated kin does not occur in the natural world, humans have the capacity to adopt and love unrelated children programmed in at the level of our DNA because: "our evolution leaves us with a rather 'open program' that enables us to adopt children comfortably" (Barash 1979, p.106). But no such "open program" can exist because, as Richard Dawkins writes, "the altruistic adoption 'strategy' is not an evolutionarily stable strategy" (1989, p.103).

This complete misrepresentation of Darwinian orthodoxy has trickled down into the popular imagination through every newspaper. The influential British science writer and science journalist John Gribbin was described by a senior editor at *Nature* as "one of the best science writers around", while the conservative political magazine the *Spectator* called him "one of the finest and most prolific writers of popular science". And yet Gribbin's sociobiology has been sold on the premiss that humans are genetically distinct from the rest of the natural world; that we have out-evolved the four-billion-year pattern of natural selection. On the back cover of the paperback edition of John and Mary Gribbins' 1993 work, a reissue and update of their previous 1988 book, Edward Wilson wrote: "The Gribbins explain the basis and paradox of sociobiology in language that can be understood by all, making clear why the subject is provocative and unpalatable to many even as it tries to provide a unified view of human behaviour". Not, note, provocative and unpalatable because it is anti-gradualist and implicitly group-selectionist evolutionary theorising.

The Gribbins tell us that we must search for natural "models" on which to base human sociobiology. Their model is the birds; birds have evolved true altruism too apparently. "Genes for helping spread through the gene pool. ... The pattern of behaviour that makes for helping at the nest of your siblings is almost exactly the same as the pattern of behaviour that makes for helping at the nest of any members of your species. As helping becomes a common activity, some individual helpers, either through confusion, inability to recognize their kin, or even as the result of a very slight mutation, will help more widely" (1993, p.238).

"This begins to show how a characteristic that starts out on the basis of kin selection can spread through a population to become, for want of a better term, general 'niceness'. And of course, such a tendency then begins to act 'for the good of the species', although it has its origins firmly in the selfishness of genes" (p.239). "We are altruistic apes" (p.246), and "the cry 'for King and country' is precisely explained in sociobiological terms" (p.297). Even patriotism, monarchism and forelock-tugging deference to our social and economic superiors is coded into our genes, according to both the Gribbins and Ed Wilson.

Unfortunately for the Gribbins, "for want of a better term, general 'niceness'" is not the distinguishing feature of birds, and for key evolutionary reasons. Should such a mutation occur, it would immediately be selected against; birds without this coding for selflessness would leave more offspring than those with such a coding. "General 'niceness'" would be bred out of the population within a very few generations. "Niceness" is not the distinguishing feature of birds; if anything murderous indifference is. It tends to be birds that are often used as models of efficient nastiness by the gene-selectionists. Dawkins tells us about blackheaded gulls within five pages of beginning *The Selfish Gene* and as a paradigm of gene-selfish behaviour. "It is quite common for a gull to wait until a neighbour's back is turned, perhaps while it is away fishing, and then pounce on one of the neighbour's chicks and swallow it whole. It thereby obtains a good nutritious meal, without having to go to the trouble of catching a fish, and without having to leave its own nest unprotected" (1989, p.5). In a later chapter we shall review some of the field study literature on birds, including gang rape within waterfowl, rapes that can be so persistent that the female subsequently drowns; "an absent male is himself usually (73%) raping another female or witnessing another rape".

And the Gribbins' claim that "Peace on Earth, cooperation, helping the sick and the weak, and all the rest is a package that has emerged through the process of natural selection" (1993, p.246), while noticeably similar to Bob Trivers' claim above, still seems extraordinary when one compares with other mammalian species, even just the primates. Again, this is Kropotkinism, not Darwinism. For example, the primatologist Frans de Waal tells us about Mozu, an oft-filmed female snow monkey, or Japanese macaque, who had survived in a National Park despite severe deformities. Yet even the openly group-selectionist de Waal must admit that "there is no shred of evidence that other monkeys have ever gone out of their way to assist her in her monumental struggle for existence" (1996, p.7).

EVOLUTIONARY PSYCHOLOGY

"There is no charity in nature."

– **Steve Jones**, *Almost Like A Whale* (p.160)

I apologise if the first part of this chapter will seem at times like a list of names and references, but readers need to understand both the context and the extent to which Option 3 has been, in effect, censored. Not only has all the academic reporting been deliberately skewed, but science journalism has relentlessly concentrated on Options 1 and 2. For over thirty years the British public, for instance, has been presented with either science journalists like John Gribbin and Matt Ridley pushing Option 2, or writers like Roger Highfield – for twenty years the *Daily Telegraph*'s science editor, plus a former editor of *New Scientist* – pushing Option 1.[3] Darwin's own understanding of human evolution, Option 3, has all but been written out of the academic and popular records, notwithstanding that it is the only answer that makes sense

---

3   In 2011 Roger Highfield produced *SuperCooperators* with the Harvard biologist Martin Nowak. When Ed Wilson decamped to the group-selectionist school in 2010, it was with Nowak that he co-wrote his position-shifting paper.

logically, mathematically, theoretically and observationally. That said, other parts of this chapter are more entertaining, so some might want to skip forward to the next section. For the rest, we must return to the somewhat depressing history.

Sociobiology largely died out in the late 1980s for a number of reasons, including Wilson and some other sociobiologists' seeming attempts to unite political philosophy and evolutionary biology under a conservative ideological banner. Wilson upset the political left when he wrote statements like "Marxism ... is now mortally threatened by the discoveries of human sociobiology" (1978 p.191). Maynard Smith, in interview with the sociologist Ullica Segerstrale, admitted the politics should have been obvious within Wilson's 1975 book, or rather its final chapter on humankind. "The last chapter – it seemed to me half-baked, silly. ... I think it is the difference between a European and an American. No European with his degree of culture and general education" would have been unaware of the obvious political leanings of the last chapter of *Sociobiology*, Maynard Smith noted. "On the other hand, I am equally disturbed, made angry by what I think is the unreasonableness of much of the criticism that has been made of Wilson. And I find that if I talk to Dick Lewontin or Steve Gould for an hour or two, I become a real sociobiologist, and if I talk to someone like Wilson and Trivers for an hour or two, I become wildly hostile to it" (Segerstrale 2000, p.241).

But the political posturing wouldn't end with sociobiology, as many evolutionary psychologists still have a weakness for grand conservative narratives if not bro-culture ideologies. The "early" Steven Pinker was somewhat known for this, but even the one-time arch neocon Francis Fukuyama (of *End of History* notoriety) would try to link evolutionary psychology with a conservative political agenda in his work *The Great Disruption*. Following the criticisms of the earlier sociobiology, even by some evolutionary psychologists, Wilson sought to "remake" himself and was highly successful in becoming a champion of biodiversity and critic of deforestation. Segerstrale has an interesting take on this. She is an historian of science and another long-time chronicler of the Darwin wars, who has interviewed at length many of the biggest names in biology across all the traditions. "So in the 1990s, a new generation of university students and environmental activists were learning about Wilson II, the 'good' environmentalist, rather than Wilson I, the 'bad' sociobiologist. ... What did all this mean? ... What Wilson had been doing during all his years of seeming exile in the rainforest was quietly bringing sociobiology back in – through the side door of environmental concerns" (2000, p.310).

For the right or wrong reasons, the sociobiology brand itself was seen as toxic by the mid 1980s. Wilson's sociobiology was "tainted", says the evolutionary psychologist Robert Wright, and "most practitioners of the field he defined now prefer to avoid his label" (1994, p.6). Wright is an award-winning science writer whose popular-level homage *The Moral Animal: The New Science of Evolutionary Psychology* left no uncertainty over where evolutionary psychologists stood on the human-morality-as-a-biological-adaptation axis. "But the evolution of sacrifice may have grown more complex with time and fostered a sense of group obligation" (p.207), and "reciprocal altruism has extended the sense of obligation – selectively – beyond the circle of kin" (p.212). "The simpler way to account for this sort of 'excessively' moral behavior is to recall that human beings aren't 'fitness maximizers' but rather 'adaptation executors'" (p.225), and "in sum, the best guess about valor in wartime is that it is the product of mental organs that once served to maximize inclusive fitness and may no longer do so" (p.391). We are right back to both unfalsifiable speculation – the explanation for something that breaks a four-billion-year mould is selection within the rules to do one job that has morphed into doing a wholly different job outside the rules – and subvertable-from-within implicit group-selectionism. And yet Steven Pinker called *The Moral Animal* "fiercely intelligent" on the book's jacket. Chimpanzees may live in that world without compassion, but gene- and individual-selectionist evolution was being argued to have left man as the uniquely group-obligated and excessively moral animal.

"What ever happened to sociobiology?" asks Wright (p.7). "The answer is that it went underground", and re-emerged in the early 1990s as evolutionary psychology, "where it has been eating away at the foundations of academic orthodoxy". But evolutionary psychology – or son of sociobiology as John Maynard Smith liked to call it – re-emerged with human sociobiology's default weakness for unfalsifiable speculation and covert group-selectionism. Key human behaviours were still seen as having evolved, but as having evolved hundreds of thousands of years ago, adapted to the way of life of Pleistocene hunter-gatherers. For evolutionary psychology, theories of human altruism needed to be only slightly changed from the earlier tradition they based themselves on: positing newly evolved "conscience modules" in our brains, humans as executors of adaptations that have "fostered a sense of group obligation", or simply fortuitous genetic expression. Steven Pinker calls George Williams' *Adaptation and Natural Selection* "the founding document of evolutionary psychology" (1997a, p.56), while Robert Wright says Williams is "perhaps the closest thing there is to a single founding father of the new paradigm" (1994, p.151). Yet despite Williams' deep mathematical scepticism, almost all evolutionary psychologists, as with all sociobiologists, hold morality to be an adaptation, albeit often an unintended adaptational by-product rather than a direct adaptation.

The discipline of evolutionary psychology is generally seen as having been ushered in by Donald Symons' 1979 book *The Evolution of Human Sexuality*, and then more forcefully by Jerome Barkow, Leda Cosmides and John Tooby's 1992 edited compilation *The Adapted Mind*, the latter becoming the bible of the field. Evolutionary psychology was to pay more attention to the psychological, and many of the originators came from psychology. As Cosmides, Tooby and Barkow put it in their introduction, "Past attempts to leapfrog the psychological – to apply evolutionary biology directly to human social life – have for this reason not always been successful" (p.3). But it was Donald Symons' contribution to the edited work, "On the Use and Misuse of Darwinism in the Study of Human Behavior", that showed evolutionary psychology as old wine in new bottles. "In fact, since the adaptations that underpin human behavior were designed by selection to function in specific environments, there is a principled Darwinian argument for assuming that behavior in evolutionarily novel environments will often be *mal*adaptive", Symons wrote, with the emphasis his (p.154). Or, to translate, the adaptation that produced behaviour A 100,000 years ago might actually manifest itself simply as behaviours X, Y or even Z, once our ancestors left the African plains. An adaptation for cannibalism across the rest of the ape world may have become just a craving for steak tartare in humans.

Recalling David Barash's sociobiological claim that adoption of unrelated kin is possible in humans because "our evolution leaves us with a rather 'open program' that enables us to adopt children comfortably", we read something surprisingly similar from two of the biggest names in evolutionary psychology, Martin Daly and Margo Wilson. Interviewed by *Scientific American*'s John Horgan in 1995 we are told that adoptive parents love their children as much as natural parents because they are often childless couples who are "more motivated to have children than many natural parents are" (p.156). Such strangers are "strongly motivated to simulate a natural family experience" (Wilson & Daly 1987, p.218). Yet it is nonsense to claim, with Daly and Margo Wilson, that our capacity to adopt unrelated children arose through natural selection. Conscious adoption of genetically unrelated children is just about the most devastatingly stupid strategy you can think of from the point of view of gene-level, or Darwin's individual-level, selection. To re-cite Richard Dawkins, "to use the language of Maynard Smith, the altruistic adoption 'strategy' is not an evolutionarily stable strategy" (1989, p.103). And because it would be, not just a pointless strategy, but a counter-productive strategy, it cannot have evolved at the genetic level. This tendency would automatically breed itself out of a population. "When, as frequently happens, people challenge Darwinians to 'explain' the love of a woman for her adopted child, say, it is often sensible not to accept the challenge. Civilized human behavior has about as much connection with natural selection as does the behavior of a circus bear on a unicycle", Dawkins and Oxford's Mark Ridley wrote in 1981 (p.32).

The LSE's Helena Cronin is an evolutionary psychologist with an unusually impressive Rolodex, as although a philosopher of science she is on friendly terms with many of the major gene-selectionist biologists and seemingly gave great assistance to a very busy Richard Dawkins with the updates for the second edition of *The Selfish Gene*. But Cronin's penchant for implicitly group-selectionist speculation is apparent when she writes that: "But for some of our genes our modern environment is likely to metamorphose their phenotypic expression from that which natural selection originally smiled upon. And genes for behaviour are the most prominent among these. An animal that is adapted to dwell nomadically in smallish bands ... much of that animal's behaviour, however, is likely to change beyond recognition" (1991, p.329). Again, we are being told to believe that an adaptation for cannibalistic opportunism across the rest of the ape world simply became a craving for slasher movies and rare steak in humans. "There is no need to assume [with Huxley] that we have to depend on cultural evolution if we are to rise above the selfishness of our genes" (p.369). Or as Cronin claimed on

BBC Radio 4's *Analysis* series in May 1997, emphasis being hers: "Now reciprocal altruism can be the font of *vast* altruism, self-sacrifice and *genuinely* societal values". No, it can't be such a font, as it would not have been evolutionarily stable, though Cronin is not famous for her diffidence or uncertainty of views. When the journalist Andrew Brown interviewed her for his book *The Darwin Wars*, he commented: "In writing about religion for ten years, I've grown to like a lot of fundamentalists ... and Helena Cronin is unnervingly like a fundamentalist cousin of mine. Both are women of great sweetness of character, to whom the world is divided into the Elect and the Damned" (1999, p.148).

Steven Pinker is another well-connected cheerleader for evolutionary psychology, and his own explanation of why we have evolved to be moral is slightly different. For Pinker, Cronin is dead wrong to suggest reciprocal altruism can be the font of vast altruism, because apparently it is Hamiltonian kin selection that is the font of vast altruism. There is a "cognitive twist" (Pinker, 2012) because humans need "environmental cues", which can include that we come to falsely view non-kin as kin, and hence Hamilton's inclusive fitness model continues to apply to these "fictive ... faux-families". "Thus people are also altruistic toward their adoptive relatives", which, remember, we have mistaken for our kin. But it is nonsense to argue that falsely viewing fictive faux-families as family through cognitive mistakes is somehow an adaptational by-product, not just because the altruistic adoption strategy is not evolutionarily stable, but also because "a long memory and a capacity for individual recognition are well developed in man" (Dawkins 1989, p.187). Yet we hear that these "extended" families and "illusions of kinship" can apply, argues Pinker, to fatherlands, fraternities and occupational brotherhoods too. Exactly as with the Gribbins we are back to patriotism, simpering monarchism, and city-dwelling being coded into our genes. Admittedly Pinker is a little more nuanced than Cronin, Trivers and Symons; you can just about read him as hedging his bets and arguing (hidden away under many, many layers) that morality is *not* a biological adaptation and may be more cultural than biological in origin. But if you want to be generous and read Pinker this way he still gets no credit for remaining firmly within the evolutionary psychology camp which holds as its central belief that we, uniquely, out-evolved a brutal four-billion-year genetic pattern.

As with sociobiology, at the popular level evolutionary psychology has always been sold on the premiss that humans are genetically distinct from the rest of the natural world. The science writer Matt Ridley wrote in perhaps the most influential pop evolutionary psychology tract, *The Origins of Virtue*, that goodness is a biological adaptation, and that "we are more like ants or termites who live as slaves to their societies" (1996, p.6). Or as Ridley commented on Radio 4's *Start The Week* in October 1996: "We are in a sense the ants of the ape family". Actually, we are not, and we will cover the haplodiploid social insects, plus the inbred eusocial naked mole-rat, in a later chapter. We're not "in a sense the ants of the ape family". We are not ants, we are apes. We are, unsurprisingly, the apes of the ape family, and must, at least at a biological level, be explained as outbred diploid apes, not haplodiploid or even inbred social insects.

By the way, a former *Economist* science editor and another *Daily Telegraph* columnist, Ridley studied zoology at Oxford, but is not to be confused with the celebrated Oxford zoologist Mark Ridley quoted earlier, who is no relation. Though Matt Ridley is another with a rather more interesting Rolodex than most evolutionary psychologists. He is nephew of Margaret Thatcher's close friend and ideological mouthpiece Nicholas Ridley, and was educated at Eton. Having been chairman during the collapse of Northern Rock bank, Ridley today has to make his money sitting as a Tory peer, and as the 5th Viscount Ridley, in the House of Lords. So Viscount Ridley, whose writing is admired by Rupert

Murdoch ("great book" – Hudson, 2012), is not wholly typical of most evolutionary psychologists, but he is probably not completely atypical either. Evolutionary psychology has always had a particular ideological attraction to many on the economic hard right, just as sociobiology previously did.

But there was to be a final twist in the saga of the implicit group-selectionism that had marked sociobiology and evolutionary psychology from the earliest days. In 2007 Ed Wilson stunned many by abandoning his supposed earlier support for Hamiltonian kin selection as the key answer to altruism when he subscribed to David Sloan Wilson's model of trait-group selection for the evolution of eusociality, or high-level social organisation, in social insects and man. Everyone seemed to conveniently misremember the fact that the group-selectionism in Wilson's original 1970s work was not just implicit, it was wholly explicit. "Curiously, the one human sociobiologist who is prepared to take seriously non-individualistic mechanisms of change is Wilson", as Michael Ruse had written (1989, p.163). It was in no one's interest to recall that both Gould's multilevel-selectionism and Dawkins' gene-selectionism had largely turned a blind eye to Wilson's original group-selectionist writings, even if the two schools had very different reasons to misremember.

In 2010 Ed Wilson and two co-authors (see Nowak, Tarnita and Wilson) went further to hammer home their argument that Hamilton's work on inclusive fitness was insufficient and that eusociality lay in multilevel selection and mutations that prescribe the persistence of the group. Patrick Abbot and 136 other evolutionists wrote a reply in *Nature*, claiming "a misunderstanding of evolutionary theory and a misrepresentation of the empirical literature" (Abbot *et al.* 2011). The attacks continued, including as the *Guardian* put it: "biological warfare flares up again between EO Wilson and Richard Dawkins" (Johnston, 2014), after Wilson described Dawkins as a science journalist. Wilson claimed he had now "abandoned" the gene-selectionism of Williams and Maynard Smith, and stated that his 2010 paper had "almost totally silenced" the gene-selectionist community. As Jerry Coyne, one of the best-known names in the list of 137, blogged back: "Wilson, who always struck me as a courtly man, a gentleman of the Southern stripe, has now overstepped his bounds and insulted a distinguished colleague. ... If Wilson can't stop touting a misguided theory of natural selection, at least he can stop calling Dawkins a 'journalist', for crying out loud. There is no need to be personal" (2014). Yet just consider the bigger picture of what was going on here. The academic generally seen as the father of Option 2, or at least the father of modern-period Option 2, was admitting that Option 2 had never been a possibility for getting away from Darwin's wager, and that Dave Sloan Wilson's Option 1 seemed to him to offer the only chance of avoiding Darwin's wager.

IT'S ALL IN THE MATHS, AND EP IS FAITH, NOT SCIENCE

But Wilson's vacillating position-taking leads us to a very interesting place indeed. Wilson had developed sociobiology with the explicit intention of arguing that "human decency is animal" (1975a) and this notion of humans as, biologically, "*the* moral animal" (Wright, 1994) remains absolutely central to evolutionary psychology, or son of sociobiology. Now in the early 1980s John Maynard Smith wrote the following, later republished in his collection of essays, *Did Darwin Get It Right?* "A few years ago, I worked through the equations in Lumsden and Wilson's *Genes, Mind, and Culture* and found them to be badly flawed". He writes that he spent "several months trying to understand the maths", before determining that their mathematical models "fail to demonstrate any synergistic effect" (1992, p.52). On three occasions, Maynard Smith continued, Ed Wilson "has found it helpful to find a mathematical collaborator. His first two were

Robert MacArthur and George Oster: he was third time unlucky" (p.91). A few important observations. Evolutionary biology has now become so technical it requires a good working knowledge of complex mathematics. It also takes a huge amount of time and effort ("*several months*") for highly competent mathematical biologists to check the assertions of colleagues. And many even senior biologists recognise that their own mathematical skills are therefore not of the necessary quality, and thus need to work alongside professional mathematicians. Although philosophical logic can certainly help us here, Darwin's wager remains in important part a question in complex mathematical modelling.

The driving ideas behind sociobiology and evolutionary psychology are all connected. These are the ideas that humankind evolved to be moral, that humankind effectively out-evolved a four-billion-year pattern, and that culture has very little (sociobiology) or relatively little (evolutionary psychology) effect on the human animal at least when it comes to key moral behaviours. But all of these connected ideas come down to mathematical biology, to Option 1, Option 2, or Option 3. These questions can therefore only be resolved by mathematical biologists. And the world-ranked mathematical biologists here at first seem to line up six against two. Because on the one side, the side saying individual-selection never broke the four-billion-year pattern of evolution to allow morality at the biological level, stand Darwin, Wallace, Huxley, Williams, Maynard Smith and Hamilton. On the other side, the side saying individual-selection did break from the four-billion-year pattern of evolution to allow morality at the biological level, stand (or stood) Ed Wilson and Bob Trivers. An important clarification before we go any further. There are of course world-ranked mathematical biologists who fall outside these eight, for example names like Fisher, Haldane, Sewall Wright and Dobzhansky who were operating on the technical language of evolution in the period largely between the 1920s and the 1940s.

The reason they are excluded is they fall outside the investigatory period for Darwin's wager, because remember what we said in the first chapter: Darwin's wager was discussed in the second half of the nineteenth century but was then lost to science until Darwinism was firmly put back at the level of the individual, and then at the level of the gene, from the 1960s. And to be as fair as we can to Wilson and Trivers we're also going to ignore for the numbers the other leading biologists that Ernst Mayr – one of the fathers of the modern synthesis of Darwin and Mendel – claims below were preparing for the "so easy" task of criticising sociobiology on purely scientific grounds, but who reportedly tore up their hostile reviews for wider political reasons (Segerstrale 2000, p.17).

So, in the world rankings it lines up six against two. Although perhaps we should exclude Wallace? Because while Wallace saw that we could not have out-evolved the four-billion-year pattern, he disappointed Darwin and Huxley by ignoring Option 3 and turning to a *fourth* option, a non-material answer. So, OK, five against two. But if we are excluding Wallace, we must surely exclude Wilson. Because Wilson's work was self-undermining as well, and he is now clearly seen as falling outside those saying individual-selection broke from the four-billion-year pattern of evolution. Wilson himself has careered back and forth between Option 1 and his part-creation of modern Option 2 without seeming to realise you just can't do this; they are effectively mutually exclusive answers, both highly controversial, and it further weakened human sociobiology every time he gave one of his ambiguous solutions.

We will also not be adding to the Darwin side of the equation the tragic story of George Price, tempting though it may be. Price, an American former chemist involved in the Manhattan Project, brilliantly reworked Hamilton's theory of kin selection. Price's reformulation, known as the Price equation, further introduced the ideas of covariance between a trait and fitness, negative relatedness, and could even give a mathematical rationale for those instances where group selection could act. In 1970 Hamilton and Price successfully schemed to get a sceptical *Nature* to immediately publish Price's updating of Hamilton's work. Price and John Maynard Smith would then together start the discipline of evolutionary game theory, jointly publishing a 1973 paper, also in *Nature*. But Price, like Hamilton and Maynard Smith, saw no way for human kindness – sociobiology's "general 'niceness'" – to have evolved through gene or individual selection. In fact Price became deeply depressed, according to Hamilton, because he could work out no way for morality to have evolved at the genetic level. Human kindness could only be, as Price's biographer Oren Harman puts it, where culture "beat out their own nature" (Judah, 2013). But Price's story is a sad one, and his depression also had roots in emotional problems and mental illness. Once a radical atheist, he would turn to fundamentalist Christianity and minute scrutiny of the Bible, and in his last years was prone to religious hallucinations, intense asceticism, and statistical mania. In January 1975 Price took his own life by cutting his throat with a pair of nail scissors. We will not add Price because we are not counting Wallace, and it is difficult not to see a parallel between the two. Alfred Wallace, that most Darwinian of Darwinians, realised morality was the antithesis of individual selection, so turned to supernatural answers. George Price, that most mathematical of Darwinians, realised morality could not exist at the genetic level, became depressed, and found meaning in the supernatural. But we will also not invoke Price because group-selectionists sometimes wish to claim Price (and by extension even Bill Hamilton) for Option 1, operative multilevel selection, not Option 3, predominant gene- or individual-level selection.

For example, Elliott Sober and David Sloan Wilson argue the Price equation, and Hamilton's promotion of the Price equation, proves group selection to be a significant evolutionary force. Sober and D.S. Wilson point to a paper by Hamilton expounding the

Price equation, and describe as "bizarre" (1998, p.78) attempts to not view the paper as Hamilton's wholehearted conversion to group-selectionism. But what the Price equation does is simply give a robust mathematical formulation to the 1964 John Maynard Smith insight that group selection can occur, but that the assumptions required are often "too artificial to be worth pursuing further". Hamilton's paper explaining the Price equation makes this clear: "I shall argue that lower levels of selection are inherently more powerful than higher levels … It reveals a group-selection component which is not zero but which is bound in an unchanging subordination to the individual selection component" (Hamilton 1975, pp.330, 335). This is not quoted to bash group selection, it is said to flesh out the earlier argument that the maths alone cannot now be enough. Because the first take-away lesson is that even Price's enchantingly short half-line equation can be interpreted wildly differently if one is so inclined, so Darwin's wager must go beyond just the mathematics. And the second take-away lesson is to note that however one views the Price equation it is, at a stretch, a political football between Option 1 and Option 3; it gives no succour to evolutionary psychology, being Option 2. The Price equation firmly rules against Trivers' conceit that humankind remained subject to Option 3 but then inverted the rulebook of Option 3.

Hence leaving Price to one side it finally lines up as five Darwinian gradualists against one evolutionary anti-gradualist. Now five can of course be wrong, and one can always be right, although we should perhaps be more cautious about the one when he is seen to be invoking macromutation and evolutionary mechanisms never before seen in the billions of years of life on Earth. But there is something else about Trivers that we have to recognise. All of the other figures on the list above genuinely investigated the alternatives. Darwin considered, and toyed with, both Option 1 and Option 2, and even Lamarckism, before finally settling on Option 3. Williams, Hamilton and Maynard Smith may be famous for savaging Option 1, but they never said Option 1 could not work, just that the conditions required were often too onerous, and Williams thought Option 1 needed "much more attention". Williams once offered to a young firebrand determined to prove him wrong about Option 1 a postdoctoral position on the spot. Even Wallace toyed with Option 1 and considered Option 2 before finally rejecting both. But Trivers has *never* considered anything other than Option 2, never toyed with anything other than Option 2, never worked with anything other than the highly questionable first principle that humankind broke from the billion-year pattern of natural selection. It is difficult not to wonder whether this inflexibility means human vanity isn't playing some role here, exactly as it was in nineteenth-century dogmatism when Herschel and Kelvin also refused to consider Option 3.

But the larger point relates to evolutionary psychology itself. "EP" is built on the core assumption that humankind's genetic code broke from the rules obeyed by the rest of nature. Whether or not this turns out to be true, it is a question that is ultimately answered through mathematical biology, notwithstanding logic and probability give good reason to be sceptical. But no major biologist will work within EP; EP can only look back to the work of the sociobiologist Robert Trivers. No one in EP is qualified to even argue for Option 2, the core tenet of EP. Let me be clear, no anthropologist and no psychologist – not Donald Symons, not Jerome Barkow, not John Tooby, not Leda Cosmides, and not Steven Pinker – is qualified to resolve the debate within mathematical biology over whether Darwin, Hamilton and Maynard Smith were correct, or whether Trivers is correct. Evolutionary psychology is therefore simply taking as an *article of faith*, not reason, that Trivers is right and that Darwin and Williams were wrong in this absolutely central supposition. EP is thus closer to metaphysics, or even theology, than it is to science. It seems extraordinary that colleges of the standing of Pinker's Harvard never worked this one out, and are today running classes in what is effectively a faith-based academic discipline. It is not that EP might not be right, but at the moment – and for the foreseeable future because biologists will not want to work in this field – it remains a discipline founded upon belief, not reason, faith, not science. *Not even wrong*, the physicists might say. And the question is not just one for Pinker's Harvard, it is one for, say, Steven Pinker as well. Who wants to work in a field where you are not qualified to reconcile, or even contribute to, the central assumption behind your field, and where the founding tenet has to be based on blind faith?

"IT SEEMS THAT MOST SCIENTISTS ARE CONTENT WITH TAKING A PASSIVE STANCE"

But nothing so far really explains why sociobiology and evolutionary psychology have been allowed to get away with claiming more for evolution than either Darwin's understanding or gene-selectionist orthodoxy would allow. Why "Maynard Smith, Williams, Hamilton, and Dawkins … have largely eschewed the deeply unpleasant task of pointing out more egregious sins in the work of those who enthusiastically misuse their own good work" (Dennett 1995, p.485). One answer does seem to be that professional evolutionary biology is a very small arena, and one must always learn to identify the real enemy.

When Helena Cronin was sent for a period by the LSE to Oxford University to help her gain background for her PhD, she began to move in the tight circle of academic gene-selectionism. She became friends with Richard Dawkins, the first book she wrote had a foreword by John Maynard Smith, and George Williams described her as a "good friend" in *Plan and Purpose in Nature*. Cronin was, above all, a hard-working ally in the war against the multilevel-selectionists. In the March 1995 issue of

The British Journal for the Philosophy of Science Paul Griffiths used a review of Cronin's *The Ant and the Peacock* to discuss various issues raised by the book. "The Cronin controversy was, and is, a dispute between two current schools in biology and the philosophy of biology", read his introduction (p.123). As Griffiths noted, group selection is the "villain" (p.132) of much of *The Ant and the Peacock*.

For the leading genic-selectionists Cronin was a loyal foot soldier helping to carry the banner of selfish gene-ery to the wider world. And if some of her thoughts on humankind were a little … *unorthodox*, well surely, the argument seemed to have gone, they posed less of a threat to orthodox Darwinism than those dreadful multilevel-selectionists? Even the always charmingly mannered George Williams would occasionally write things like group selection needs more attention "but not with the stupidities published by people like Steve Gould" (letter, 2 September 2003). Up to his death George remained great friends with David Sloan Wilson, still one of the most influential multilevel selection theorists, so for someone known as one of the nicest guys in biology to use incautious language like "stupidities" about friends of friends explains how quickly things could and did blow up.

Although the leading gene-selectionists had always feared the damage that the sociobiologists and evolutionary psychologists are doing to Darwinism, they feared losing ground to the multilevel-selectionist tradition even more. Sociologist Ullica Segerstrale writes that Ernst Mayr, one of the fathers of the modern synthesis of Darwin's work with the genetics of Gregor Mendel in the early and mid twentieth century – and co-recipient with Williams and Maynard Smith of the 1999 Crafoord Prize – admitted to her that it would have been "so easy" to criticise sociobiology on purely scientific grounds. "Perhaps even more damaging to the potential scientific debate about sociobiology was the absence of any serious critical reviews in scholarly journals. There was a clear reason for this. According to Mayr, just because of the political criticism, several people who had been severely critical of sociobiology and had taken their time preparing reviews for scientific journals, now simply tore them up. They did not want their genuinely scientific disagreements to be seen as in any way supportive of the [Gould and Lewontin left-leaning] Sociobiology Study Group's political attack on sociobiology. Mayr knew of at least three such cases" (2000, p.17). Segerstrale even draws a parallel with other examples from the history of science where few take on the responsibility to correct others' mistakes. "And fewer still regard it as their task to enter the controversy in order to increase mutual understanding between parties in a polarized situation. It seems that most scientists are content with taking a passive stance, from which they watch the show while they get on with their *own* research" (p.245).

This perceived need to constantly attack, or at least never support, those within the multilevel selection tradition can reverberate throughout other disciplines. The Cambridge palaeontologist Simon Conway Morris produced an influential book in the late 1990s analysing and interpreting the fossils from the famous Burgess Shale in British Columbia. So it was fascinating to come across Richard Fortey's take on things. Fortey was a senior palaeontologist at the Natural History Museum in London, and his wonderful book on the trilobite, subtitled *Eyewitness to Evolution*, remains a real eye-opener in many ways. In *The Crucible of Creation* Conway Morris had savaged Stephen Jay Gould's account of the Burgess Shale investigations and the supposed Cambrian explosion of life. Savaged is probably the right term; Fortey wrote that he had "never encountered such spleen in a book by a professional; I was taken aback" (2000, p.136). At least according to Fortey the venom was undeserved by Gould who, he claimed, had been nothing but honourable in his treatment of Conway Morris. But what really grated with me was Dawkins' subsequent lauding of Conway Morris – a devout Christian, so not normally to be defended by Dawkins – simply because he was attacking Gould. Fortey certainly appeared to believe that some of those, like Richard Dawkins, who drew attention to Conway Morris's criticisms of Gould may not have been fully grounded in the history of the Cambrian explosion-of-life opinions. Opponents of Gould in other arenas, Fortey wrote, they appear to have used the book as a stick to beat him, "operating on the principle: 'my enemy's enemy is my friend'" (p.138).

For the sociobiologists and evolutionary psychologists both the friendships and, more importantly, the ally status would reap rewards. In 1992 and 1993 "The Cronin Controversy" erupted in the pages of the *New York Review of Books*, where so much of the Darwinian vitriol tended to appear while Gould was still alive. Gould slammed Cronin for both being a gene-selectionist and for jealously co-opting human explanations into orthodox gene-selection. Yet Cronin's teachers could see only another attack on selfish gene-ery. Maynard Smith and Dennett both leapt to the defence of gene-selectionism, while the fundamental question of what Darwinism can tell us about the human animal – for Darwin, remember, "the highest & most interesting problem for the naturalist" – was almost ignored. Maynard Smith did admit he had important reservations over Cronin's human interpretations: "As it happens, I agree with [Gould] that there is more to the evolution of human altruism than kin selection: once a species has acquired language as a second method of passing information between generations, new mechanisms of change become possible" (1993, p.43). Nevertheless this important point was again lost in the same tired ding-dong altercation between gene selection and multilevel selection where circling the wagons, and not furthering human self-understanding, appears to be the prime objective. As an example of events on the ground, Segerstrale writes that when critic of gene-selectionism Steven Rose ("Britain's Lewontin" – 2000, p.7) threatened in 1985 "to sue Dawkins for libel … there was quite a flurry of activity at the time to protect Dawkins" (pp.191–2). Bill Hamilton reportedly approached E.O. Wilson in order to get Segerstrale's PhD thesis for use in a possible legal defence, and Dawkins himself contacted Segerstrale for background information. And such political manoeuvring is a large part of the reason why Option 3, being Darwin's own interpretation of human evolution, has never been publicly debated.

And yet in one sense the shift from human sociobiology to evolutionary psychology – an at least nominal shift from saying that human differences are largely genetic to saying that human differences are largely cultural – is considerable. But credit for causing this shift sits exclusively with the multilevel-selectionists; precious little help was forthcoming from the leading gene-selectionists. The journalist Andrew Brown put it nicely in his book *The Darwin Wars*. "The development of evolutionary psychology from sociobiology can be understood in two ways. Looked at purely ideologically, it is a triumph for Gould and Lewontin, who have seen almost all their original objections incorporated into the project". But it came in a context of unremitting personal hostility, Brown continues, with Gould himself "particularly loathed" (1999, pp.147–8). As an example of what Gould was up against before his early death in May 2002 see the evolutionary psychologist Robert Wright's December 1999 piece "The Accidental Creationist: Why Stephen Jay Gould is Bad for Evolution". And this is even though some of Gould's criticisms of Wilson's original sociobiology "are now accepted even by its sympathisers", says Brown, interviewing Cronin, who reportedly commented that parts of *Sociobiology* "were not even testable" while others were "simply false, and, interestingly, bad Darwinian theory" (1999, p.148).

		Requires a change to the template of evolution?	Fails the parsimony test?	Invokes new evolutionary processes?
Option 1	Multilevel-selectionism / Group-selectionism	YES	YES	NO
Option 2	Sociobiology / Evolutionary psychology	YES	YES	YES
Option 3	Darwin's Wager	NO	NO	NO

So who is the "accidental Creationist" here? Gould or Wright himself? Because at least Gould was invoking a recognised, if rare and slow, biological mechanism. Group selection can exist, it is just that it is "usually too weak to produce noteworthy effects" as George Williams wrote. Gould and others were using group selection models to effectively resurrect Peter Kropotkin's thesis that uncalculated benevolence is widespread in nature, but at least they were conjuring with a known, if anaemic, scientific mechanism. Lord Kelvin criticised Darwinian theory, and while he may have been a devout Christian and inherently hostile to Darwinian gradualism he least used the accepted science of his day to bed his criticism, even if that accepted science would later be overturned with the discovery of radioactivity. In contrast, Darwin's former friend Sir John Herschel stepped outside the science of the day when he simply admitted he needed to see guided evolution, and an intelligence behind the direction of human evolution. And it is the sociobiologists and the evolutionary psychologists, and not Gould and notwithstanding his other faults, who step outside the science of their day. It is sociobiology and evolutionary psychology that invents new processes – such as indirect reciprocity, metamorphosed phenotypic expression, "*mal*adaptive" evolution, or Robert Trivers' "multiparty altruistic system in which altruistic acts are dispensed freely" – that we do not need, and indeed cannot use, in the explanation of all other life on Earth. Gould is the Lord Kelvin figure here, but Bob Trivers is the Sir John Herschel figure. If there is an accidental Creationist that has to be identified, it is Steven Pinker more than it ever was Stephen Jay Gould. It is evolutionary psychology and not multilevel-selectionism, Option 2 not Option 1, that invents completely new biological processes not needed to explain all other life on Earth.

> "My initial interest in Darwinian theory was roused by philosophers' criticisms – not because I thought that they were right but because I was convinced that they must be seriously wrong."
>
> – **Helena Cronin**, *The Ant and the Peacock* (p.xii)

But it is also hostility from outside biology that has created what Dennett in *Darwin's Dangerous Idea* called a "siege mentality" within orthodox gene-selectionism and that has led the leading theorists to eschew their "duty" (p.485) to expose the sins of their less orthodox disciples. There is little love lost between scientists and philosophers, with a number of the gene-selectionist biologists having been particularly hostile. In 1979 the late philosopher Mary Midgley wrote a paper for the journal *Philosophy* criticising, amongst other things, Dawkins' use of metaphor, a device he often uses to get a larger message across. The paper was quite extraordinarily unfriendly; *Philosophy* permitted Dawkins a reply, and his bitterness was manifest. "Such transparent spite ... so rude ... I deplore bad manners ... it is hard for me not to regard the gloves as off" (1981, p.556). Midgley, wrote Dawkins, raises the art of misunderstanding to dizzying heights, and had "so pathetically misunderstood" the mechanism of reciprocal altruism (p.571). But in his renunciation of such philosophical criticism, Dawkins was quick to defend sociobiology and "our field (it wasn't called sociobiology then)". Time did not heal these wounds and, according to the journalist Andrew Brown, in 1992 Dawkins was still so offended by Midgley's review of his work thirteen years before that he withdrew from a conference to which he had been invited "when he heard that Midgley would also be present. 'I wouldn't want to see her over breakfast,' he told the organiser" (1999, p.87).

John Brockman's *The Third Culture*, mentioned in the opening chapter, was a book with essays not only from biologists, but with contributions from giants within particle physics and astrophysics like Murray Gell-Mann, Roger Penrose and Alan Guth. The title for the book was a reference to C.P. Snow's famous identification of the two cultures of literary intellectuals versus scientists, and then Snow's later identification of a third culture that might bridge the lack of communication between the two. Brockman was adamant that his third culture was different from Snow's, though. "Literary intellectuals are not communicating with scientists. Scientists are communicating directly with the general public" (1995, p.18). The whole point of *The Third Culture* was to show, as the book proclaimed loudly on its cover, that "literature and philosophy have shifted into the background", that scientists represent "the intellectual culture of today", and that only scientists have anything interesting to say "on the important questions facing mankind". This sort of at least partly ignorant claim does not exactly go down well with philosophers, and to say that biologists and physicists generally dislike and denigrate philosophy is an understatement. In the *New York Review of Books* the geneticist Steve Jones once compared science to real sex while philosophy was, he said, just masturbation: "For most wearers of white coats, philosophy is to science as pornography is to sex: it is cheaper, easier, and some people seem, bafflingly, to prefer it" (1997, pp.13–14). In similar language the theoretical physicist Lawrence Krauss – whose writing Richard Dawkins bizarrely compares to *Origin Of Species* in its frame-changing importance – has more recently compared philosophers with gym teachers: "Philosophy is a field that, unfortunately, reminds me of that old Woody Allen joke, 'those that can't do, teach, and those that can't teach, teach gym'", in interview with Ross Andersen (2012).

"There has been a fair amount of sniping between these two disciplines over the past few years. Why the sudden, public antagonism between philosophy and physics?", Andersen asks Krauss. There is a "natural resentment" on the part of philosophers, Krauss believes, who "feel threatened, and they have every right to feel threatened, because science progresses and philosophy doesn't". Philosophy "hasn't progressed in two thousand years". Really? When it was philosophers, not scientists, who a couple of decades ago were able to give us probably the only objective moral fact that humankind can ever know? When it was scientists, not philosophers, who sold Darwin down the river? And when it is philosophers, not scientists, trying to keep Darwin's wager alive? Scientists are "really happy" when they get things wrong, says Krauss, whereas philosophers presumably don't admit to their mistakes. And when philosophers comment on Krauss's writing with anything but glowing praise they risk being referred to as "moronic" (Andersen, 2012). But while I have some sympathy with Krauss's general line of argument, and while Krauss himself has no time for scientists who defend the falsehood of free choice, we must certainly take issue with this idea that scientists, and the scientific community, are "really happy" to draw attention to their own mistakes, or willingly change their minds. Max Planck, a physicist so influential his name is given to a constant, a length, a unit of time, and a law, recounted in his biography that "a new scientific truth does not triumph by convincing its opponents and making them see the light, but rather because its opponents eventually die, and a new generation grows up that is familiar with it". Krauss himself is not swift to call attention to the misstatements of scientists from E.O. Wilson to Bob Trivers, and from Roger Penrose to Brian Greene, or to the damaging mysticism, obscurantism and even dishonesty of past scientific giants like Alan Turing, Wolfgang Pauli, and Niels Bohr.

"SHRINKING BREASTS", SOFT SCIENCE, AND P-VALUES

While some of the early names in the development of evolutionary psychology, such as John Tooby, Donald Symons and Jerome Barkow, were anthropologists – anthropology is a "soft", or social, science – many others, such as Leda Cosmides, Martin Daly and Margo Wilson, were psychologists by training, and psychology is also a soft or social science. Today evolutionary psychology is largely run out of psychology departments and psychology journals. The journal *Psychology Today* hosts one of the main evolutionary psychology websites; it has published blogs in the recent past on how much diversity we can handle, whether being shown baby photos increases the desire for marriage, that income inequality doesn't really make people unhappy, and The Shrinking Breast Fashion ("modern women are less focused on extreme sexual signals"). It may seem unfair that biologists see themselves as involved in the "hard" sciences, and so wish to minimise contact with soft sciences like psychology and anthropology, but this is also an important defence mechanism to try to maintain the rigour of the hard sciences. It is notoriously difficult to interpret human responses and behaviour. It is easy to be mistaken, to misformulate an experiment, to get carried away, or even introduce a multitude of experimenter and subject biases. And while bias, and even actual fraud, is possible, and does occur, in the hard sciences, biologists are very aware of the significant new dangers that come with studying the human animal. Plus the social sciences, and particularly large parts of psychology, have earned a reputation for not understanding statistical relevance, at least according to statisticians, and despite statistical competence supposedly being a crucial part of published psychology studies.

So, for example, a 2016 article by the Turing Fellow, theoretical physicist, and Oxford data scientist Taha Yasseri is entitled "P-values Are Widely Used in the Social Sciences, But Often Misunderstood: And That's a Problem". P-values, probability values, are a measure of statistical significance, with a p-value less than 0.05 (1 chance in 20) usually taken as the hurdle for significant results against a null (no correlation) hypothesis. But what is called "p-hacking" is a common worry in the social sciences, as getting a result of 0.05 is not difficult if data is improperly sorted. As Brian Resnick and Julia Belluz commented in *Vox*, stopping an experiment when a p-value of 0.05 is achieved is an example of p-hacking, and another is collecting data on a large number of outcomes but only reporting the outcomes that achieve statistical significance through chance alone. "A 2012 survey of 2,000 psychologists found p-hacking tactics were commonplace. Fifty percent admitted to only reporting studies that panned out (ignoring data that was inconclusive). Around 20 percent admitted to stopping data collection after they got the result they were hoping for. ... Many thought p-hacking was a way to find the real signal in all the noise" (Resnick & Belluz, 2018). *Vox*, which has regularly reported on p-hacking and data-dredging, noted that the "publish or perish" mindset in modern academia was a major driver. "One young scientist told us, 'I feel torn between asking questions that I know will lead to statistical significance and asking questions that matter'".

But the problems with this social science p-values mentality goes deeper. A p-value of less than 0.05 does *not* mean that there is only a five per cent (1 in 20) chance of the result being a false positive, nor that there is less than a five per cent probability the experimental result is due to chance. It only means there is less than a five per cent chance of getting this result in a situation where the null hypothesis is true, which is a crucial difference. In fact the statistician Valen Johnson, one of the best known names among the seventy-two statisticians and other data scientists who in September 2017 made a high-profile call for a higher threshold of statistical significance, has used more rigorous Bayesian analysis to show that at the p-value threshold of 0.05 there may be closer to a thirty per cent (1 in 3.3) chance of getting a false result: "these analyses suggest that the range 17–25% underestimates the actual proportion of marginally significant scientific findings that are false" (2013, p.19316). And David Colquhoun published a *Royal Society Open Science* review article in 2014 calculating an inaccuracy, or false discovery, rate above thirty per cent, while Yasseri's article above links to those who have found even higher rates.

So great are statisticians' concerns over p-values – some now refer to "p-trash", and "p-dolatry" – that in March 2016 the American Statistical Association released a statement on the statistical significance of p-values "intended to steer research into a 'post $p<0.05$ era'". Although a p-value of less than 0.05 does not mean that there is less than a five per cent probability the experimental result is due to chance, surveys show that most social scientists appear to mistakenly think it does mean that. Hence the ASA statement actually had to spell out to the social science community that "P-values do not measure the probability that the studied hypothesis is true, or the probability that the data were produced by random chance alone" (ASA, 2016). The ASA commented upon the value of additional, and more robust, measures, such as confidence intervals. Many of the hard sciences work to much higher statistical significance tests. In particle physics, for example, the 2012 discovery of the Higgs boson satisfied a test of five-sigma, or five standard deviations, equivalent to a null hypothesis p-value of not one chance in 3.3, not one in twenty, not the one in one hundred sometimes already used ($p<0.01$), not even the one in 200 ($p<0.005$) called for by Valen Johnson and colleagues, but one in over 3.3 million ($p<0.0000003$). In other words, *if* the Higgs does not exist, the data collected would have been expected to have been seen through background fluctuations in just one experiment in around three million. High-energy physics tests to five-sigma because a number of three-sigma events have later turned out to be nothing more than statistical anomalies, background noise. Incidentally, *New Scientist* may have inadvertently misguided its readers over the statistical meaning of the evidence behind the Higgs, so even without bias the best intentioned often fail to understand experimental relevance.

The observational and data risks within the social sciences have very much been highlighted recently, and psychology is currently going through what has been called a crisis of confidence, which in part led to the 2016 ASA statement. The Reproducibility Project started in 2011, led by the Center for Open Science but under Brian Nosek and colleagues at the University of Virginia – Nosek was one of the seventy-two authors on the July 2017 statistical significance call above – and was a collaboration of 270 contributing authors to "reproduce" the findings of around 100 published psychological studies, and reporting in August 2015. After the Reproducibility Project announced its results, the headline in the journal *Nature* was "Over Half of Psychology Studies Fail Reproducibility Test", before going on to say "in fact, two thirds" of what you read in the psychology literature "should probably be distrusted" (Baker, 2015).

Yet evolutionary psychology faces even more problems than other parts of psychology, given the largely untestable "Just So" stories of sociobiology and EP; pure speculation against unproven, and often unprovable, assumptions. Recall Helena Cronin's untestable hypothesis "but for some of our genes our modern environment is likely to metamorphose their phenotypic expression from that which natural selection originally smiled upon", Donald Symons' equivalent "there is a principled Darwinian argument for assuming that behavior in evolutionarily novel environments will often be *mal*adaptive", and Robert Wright's similar "the best guess about valor in wartime is that it is the product of mental organs that once served to maximize inclusive fitness and may no longer do so". And when you start with the hypothesis that major human behaviours evolved hundreds of thousands of years ago adapted to the way of life of Pleistocene hunter-gatherers it becomes a bit difficult to rigorously test against it without a time machine, and even assumptions are then just a matter of fancy. *P*-dolatry starts to look positively robust when untestability is your standard operating procedure.

Buried in an endnote to the second edition of *The Selfish Gene* Richard Dawkins fumes briefly at the criticism that "comes from doctrinaire sociobiologists jealously protective of the importance of genetic influence" in the human animal (1989, p.331). But that is the point; the genetic hypotheses that are regularly used to try to divide (albeit occasionally unite) human beings are not being openly challenged when they should be, and not only because evolutionary psychology is ultimately faith-based, and hypotheses often untestable. Notwithstanding the efforts of statisticians, and more robust auditing like the Reproducibility Project, "most scientists are content with taking a passive stance, from which they watch the show while they get on with their *own* research".

4

"ATLANTIS IS REALLY SICILY"

"The disagreement between Dan and myself is essentially this: it's like we're living in a world where most people believe in Atlantis. And they believe in the underwater kingdom, and they read Plato closely trying to figure out where it was. And I want to say, Atlantis doesn't exist, it didn't exist, people are confused about Atlantis. Dan wants to say that Atlantis is really Sicily."

– **Sam Harris**, "On arguing free will with Dan Dennett" (2012a)

But for the moment biological evolution must go back on hold. We will now come at Darwin's wager through a back door, by examining the free will debates. Remember from the introduction that what matters here is free will defined as freedom of choice, because then what we find lying at the heart of the debates is the issue of lack of opportunity and undeserved dumb luck. "Although others may define differently, this paper is concerned solely with the free will debate *as it relates to* freedom of choice, or the possibility that an individual could ever have done otherwise. ... Furthermore, this paper is defining determinism as the recognition that everything that happens is determined by that which preceded it" (Miles 2013, p.206). A deterministic universe is a universe where all current and future events – at least from the point of view of human action – are necessitated by past ones. It is the understanding that all events in the quasiclassical or non-quantum universe have a cause. Determinism is contrasted with indeterminism which recognises events with no cause, as arguably (because this is still much debated) in the quantum world. As the philosopher Paul Russell put it in *Freedom and Moral Sentiment*, what is called the dilemma of determinism goes as follows. "One horn of this dilemma is the argument that if an action was caused or necessitated, then it could not have been done freely, and hence the agent is not responsible for it. The other horn is the argument that if the action was not caused, then it is inexplicable and random, and thus it cannot be attributed to the agent, and hence, again, the agent cannot be responsible for it" (1995, p.14). As Russell goes on to note, the dilemma of determinism has stark implications because if our actions are caused, then we cannot be responsible for them, but if they are not caused, we cannot be responsible for them. "Whether we affirm or deny necessity and determinism, it is impossible to make any coherent sense of moral freedom and responsibility."

We are defining free will in relation to freedom of choice, or the possibility that a specific individual could ever have done otherwise. When you define free will this way the table below effectively summarises everything that has ever been written by academic philosophers, scientists and theologians in defence of the notion of free will. But the table also highlights that the dilemma of determinism raises a very obvious problem, and a problem that – unlike perhaps with the definitions of freedom and responsibility – we should not logically be able to dispute over. This is called *the problem of moral luck*. If there is no freedom of choice, no true ability to have done otherwise, then success or failure in life can only, everywhere and always, be the result of undeserved dumb luck; be that biological luck ("birth"), environmental luck ("upbringing"), or whatever combination of birth and upbringing. Some of us just happen to have been luckier than others in our biology and upbringing, through no credit to ourselves, and through no discredit to them. And failure to at the very least acknowledge this unalterable truth would mean that all we have is winner's justice, and the lucky setting the rules by which the unlucky must play, notwithstanding that they are the rules that *only* the lucky can obey, and that the unlucky *cannot help* but disobey.

In a later chapter we shall look at the implications – social, political and particularly economic – where a world reduces to nothing more than undeserved dumb luck, and even some of the motivations for why philosophers might, in a world where success or failure comes down to nothing more than undeserved dumb luck, wish to play down such knowledge. But, for now, and in this chapter, we shall only concentrate on the question of whether success or failure in life truly comes down to nothing more than undeserved dumb luck. And why is this so important to cover in this book? Because Darwin wagered that humankind is not born moral, that we must learn morality, yet it is logic related to the above that will back up Darwin's insight by demonstrating that the great majority of humans who have ever lived have not been moral, just or fair beings.

*

LIBERTARIANISM – FREE WILL AS ERROR

In free will theory metaphysical libertarianism is the belief that freedom of choice is actually possible.

	Can free choice and determinism co-exist?	Is determinism true (at the human level)?	Do success and failure reduce to undeserved dumb luck?
1. Libertarianism	No	No	No, but we have no proof of this
2. Compatibilism	No	Yes	No, as there are no less fortunate in life
3. Illusionism	No	Yes	Yes, but "maintaining human dignity depends on … degrading fellow people"

If it all comes down to biology and environment our behaviour would be said to be deterministic – would be an inevitable outcome – because biology and environment are themselves recognised as deterministic systems. Libertarian free will is the idea, the hope, that humans are *not* fully determined beings; that although we generally appear to exist within a deterministic universe we somehow manage to break free from this causal chain. For libertarians an individual is truly the ultimate – the originating – cause of his or her actions. The idea is that humans cannot, as above, be the product of only two things – biology and environment – but somehow must be the product of three things: biology, environment, and free choice which exists away from the dictates of biology and environment.

By the way, absolutely no apologies if this chapter seems at times a little technical, because remember the stakes we are playing for. As one leading free will apologist philosopher puts it, life is "a masquerade in which maintaining human dignity depends on … degrading fellow people" (Smilansky 2000, p.278). Through the myth of free will we degrade the least fortunate so that the more fortunate can maintain their supposed "human dignity". And the more cultures subscribe to the myth of free will, the more we will see that their economies are structured to let the poor get poorer, the wider the divide between the top and the bottom, the weaker the commitment to equal opportunity, the less social mobility they offer, and the more they allow the one per cent to control the rest of society. We steal away any real opportunity from the least fortunate, we mutilate people, we put others to death, largely because the myth of free will enables it and makes the more fortunate feel better about themselves. "Inflicting … rape" will even be seen to be part of the cost of the free will myth. So no, there will be no apologies for when this chapter has to get complicated.

The immediate problem for a libertarian view of human action is that it flies directly in the face of both our logical and scientific understandings, and for this reason has tended to be viewed with a profound scepticism by modern thinkers. Dan Dennett tells us that a 2009 *Philpapers* survey found that only around 14% of modern philosophers now believe that anyone has freedom of choice (Dennett, 2014). That survey, by the Australian philosophers David Bourget and David Chalmers, canvassed ninety-nine leading departments of philosophy and targeted almost 2,000 philosophers, and reported that while 13.7% of philosophers identify themselves as libertarian, only 7.7% are fully convinced of the possibility of free choice, while the other 6.0% "lean towards" belief in the possibility of free choice. The study also reported that 14.6% of philosophers subscribe to theism (10.6% fully accepting, 4.0% leaning towards), and Bourget and Chalmers (see 2014) ended up lumping these characteristics together as "anti-naturalism" in their findings. Neither determinism nor indeterminism can give us freedom of choice, and anti-naturalist philosophers have traditionally made little or no attempt to offer a coherent explanation for how ultimate origination could even be possible, or for how we might get to stand outside biology and environment at any moment.

A few libertarians have tried to found free choice on some form of quantum interaction, specifically some form of indeterminism, but that brings its own problems. The macroscopic universe we inhabit seems to obey deterministic laws because of a phenomenon known as decoherence, which effectively reinstates classical mechanics at the level of systems above the very, very small. This is an effect of universal entanglement that arises from the unavoidable interaction of quantum systems with their environment, and quantum indeterminacy would have no implications for human action because we inhabit the macroscopic universe. This is largely irrelevant, though, because *even if* quantum theory held implications for human action, quantum effects cannot give us the freedom of choice that libertarians need to rule out the problem of moral luck.

The hypothesised random chance of quantum theory has no connection whatsoever to the concept of ethical freedom: the freedom to *choose*, the freedom to *will*. Doing something because a subatomic particle may randomly move inside your skull offers no more freedom than doing something because genes or culture dictate it. The quantum event may be uncaused, but your resulting action would itself be caused by the quantum event. The action is therefore not uncaused, and it is most certainly not chosen or willed. Self-evidently we have no control over quantum indeterminism; it produces by definition truly random events that admit no causes, so cannot be identified with the will, or even with the person's desires or character. As the celebrated mathematician Norbert Wiener famously said, the chance of the quantum-theoretician is not the ethical freedom of the Augustinian.

The logic of the physical universe – indeed, any possible universe, deterministic or indeterministic – rules out free choice. Why? Because who a person happens to be from a moral point of view cannot possibly be under his or her own control. To be responsible for how they act they would have to be responsible for how they are, and to be responsible for how they are they would have had to have created themselves, and no one can be the *causa sui*, the ultimate cause of him- or herself, because in order to do so he or she would have to be in every sense his or her own author. But self-authorship is a nonsensical idea. As Nietzsche put it, "the *causa sui* is the best self-contradiction hitherto imagined, a kind of logical rape and unnaturalness. ... For the desire for 'freedom of will' ... is nothing less than the desire ... to pull oneself into existence out of the swamp of nothingness by one's own hair" (1886, pp.50–1).

Ultimately for libertarian free will you need an initial creator self, a "prime mover" self, which is impossible to get to because how would it have come into existence? Determinism cannot give man freedom of choice, because if we act as we do because we are the causal products of biology and environment we had no possibility of doing otherwise. Determinism cannot give man freedom of choice, but neither can indeterminism, because if the mind is – at least in part – undetermined, then some things "just happen" in it outside the laws of causation for which, by definition, nobody and nothing is responsible. To be freely choosing, an individual would have to be free from both deterministic effects and indeterministic effects; free from both A and not-A. To be freely choosing you cannot have A, but you cannot have not-A either: free choice requires something that cannot logically exist in this or any possible universe.

My friend the philosopher Richard Double (1990) has pointed out that few libertarians even purport to be able to provide evidence that people actually make free choices. While this is not an argument against the existence of free choice, Double has raised the moral ante by asking how much epistemic justification a reasonable libertarian should need before starting to claim that people make free choices, with all the attendant contempt, loathing, blame, violence, revenge, suffering and retribution this normally entails. "If the practices sanctioned by libertarianism are morally objectionable, the charge of lack of moral conscientiousness seems to apply to libertarian theory" (2002, p.227). Double has called this the "moral hardness" of libertarians, being their unwavering faith in the righteousness of their world view no matter the lack of any objective evidence and irrespective of the harm caused to others. As Double puts it, "fallibilism about one's views is a desirable quality in general, but it is morally obligatory when dogmatism has potentially harmful repercussions for persons" (p.231).

Kant called free choice an "antinomy", from the Greek *nomos* meaning law – and thus antinomy, meaning in contradiction of the universal law; in contradiction of the rules that run the universe. In other words a paradox, the seemingly impossible, although of course only a paradox for those who try to cling to belief in free choice, for those who try to cling to the impossible. Everything that exists in nature, in the empirical world, is bound by the laws of causal necessity, and yet we think of ourselves as free. And, in the more than 200 years since Kant was writing, libertarian theory has been no more successful at making the idea of free will at all meaningful. Peter van Inwagen is one of the leading modern libertarian philosophers but in his book *An Essay on Free Will* he bases his belief in libertarian free will on the premiss that we "know" we have moral responsibility for our actions. "To deny the free-will thesis is to deny the existence of moral responsibility, which would be absurd ... therefore, we should reject determinism", says van Inwagen (1983, p.223), which is just begging the question, not proving the assertion.

Such an assertion is the logical equivalent of suggesting that we "know" God exists so to reject belief in God's existence would be "absurd". Our "knowledge" of God's existence would become the proof of God's existence. It is empty circular reasoning where the conclusion is already built into the premiss.

Another example of the degree of faith necessary to hold to the standard libertarian picture is given by the libertarian philosopher John Searle, probably the best-known academic advancing claims for supposed "gaps" in human consciousness that might leave room for free will. There are different versions of this argument, and often they will invoke some distinction between what they call bottom–up, top–down, and even left–right consciousness and causality. Searle is generally held to be the leading exponent of this type of writing. And yet, in one paper, Searle sought over almost two dozen pages to prove free choice before admitting that ... er ... he couldn't prove it. "I have not tried to solve the problem of the freedom of will", Searle wrote, after nineteen pages of trying to solve the problem of the freedom of will. The flaw with each of his arguments, Searle admitted, is "to see how the consciousness of the system could give it a causal efficacy that is not deterministic" (2000, p.21). No guff, Chet.

Given the widely recognised illogic of the metaphysical libertarian position, it is interesting to note that probably the most commented-upon recent development within libertarianism has been the work of Robert Kane, who argues for a form of self-creation, but not in a way that allows for choice or the ability to have done otherwise. A degree of self-formation is possible for Kane, but it only exists on the edge of quantum indeterminism, when we are torn between two courses of action we struggle to resolve. Kane (2002, 2007) hypothesises a situation where we are in two minds as to whether we undertake a course of action. Either course is one that we could identify with (i.e. is within our personality profile) but instead of a deterministic resolution

– of biology and/or environment forcing our hand – it is an indeterministic event that ultimately forces our hand. Kane is not trying to argue for could-have-done-otherwise, but is still trying to offer us a self-formed character for our subsequent decisions.

Kane's influential model, though, is not giving us any form of decision that people are responsible for in the sense of having made a free choice. All Kane is giving us is a deterministic system with a little bit of arbitrary randomness thrown in on top. As many have noted, if what finishes the act is separated off from our existing determined character then what makes the final choice – what completes the act – isn't really "us" anyway. Kane's model gives us no basis to attribute real freedom of choice and blame, as Kane often seems to recognise. Whatever the actor gets to do here, the cards were either stacked against him or her or stacked for him or her, and the deck doesn't stop being stacked if occasionally indeterminism gives the actor a slightly luckier (or slightly less lucky) hand than he or she might otherwise have played. Luck continues to swallow everything. But Kane's work is valuable not only because it is more robust and thoughtful than almost all previous libertarian theory but also because Kane is driven to positing such constrained free will. And due to this recognition Kane has been forced to reflect upon the moral dangers to the belief in standard libertarian free will, and has been willing to draw attention to those downsides, actually distancing himself from such colleagues.

Libertarian free will – freedom of choice, freedom to have done otherwise – is, in all its guises, an inherently illogical and erroneous concept. And because libertarian free will is an inherently illogical concept, luck swallows everything in human life.

*

COMPATIBILISM – FREE WILL AS MISDIRECTION

Metaphysical libertarianism argues that success and failure, virtue and vice, do not reduce to undeserved dumb luck because a third factor frees us from birth and upbringing, yet libertarian freedom to choose is wholly irrational. But since libertarianism is incoherent, how can philosophy possibly sidestep the problem of success and failure coming down to nothing more than undeserved dumb luck? Philosophy really has two answers. The first, compatibilism, and subscribed to by over fifty-nine per cent of philosophers (Dennett, 2014), effectively tries to argue that all humans get the same opportunities in life. The second, illusionism, will argue that while such luck certainly exists the unlucky must be sacrificed for the lucky. Let us start first with the former answer.

	Can free choice and determinism co-exist?	Is determinism true (at the human level)?	Do success and failure reduce to undeserved dumb luck?
1. Libertarianism	No	No	No, but we have no proof of this
2. Compatibilism	No	Yes	No, as there are no less fortunate in life
3. Illusionism	No	Yes	Yes, but "maintaining human dignity depends on … degrading fellow people"

Philosophical compatibilism dates back to the early Stoics, and is supposed to be the idea that free will is compatible with a fully deterministic, choiceless, universe, and that free will can coexist with the understanding of humans as fully determined persons lacking choice or the ability to have done otherwise. As we already know, for humans you can fit quantum indeterminism into a deterministic picture of actions because the quantum event may be uncaused but our resulting actions would be caused by the quantum event. But how can free will be compatible with, at the human level, a fully determined universe? The answer is that, for free will compatibilists, free will is redefined as being something other than freedom of choice, something other than freedom to have done otherwise, something other than freedom to have willed otherwise.

So, for example, Susan Wolf has redefined free will to mean sanity, whereas others have redefined it as freedom from constraint, as unpredictability, or as acting in accordance with Reason (with a capital R). Possibly the most influential – and certainly the most widely read – compatibilist, the philosopher and evolutionist Dan Dennett, has defined free will as mechanical self-control (1984). Dennett has thus written that the Viking spacecraft had free will as soon as it got so far from Earth that NASA left it to float freely into the beyond (1995, pp.366–7). Free will, according to Dennett, is possessed by yeast, chrysanthemums and some plastic toys. Under Dennett's formulation were you to take your son's toy car, put in new batteries and then set it to race away, it would not have free will. However, as soon as you turn your back and walk away from it never to return, you have blessed it with free will. In other words, free will has deliberately been defined so generously that it becomes almost a meaningless term, a morally empty concept; a capacity we can share with both the Energizer Bunny and fungal infections. This is why Kant in 1788 called compatibilism a "wretched subterfuge ... petty word-jugglery" (pp. 189–90), why William James in 1884 called compatibilism "a quagmire of evasion" (p. 149).

But although Dennett argues we have "free will" and a form of moral responsibility on the basis of nothing more than the mechanical self-control we share with the Energizer Bunny, surely he, and all other compatibilists, must nevertheless acknowledge the problem of moral luck? Must nevertheless accept that luck swallows everything? Er, no ...

*

DAN DENNETT, AND WHY THE UNLUCKIEST 25% DO NOT MATTER

It is important to understand that the problem of moral luck is so overarching in philosophy, and so unanswerable, that almost all compatibilists seek refuge from it by becoming – at least temporarily – metaphysical libertarians. Dan Dennett for example writes erroneously that when we are making important decisions we undertake an internal monologue or debate but at some point we stop the deliberation "in the full knowledge that I could have considered further" (1978, p.297). Yet as my colleague Bruce Waller notes, the "glib suggestion" that everyone, no matter what their capacities and resources, could have carried out the same level of self-deliberation, internal monologue and self-criticism "is both shallow and false" (2011, p.163). Our internal monologue is the product of the determinism of biology and the determinism of upbringing, so no one could ever have considered further than they actually did, and it is wholly misleading for Dennett to suggest otherwise.

Dennett is not unusual in straddling the divide between compatibilism and libertarianism. Gary Watson is another leading compatibilist who will suddenly write: "The force of the example does not depend on a belief in the *inevitability* of the upshot. Nothing in the story supports such a belief. The thought is not 'It had to be!'" (2004, p.243). But Watson is simply wrong where he is here trying to suggest that the person was not the inevitable product of biology and environment. The thought is wholly the inevitability of the upshot. The thought is *only* "It had to be!". The influential philosopher Jonathan Jacobs is another ostensible naturalist who tries to sneak in self-creation, as when he writes that "the inability of the ethically disabled agent to overcome that condition is not exclusively a matter of bad constitutive luck" (2001, p.81). But, unless you are a (mistaken) libertarian, it is *exclusively* a matter of bad constitutive luck, as everything in life comes down to the lottery of biology and upbringing.

Bruce Waller (2011, pp.115–31) provides a whistle-blower list of other examples of supposed naturalists and philosophical compatibilists ultimately espousing a form of voodoo libertarianism and self-creation, including such major theorists as Charles Taylor ("self-resolution in a strong sense … is within limits always up to us"), George Sher (we can only not talk about desert "if the difference between them has made it impossible for N to achieve as much as M. However, differences … are rarely so pronounced as to have this effect"), and Nancy Murphy and Warren Brown ("there is no limit, other than lack of imagination, to the ability of the agent to transcend earlier conceptions"). But Dennett and Watson's influential writing takes us into darker places than just libertarians hiding out as compatibilists. For Dennett and Watson the importance of denying the problem of moral luck is so overriding that they are prepared to accept either that life doesn't have to be fair (Dennett) or that the unlucky are not our equals and should have lesser rights to consideration (Watson).

So Dennett has claimed that "there is elbow room for skill in between lucky success and unlucky failure" (1984, p.97). But it is utterly disingenuous for a self-proclaimed Darwinian like Dennett to state that there is elbow room for skill between good luck and poor luck, which is exactly equivalent to arguing that $1 + 1 = 3$. According to Dennett there seems to be something *left over* when one takes away the lottery of biology and environment. You can have good or bad fortune in internal causes (biology), and you can have good or bad fortune in external causes (environment) but, for Dennett, there is something beyond normal causation – some form of uncaused skill, or ghost elbow. Similarly, Dennett has written that: "Yes, luck plays a role but so does skill; we are not *just* lucky" (2014). It is insincere for a Darwinian to pretend that skill lies outside the realm of luck. Skill, too, comes down solely to the luck of biology (natural or innate skill) and/or the luck of environment (learned skill).

> "Is [the system] fair enough not to be worth worrying about? Of course. After all, luck averages out in the long run"
>
> – **Dan Dennett**, *Elbow Room:*
> *The Varieties of Free Will Worth Wanting* (p. 95)

As Bruce Waller puts it: "Dennett does not argue that our moral responsibility system is fair; rather, it is *fair enough* … Dennett seems comfortable with 'fair enough', and he can champion such a system and not blink" (2012). But how exactly does Dennett define *fair enough*? Dennett defines it as *the interests of the lucky*. "In fact, I will argue, it is seldom that we even *seem* to care whether or not a person could have done otherwise", Dennett has written (1984, p. 133), arguing that we must be blind to the lack of opportunities some receive. "Waller … dismisses as absurd my claim that it is fair because luck averages out in the long run. … The luck averaged out in ninety-nine percent of the population. … If anything like that were true, my claim would not be absurd at all" (Dennett, 2012). This comes from an example where Dennett tells us to consider a population of 300 million – i.e. around the population of the United States at the time – and to realise that ninety-nine per cent of the population get exactly the same opportunities. For Dennett the system is "fair enough" because it worked out for the vast majority. The fact it was manifestly unfair to the small minority, being just a paltry couple of million, doesn't even impact on Dennett's consideration. Dennett's argument here that we are still treating the unlucky one per cent fairly – the system is "fair enough" remember – is that the system is to the benefit of the other 99%. Because luck averaged out "in ninety-nine percent" of the population, those it didn't work for are *obliged*, according to Dennett, to regard it as a universal averaging-out.

The question is: *Are we treating X fairly?* Dennett's evidence that we are treating X fairly isn't provided by investigating our treatment of X, but instead by investigating treatment of a completely unconnected and extraneous Y. Fairness to the bottom one per cent, for Dennett, is not to be judged by reference to that one per cent; according to Dennett, the fact that it doesn't work to the benefit of that one per cent is unimportant and meaningless. That 99% have a good deal is enough to completely excuse the fact that one per cent get a raw deal. "Is it fair, he keeps asking, to hold both of them responsible? Life isn't fair" (Dennett, 2012). Luck *does* average out, says Dennett, because we can write off those it doesn't average out for. Hence we not only have the most extraordinary attempt to get around the problem of moral luck, but we also have the situation where this attempt makes life's unfortunates wholly responsible for their ill fortune, as all luck and misfortune has (for Dennett) disappeared from the system over the longer term. This is of course an absurdly unjust argument, but even for the supposedly lucky 99% his argument is extraordinary and wholly unrealistic. Please understand he uses this as an example of a modern state, in fact America. We are supposed to believe that America is "fair enough" as around 99% are, overall, lucky. Really? Only one per cent unlucky? When 44 million Americans at the time when Dennett wrote this had no health insurance, and another 38 million inadequate health insurance? That's twenty-five per cent of the population, not one per cent, who are not only unlucky at the moment, but unless things radically change in America are unlikely to get much luckier.

Dennett has written that although people are born with different opportunities and then get different breaks ("luck") throughout life, this means nothing over the longer term. Over the long term the differences we are born with, and are raised with, confer "such a relatively small initial advantage" as to "count for nothing" (1984, p.95). But Dennett's suggestion that the differences we are born with, such as physical beauty, skin colour or wealth, count for nothing, while "many of the differences that survive are, in any event, of negligible importance" (2003, p.274), is both intellectually false and morally obnoxious. First off, biological luck does not average out. Some genetic disorders can simultaneously engender benefits, such as sickle-cell anaemia which has survived in the human population because it protects against the worst effects of malaria, but poor biological luck is rarely averaged out by bringing simultaneous biological or environmental opportunities There are vastly more ways for a random genetic mutation to hurt the body than to help it. Secondly, environmental luck does not average out. As the Oxford philosopher Neil Levy writes in *Hard Luck: How Luck Undermines Free Will and Moral Responsibility*, Dennett is just plain wrong to argue that environmental luck averages out, because luck "tends to ramify" (2011, p.199) both the bad and the good. If you start off with a poor environmental hand, it will largely follow you and limit your future opportunity, particularly in countries like America and Britain. Levy tells us that sixty-three per cent of black Americans born into the bottom income quartile will die in that quartile.

The problem of moral luck is very real, and Dennett's attempts to deny this by claiming that unfairness to some does not matter, that we all start out with the same advantages in life, and that luck will almost always average out for those who didn't start out with such advantages are, to be blunt, shameful. Oh, and in *Elbow Room*, Dennett's argument for suggesting that people could have done otherwise, and "within limits we take care not to examine too closely", is that "we are rewarded for adopting this strategy" by the greater number going on to display responsible behaviour (1984, p.164). The benefit of doing what even Dennett seems to recognise as injustice to the minority is supposedly inculcating responsibility in the majority. Is this not an extraordinary assertion – that the majority learn responsibility through deception and the practice of injustice towards the minority?

*

GARY WATSON, AND THOSE WHO ARE NOT OUR EQUALS

So if Dennett fails to undermine the recognition that in human life luck swallows everything, isn't the game over for the compatibilists? Well, not if you now change the argument such that the unlucky no longer count within the fairness equation. Dennett tried to show the equation balanced by in effect keeping a thumb on one side of the scales. Gary Watson, a highly influential free will apologist at USC, the University of Southern California, will try something different; he will delete multiple people from one side of the moral luck equation until it does start to balance. Unlike as with Dennett, the unlucky are still acknowledged as being there, but we no longer have to count them. They are henceforth to be seen as having lesser rights to consideration, and thus are not part of the fair play equation.

Gary Watson is an "essentialist", as this philosophical school is called, and essentialists believe that they can bypass the problem of moral luck by giving us an argument based on *essential human differences*. Experiments in social psychology such as the famous work of Stanley Milgram have always raised challenging questions about the nature of good and evil, and of the human predisposition to both good and evil depending on situation. Abraham Lincoln, the emancipator of millions and that great critic of the conceit of free will, once said that Northerners couldn't feel too morally superior to Southern slave holders because "if we were situated as they are, we should act and feel as they do; and if they were situated as we are, they should act and feel as we do; and we never ought to lose sight of this fact in discussing the subject" (Guelzo 2009, p.39). Yet many are deeply uncomfortable with such considerations, almost taking as a personal slight the thought that they might have been raised to be different people, perhaps even racists and slave owners. Gary Watson, for example, has admitted to "an ontological shudder" and even a (to him) "troubling … sense of equality with the other", to the troubling thought that "I too am a potential sinner" (2004, p.245), when he ruminates upon, but quickly rejects, the possibility that he might have been raised to be a quite different, and quite nasty, person. But even Lincoln, Honest Abe or the Great Emancipator, a man known for his humility yet incongruously memorialised in Washington as 28 feet of white marble, was still a product of his time and his place. Lincoln possessed no essential virtue, no essentialist human difference. Because Lincoln may have freed the slaves, yet he was still a nineteenth-century Northern racist, and white supremacist, at heart, as were almost all American whites of the period. In September 1858, just a few years ahead of his Emancipation Proclamation, he said the following: "Ladies and gentlemen … I am not, nor ever have been in favor of bringing about in any way the social and political equality of the white and black races. … While they do remain together there must be a position of superior and inferior. … I say upon this occasion I do not perceive that because the white man is to have the superior position the negro should be denied everything. I do not understand that because I do not want a negro woman for a slave I must necessarily want her for a wife" (Lincoln, 1858). And while his views did ameliorate to a small degree before he died, and over the single political issue of – very limited – black male suffrage, he never withdrew his comments that black people should not be allowed by law to intermarry with whites, or serve on juries, or hold office.

Yet notwithstanding the above, essentialists are theorists who want to argue, who want to believe, that there is something essential in them that means that even with the most terrible of upbringings they would still have turned out virtuous, or at the very least lacking in vices and what Watson likes to call "sin". Essentialists, in other words, like to suggest that they, and indeed most of the American upper middle class, somehow stand *outside* any real lottery of biology and environment and that, at least to an extent, they were always destined to win in life. Discussing the case of one American serial killer – who was tortured by his sadistic and wholly unpredictable father (who believed the boy was not his natural son), hated by his mother because she blamed her son for the beatings she received at her husband's hands, and bullied by merciless classmates, before being incarcerated in an American prison for children where he was repeatedly raped from the age of fourteen – Gary Watson tells us that had *he* ever been subjected to such hate, torture, indifference, injustice, and rape as a vulnerable child, he might very well *not* have become a scarred, angry or violent person. "There is room for the thought that there is something 'in me' by virtue of which I would not have become a vicious person in [these] circumstances. And if that factor were among my essential properties, so to speak, then that difference ... would not be a matter of moral luck on my part" (2004, p.248).

Watson is arguing that he would never have behaved badly in either a good or bad environment (he was in effect *fated* to be a good, or at least non-sinful, person), while others are effectively *doomed* to be a bad person, at least in a bad environment. In Watson's view, or at least Watson's essentialist view, the world is *clearly and permanently divided* into the non-sinning (who owe no gratitude for their fine upbringings but simply possess better, non-toxic, biologies) and the sinful and violent who – no matter what environment we give them – will always be marked out for suspicion because they are carrying those worse, toxic, biologies. But although he has divided humankind into two forms, will Watson actually go so far as to deny to one form the consideration and rights he claims for the other form? Yes, he will. Recall Watson telling us that he has a sudden "sense of equality" with "the other", a sense of equality that disappears once we split humanity into two forms; a sense of equality that disappears as soon as he can convince himself that he could never have been like that. Watson then adds to this, and tells us that although sympathy, along with outrage, is the appropriate emotional and moral response to "the other" – which justice demands that we *simultaneously* view with sympathy and outrage – he has found a reason to deny the other the sympathy that would otherwise be his moral due. The other "violates the criteria" (p.244) for equal consideration. There is no longer that "troubling ... sense of equality with the other". The other is not owed that sense of equality. The other in effect has lesser rights to respect and sympathy, and thus to legal and moral consideration. Skin colour and nose shape do not drive this ghettoisation, but biology still does.

In fact Watson goes even further, and bizarrely suggests that benign biology, and by implication malign biology, is somehow deserved – "but a matter of who we essentially were ... [and] this difference still might explain what is to my credit" (2004, p.248). Essentialism comes down to pure biology for Watson, but if you can find credit in the biology you are born with, the corollary can only be that others should take the blame for the biology they were born with. The whole point of essentialism is to deny moral luck, and as Watson is trying to find an argument that good biology is not just down to luck and must be somehow deserved, the corollary must be that bad biology is not just luck either but is also somehow deserved. For Watson and philosophical essentialism life does not come down to moral luck; not because there is no lottery of biology and environment, but because humans are divided into two biological forms, as distinct as Morlocks and Eloi, and the luckier form need sense no fellow-feeling (no "troubling ... sense of equality") with the unlucky form.

As he is discussing biology Watson, a non-biologist, will try to ground his views in evolutionary psychology, but evolutionary psychology can actually give Watson little comfort. Even putting the telling example of Lincoln to one side, most if not all evolutionary psychologists are descended from ancestors who behaved in extraordinarily brutal and unjust ways, which immediately begins to unravel the essentialist world view. Watson is a fan of the Harvard evolutionary psychologist Steven Pinker, who likes to talk about a universal human nature. But exactly what is this nature supposed to be? Pinker is himself descended from ancestors whose "atrocities had 'lit up hell-fires in Christendom'", according to Charles Darwin (Desmond & Moore 1991, p.377). So the question must then arise: is the socially liberal, though economically conservative, Steven Pinker displaying that "real" human nature he likes to talk about while it was his ancestors who were the culturally twisted freaks, or were his ancestors displaying that "real" human nature while Steven P. is the culturally distorted atypical one? Pinker supports gay rights, but he is descended from people who screamed their hatred as they stoned homosexuals to death. If you were to judge over human time frames and take evolutionary psychology at its word it would be Pinker's vile and thuggish ancestors who were displaying our "true" biological human nature, because atrocities and prejudice have a much longer pedigree within both oral and written history than does our opposition to violence and discrimination. We are all descended from ancestors whose barbarities lit up hell-fires in Christendom if you go back far enough and, *pace* Watson, there is nothing in orthodox biology to suggest we carry a genetic code dissimilar to those ancestors. There is nothing in orthodox biology to suggest "that there is something 'in [us]' by virtue of which [we] would not have become" like them under the right circumstances. Watson's essentialism – and evolutionary psychology's benign universal human nature – is pure pseudo-science.

And often you do not even have to look back particularly far to get to our thuggish ancestors. It was only a handful of years ago that the UK Treasury finally paid off a giant loan it had taken out in 1833 to compensate British slave owners for the emancipation of their "property". Parliament had previously regarded black slavery as lawful and just, and while 800,000 slaves received not a penny, slave owners – who had been party to a global system of terror, kidnapping, dehumanisation, torture, mutilation, rape and murder – were fully compensated for their economic distress. The father of William Gladstone, William being four times prime minister and one of the greatest names in the history of British political and social reform, received the equivalent of tens of millions from the state. In the three year period to 1820 John Gladstone had worked to death fifty-three men, women and children, a thirteen per cent mortality rate, at just one of his plantations in former British Guiana. Billions were to be paid out to the 45,000-odd claimants, and a relative of more recent Prime Minister David Cameron received the equivalent of £3 million. But it wasn't just the tens of thousands of families who received reparations who were party to slavery; until at least the mid nineteenth century the British, American, Dutch, Spanish and Portuguese economies had to a large extent been built on this system of global terror and mutilation backing monopolies in commodities like sugar.

It is somewhat bizarre to hear "innate goodness" essentialist views being voiced by a white professor of philosophy living and working under the protection of a country, and indeed a federated state, that was built on the extermination of indigenous non-white people, the enslavement and dehumanisation of trafficked black people, and the wholesale theft from Mexican people. We like to think Watson's California is one of the more enlightened US states, but it actually has a history as savage as any. California was stolen as part of President James K. Polk's vicious land-grabbing war of aggression with Mexico between 1846 and 1848. Ulysses S. Grant served with distinction in that war, and would himself become US president, but Grant later notoriously said that, "I do not think there was ever a more wicked war than that waged by the United States on Mexico". Polk was a racist and a slave holder, and the land grab was part of the American belief in "manifest destiny"; the conceit that only the white Anglo-Saxon Protestants of the United States should control land across the American continent. In fact the war, or rather invasion, would give us the term "Latin America", to distinguish from "Anglo-America", as although the US had initially been treated as another republic resisting brutal empires, after the invasion the US was seen as just another barbarous land-grabbing empire. And after the US took California, there began a systematic extermination of Native Americans. From 1850 the state of California targeted indigenous Americans in what historians admit was a deliberate policy of genocide. Almost ninety-nine per cent of the Comanche who had been living in the decades before the Mexican–American War were dead by 1875.

White upper-middle-class educated Americans have always had a dangerous fondness for drawing biological distinctions between human beings, with them of course at the top and others at the bottom, and white America embraced eugenics and forced sterilisation as enthusiastically as any group in the early twentieth century. It is always informative to be lectured on the innate goodness of upper-middle-class Americans, and the innate wickedness of other Americans, by white philosophers. Watson's own USC, for example, was established just as California was completing its genocide of Native Americans. USC was able to set up its geographic footprint in what was now deemed to be *terra nullius*; after all, how much land did Native Americans really need when almost ninety-nine per cent of them had been exterminated? In *The Barbarous Years*, Bernard Bailyn, the nonagenarian double Pulitzer Prize-winning Harvard historian, argues that the horrors of American slavery were a by-product of the physical and intellectual "savagery" (Bailyn's term) of the white Christian European-descended settlers and their intolerant apocalyptic world view. Which may help to explain the homophobia, anti-Semitism, misogyny and casual racism of the vast majority of white American males until at least the 1950s. Even in California. Especially in California.

Watson's conceit that there may be some "essential" and unchangeable biological goodness in him, yet not in many other humans, is punctured as soon as one remembers that even evolutionary psychology would have to put a tendency towards slavery and segregation at the heart of human nature. But there is another reason why essentialism is both morally and intellectually vacuous, and that is its apparent attitude towards the poor. Essentialism is a form of blanket free will apologism, but the conceit of free will is used as much against the poor as it is against offenders. By refusing to acknowledge that the poor are poor through nothing more than undeserved dumb luck, while the rich are rich through nothing more than undeserved dumb luck, essentialism seems to be extending to the realm of poverty its belief that "that difference ... would not be a matter of moral luck on my part". One can only refuse to talk about the dumb luck that separates the rich and the poor if one believes that it is not dumb luck that separates the rich and the poor, but rather "a matter of who we essentially were". There all too often seems to be an absence of any "troubling ... sense of equality with the other" when it comes to poverty as well.

*

OTHER COMPATIBILISMS: REACTIVE-ATTITUDINISM AND SEMI-COMPATIBILISM

There are other lesser "flavours" of compatibilism that attempt to circumvent the problem of moral luck, though mainly by avoiding addressing the issue completely. For reactive-attitudinists our practices are expressions of our underlying moral attitudes. While in many ways an outgrowth from earlier forms of compatibilism, the late Peter F. Strawson is generally seen as having originated the tradition of reactive-attitudinism in the 1960s. (The free will apologist P.F. Strawson should not be confused with his son the anti-free will philosopher Galen Strawson mentioned previously.) As Peter Strawson put it in his 1962 classic *Freedom and Resentment*, our current practices express our natural human reactions, including the "reactive attitudes", and there is no deeper need to justify concepts such as contempt and retribution through recourse to ideas like self-origination, could-have-done-otherwise, free choice, or indeed a need to solve the hard problem of moral luck. To attempt to suppress the natural reactions – through (for example) dwelling on the fact that people cannot choose to do otherwise – is to undermine normal human relations. Thus the reactive attitudes of praise and blame are the only justification needed for praise and blame: they are their own justification. Contempt, revenge and the infliction of suffering are morally justified by the need for contempt, revenge and the desire to inflict suffering. While not firmly ruling out the possibility of free choice, irrespective of the truth of free will, Strawson said, we can feel confident that people should and will be prepared to continue to "acquiesce in that infliction of suffering" on others (reprinted as 2008, p.34/77).

In *Freedom and Resentment* Strawson went on to introduce the idea of different "types" against which to assess the appropriateness of the reactive attitudes. The point here was to describe and justify what philosophers term exempting conditions. But as Pereboom (2001) has shown, both in relation to attitudinism and more widely, there is no coherent moral or intellectual rationale to exempt some but not others. Strawson had noted that the agent who was "peculiarly unfortunate in his formative circumstances" (2008, p.25/66) is set apart and not an appropriate object of the normal reactive attitudes, being one who "tends to promote, at least in the civilized, [sympathetic] objective attitudes". Yet, every time and always, success and failure in life come down to nothing more than undeserved dumb luck, and Pereboom makes the point that it is a feature of our system of morality that when there is no relevant moral difference between two agents you cannot hold one responsible if you are excusing another (2001, p.99). Such "peculiarly unfortunate" circumstances self-evidently apply across the board with offenders (and, likewise, the undeserving poor), as otherwise they would not be offenders (or poor) in the first place. Strawson's thesis is all about the justification for resentment when one person is injured by the action of another – people whom he labels "offended parties" (2008, p.21/62). But in a world without origination there is a deep ontological problem with simplistically dividing a world, a world where everything comes down to biological and environmental good and bad luck, into the offenders and the offended-against. As such, attitudinism wholly fails to address, and avoid, the problem of moral luck.

And semi-compatibilism was developed by John Martin Fischer and Mark Ravizza as another breakaway movement from compatibilism. Bothered by the quickly expanding potential problems of trying to argue for the existence of free will (however defined) in a universe deterministic at the human level, and by the accusations of misdirection and word-jugglery, Fischer and Ravizza (e.g. 1998) formulated their argument that while free will may or may not be compatible with determinism (or indeterminism for that matter), moral responsibility and blame certainly still were. Semi-compatibilism – at first as advanced by Fischer and Ravizza, but for the last decade largely as advanced by John Fischer alone after Ravizza was ordained into the Church as the Jesuit Father Ravizza – holds that moral responsibility and blame do not require self-origination or alternate possibilities. Moral responsibility requires only that a person is moderately responsive to reason.

But we are here interested in the problem of moral luck, not moral responsibility as such, and semi-compatibilism makes no attempt to address the problems of fair play and moral luck. As well as accusations of subjective bias and discrimination (see Miles 2015), semi-compatibilism leaves itself open to the charge that the system is winner's justice; the lucky setting the rules by which the unlucky must play, notwithstanding that they are the rules that only the lucky can obey, and that the unlucky cannot help but disobey. Peter Strawson sought to divide the world into types to try to allow himself protection (though still subjective protection) of certain at-risk groups; Fischer has abandoned even this level of protection. For Fischer, and originally Ravizza, life is divided into the lucky winners and the unlucky losers, and the winners not only have no duty to help the losers, they have a right to make the unlucky losers suffer *for being* unlucky losers. Fischer tells us he "is not troubled by" issues of moral luck, winners' justice, and the lack of the ability to have done otherwise. He asks, "why be disturbed by" such concerns? (2007, pp.69–70). After all, says semi-compatibilism, there are no "less fortunate" once one prevents oneself being disturbed by – "why be disturbed by?" – questions of luck, lack of opportunity, and winners' justice.

*

ILLUSIONISM – FREE WILL AS SACRIFICING THE LESS FORTUNATE

Though compatibilism and libertarianism can be shown to have pedigrees back as far as the ancient Greeks, free will illusionism as a recognised tradition has a relatively recent history. There have been earlier instances of the Christian Church expressing a desire to keep the truth on free will from the public. The great sixteenth-century Catholic theologian Erasmus wrote that if there should prove to be no free will then only an educated elite should be allowed to possess such dangerous knowledge. While this knowledge "might be treated in discourses among the educated", the lay folk were too "weak", too "ignorant", and too "wicked" to handle such an understanding (1524, pp.11–12). Notwithstanding such instances, open deception on the issue of free will only really entered intellectual thought a couple of decades ago in the tradition best represented by the work of the philosopher Saul Smilansky. According to Smilansky, you the public are "fragile plants" who need to be "defended from the chill of the ultimate perspective in the hothouse of illusion" (2011, p.436).

Smilansky has himself admitted to concerns about the deception underlying all illusionist defences of free will, but he nonetheless thinks he can find both ethical and democratic grounds (though not, please note, arguments based in fairness or justice for the individual) for such deception. Free will illusionism assumes

	Can free choice and determinism co-exist?	Is determinism true (at the human level)?	Do success and failure reduce to undeserved dumb luck?
1. Libertarianism	No	No	No, but we have no proof of this
2. Compatibilism	No	Yes	No, as there are no less fortunate in life
3. Illusionism	No	Yes	Yes, but "maintaining human dignity depends on … degrading fellow people"

the illusion of free will, and building social, economic, and legal systems upon such illusion is a necessary step, and irrespective of the unfairness and injustice this creates for the victims of such a fraud. Unlike the compatibilism of Dennett and Watson there is no attempt to argue that the problem of moral luck has been solved, and from Smilansky we get instead a justification of the otherwise unanswerable problem of moral luck. For Smilansky because, he says, admitting that free will does not exist would undermine the very possibility of settled existence, we must be willing to pay any price not to let that happen. Even at the cost of sanctioning deeply unjust practices. "In practice we commit horrendous injustice on a daily basis, and must do so. … What could be more absurd than the moral necessity of belief in the justness of deeply unjust practices, practices that ought largely to continue and flourish?" (2000, pp. 256, 279).

For Smilansky, the necessity of the free will fraud means there can never be fairness for the less fortunate. Fairness, and justice, can only ever be defined in terms of groups and the wider society, and only ever in terms of stability. Rather than arguing alongside Dennett, Watson and Fischer that it can ever be just to individuals to suppress the knowledge that luck swallows everything in human life, Smilansky acknowledges the unfairness they try to bury or refuse to talk about, but claims a larger exoneration. There is no room for a truly just world here, because under this view the weak and unlucky must of necessity be sacrificed to a stable society, no matter how disgusting ("astounding and grotesque" – p.278) this would objectively appear to be. For Smilansky profound injustice creates the stability that then excuses it. If human communal living *requires* the myth of free will then Smilansky wants to argue that this *excuses* the problem of moral luck and any injustice from the community that is directed towards the individual. Our cultures have no right to claim a foundation on truth and individual fair play, writes Smilansky, and yet we cannot admit this publicly for fear of undermining the free will illusion that keeps society together. According to Smilansky, Darwin's wager is not only correct to say we're not born moral, but Darwin underplayed his hand, because neither biology nor culture can make us moral, as morality and justice are conceited fantasies only there to allow us to be able to look ourselves in the mirror.

Smilansky has defended illusionism in a number of places, but in his 300-page *Free Will and Illusion* he nowhere mentions that the victims of the illusion might include more than just offenders. Yet once you admit that the conceit of free will is being actively used to the detriment of one minority group there is a real problem with failing to research and acknowledge that the myth of free will may be being used against a wider pool of the unlucky, for example the "undeserving" poor. Smilansky has developed a theory of illusion that by its own admission both recognises and justifies scapegoating, yet without having considered the wider effects of that illusion, and the full extent of the scapegoating. One overarching problem here comes from the fact that Smilansky's utilitarianism is based on supposed calculation, the greatest happiness of the greatest number, but how can Smilansky – or Dennett, or Watson – even begin to correctly calculate the balance if one is not adequately summing on both sides of the equation (or is, like Dennett, keeping a thumb on one side of the scales)?

Smilansky has suggested that free will is the only fraud that should be perpetrated on the American public, in part because "the threat of political manipulation and the like is less acute here" (2000, p.271). Really? Smilansky even suggests that he can give us what is independently "a reasonably just social order" and "a decent socio-political order" (pp.258, 268). But Smilansky's "reasonably just" is identical to Dennett's "fair enough", or what Dennett elsewhere gives as his indifferent "Is it fair ...? Life isn't fair" maxim. Fairness for the majority can be bought at the cost of unfairness to and discrimination towards the minority, and is anyway to be judged only by the lucky.

*

Freedom of choice is a wholly illogical concept in this or any possible universe, and as soon as we reject what Darwin called the "general delusion" (Barrett *et al.*, 1987, p.608) of free choice, we come up against something that we should not, logically and rationally, be able to debate or deny: the overarching "problem of moral luck". That success or failure in human life comes down to nothing more than undeserved dumb luck. That some of us just happen to have been *luckier* than others in our biology and upbringing, through no credit to ourselves, and through no discredit to them. And a failure to at least acknowledge this stark fact makes morality, fair play and justice simply impossible, because it leaves us with the lucky setting the rules by which the unlucky must play, notwithstanding that they are the rules that only the lucky can succeed at, and that the unlucky cannot help but fail at. So for most of human history morality, fair play and justice have been the exception, not the rule. As Darwin realised, we are not born the decent animal, although maybe some of us can learn to be the decent animal.

5

DNA NEITHER KNOWS NOR CARES

"The universe we observe has precisely the properties we should expect if there is, at bottom, no design, no purpose, no evil and no good, nothing but blind, pitiless indifference. ... DNA neither knows nor cares. DNA just is."

– **Richard Dawkins**, *River Out of Eden* (1995, p.133)

In his book *Plan & Purpose in Nature*, George Williams notes that it was the anthropologist Sarah Blaffer Hrdy who was the pioneer in bringing the prevalence of monkey infanticide to the attention of both biologists and the general public. Hrdy found infanticide to be the "single greatest source" of the up to eighty-three per cent infant mortality rate amongst the langur monkeys she studied at Abu in India, and her 1977 article, "Infanticide as a Primate Reproductive Strategy", was greeted says Williams "with outraged disbelief by many readers who refused to believe that adult males' attacks on infants could be adaptive and normal" (1996, p.218).

Hrdy's groundbreaking paper on monkey infanticide argued that infanticide by males could no longer be dismissed as abnormal. Her own observations on langur monkeys allied to the work of others "led me to reject my initial crowding hypothesis in favor of the theory that infanticide is adaptive behavior, extremely advantageous for the males who succeed at it" (1977, p.43). Infanticide was the single dominating source of the very high infant mortality rate, but equally shocking to her were the instances of mothers abandoning their butchered infants soon after or even before death. In the paper Hrdy considered whether, as some had suggested, this was caused by a mother's fear, but rejected that answer in favour of the more hard-nosed gene-selectionist understanding around since the late 1960s: "It is far more likely, however, that desertion reflects a practical evaluation of what *this* infant's chances are, weighed against the probability that her next infant will survive" (1977a, p.286).

While cannibalism subsequent to infanticide is still rare in primates, ape researcher Mariko Hiraiwa-Hasegawa notes that the frequency of cannibalism in chimpanzees is now known to be "exceptionally high" (1992, p.329), and that a female chimpanzee and her adolescent daughter initiated three separate acts of cannibalism as witnessed by Jane Goodall and colleagues in Gombe National Park between 1975 and 1976. As Hrdy put it back in 1977: "we are discovering that the gentle souls we claim as our near relatives in the animal world are by and large an extraordinarily murderous lot" (p.46).

Sarah Hrdy's paper also cited others' recent findings, from Dian Fossey's observations of infanticide in African gorillas to David Bygott's graphic recounting of cannibalism in Tanzanian chimps that we saw earlier. "This female and her infant were immediately and intensely attacked by the males. For a few moments, the screaming mass of chimps disappeared from Bygott's view" (p.47). Hrdy recorded that when Bygott managed to relocate them, the strange female had disappeared, before one male reappeared holding the struggling infant. In contrast with normal chimp predation, this assaulted and butchered infant, and cannibalised corpse, was nibbled by several males but never actually consumed, Hrdy wrote.

Bygott's paper in *Nature* in 1972 was one of the very first to catalogue chimpanzee cannibalism, and it detailed also the levels of extreme violence against females, and how even low-ranking group members indulged in such behaviour. "Without apparent warning", the older of the two females was viciously "attacked by the five adult males in my group" (1972, p.410). Times have changed in biology, partly due to better field research, but also through a fuller appreciation of the sorts of behaviour selection at the level of the gene can be expected to code for. DNA neither knows nor cares. Only a decade after Bygott was writing, the geneticist Steve Jones would report in *Nature* that cannibalism had by then been recorded in more than 1,300 species of animal and was often the primary cause of mortality: "there has grown up in biology the comforting supposition that nature is not really red in tooth and claw" (1982, p.202). As George Williams concluded in his own review with James Paradis, "simple cannibalism is the commonest form of killing, and Polis's 1981 review indicates that it can be expected in all animals except strict vegetarians" (1989, p.202).

"July 24, 1990: ... *Ntologi* had in his hand the 5-month-old infant of *Betty*, a primiparous immigrant. The infant was still alive. *Ntologi* began to bite on the fingers of its right hand. He struck the infant against a tree trunk, and also dragged it on the ground as he displayed. As a result the infant was finally killed. After a while, *Musa* began to feed on the fingers of the left hand, and *Bakali* and *Lukaja* fed on the toes. *Musa* pulled at the legs, while *Ntologi* pulled the upper part of the body, and consequently the body was split apart. ... In total, ten adult females and eight adult males came to eat."

– **Hamai** *et al.*, "New records of within-group infanticide and cannibalism in wild chimpanzees", *Primates* (1992, p.153)

"The story of the forest or coral reef is a tale of relentless arms races, misery, and slaughter", writes Williams (1996, p.214), and he has noted that other wild animal populations are many *thousands* of times more likely to kill than are humans from even the most murderous of American cities. Stephen Jay Gould had the same point to make in his essay "Ten Thousand Acts of Kindness". Ethologists, Gould noted, describe organisms as peaceful if tens of hours go past with only one or two aggressive encounters. Consider the many millions of hours we can log for most people on most days with nothing more than a raised middle finger every once in a while, he wrote. "*Homo sapiens* is a remarkably genial species" (reprinted in 1993, p.281).

"Mountains of data on parasitism and predation (including cannibalism) in nature could be amassed to document the enormity of the pain and mayhem that arise from adaptations produced by natural selection", says Williams (1996, p.216). In his academic work Williams has been more detailed, and in one paper he devoted over seven pages simply to documenting the data already collected by field researchers. "Besides adultery and rape, just about every other kind of sexual behavior that has been regarded as sinful can be found abundantly in nature. Brother–sister matings are the rule in many species (Hamilton 1967)" (1988, p.395). Gone is the bright optimism of Darwin's day where some could still argue that nature might teach moral lessons to man. "With what other than condemnation is a person with any moral sense supposed to respond to a system in which the ultimate purpose in life is to be better than your neighbor at getting genes into future generations, … in which that message is always 'exploit your environment, including your friends and relatives, so as to maximize our (genes') success', in which the closest thing to a golden rule is 'don't cheat, unless it is likely to provide a net benefit'?" (1996, pp.213–4).

Williams notes the differential infanticide strategies nature has developed in ground squirrels. "A male may raid a nest to kill and eat one of the young. A female may raid the nest of a competitor and kill all the young (but not eat them)" (Paradis & Williams 1989, p.202). While it is always more difficult for a male to keep track of which offspring he has fathered, even usually in species where adults pair for life, it is much simpler for the female to identify the threat posed to the hegemony of her genes and do something about it. And rape was a strategy that was widely expected by selfish gene theorists even before the observations began flooding in. In one of the earliest detailed papers on avian rape, Pierre Mineau and Fred Cooke noted in 1979 that even the briefest absences by her mate could make the female snow goose vulnerable to rape by neighbouring males. Rape makes "sense" in an animal kingdom when the only thing that drives life's algorithm is the need to get your sperm to fertilise as many eggs as possible. Nature has made males cautious about leaving their mates unguarded for long, because in addition to rape he runs the risk that she will seek a finer gene pool than is offered by his seed. Two can play the game of enhancing gene survival.

Such behaviours are not *by-products* of naturally selected behaviour, they are the *dynamics* of natural selection. An animal that is busy protecting its mate from rape this season will be busy raping others' mates next season. As Mineau and Cooke noted of their snow geese, personal status, familiarity and coupling matter little in the game of gene preservation. This is the universal genetic logic of natural selection where only opportunity matters. "The rapist also was usually a known territory holder (84 percent), commonly a neighbour. Rapists seem to capitalize on attendant male absenteeism. ... An absent male is himself usually (73 percent) raping another female or witnessing another rape. Indeed, 'gang rapes' usually occur when spectators at a rape attempt use the disturbance to join in the melee. Up to 80 spectators have been seen at a rape attempt" (1979, pp.282–3). As Williams adds, "an unguarded female mallard may be attacked so persistently by gangs of males that she drowns" (1988, p.394).

And domestication, like civilisation, is a thin veneer. Even untold generations of intense artificial selection in the descendants of the wolf have been barely able to mask the amorality/ immorality of the natural world. What has been termed dogs' hypersociability, or exaggerated gregariousness, has been linked to molecular mechanisms for "the extension of juvenile behaviors into adulthood" and enhanced bonding (vonHoldt *et al.* 2017). But as Steve Jones notes in *Almost Like A Whale*: The Origin of Species *Updated* "by owning a dog, any dog, men welcome into the home a beast that preserves much of its primordial self. Overgrown juveniles though they are, evolution by human choice has not removed the instincts of their ancestors. ... Like wolves, dogs attack the weak, be they children, old, or drunk. Packs of feral animals have pulled infants from bicycles and eaten them, and a mere half-dozen beagles, dachshunds and terriers once devoured an eighty-year-old woman. The homicidal packs relive their past" (1999, p.41).

Cannibalism is not a homogeneous act, and zoologists must make a distinction between heterocannibalism of unrelated individuals, and sibling and filial, or parental, cannibalism. All of these forms of cannibalism can occur in different species, and have a range of alternative explanations. Cannibalism, note Elgar and Crespi (1992), occurs in a variety of contexts, including infanticide, mating and courtship, adult–adult cannibalism, and competitive interactions. One obvious feature is that cannibalism tends to be associated with an asymmetry between cannibal and victim. Generally the victim is at a more vulnerable stage of its life cycle, so while cannibalism between adults does occasionally occur, cannibalism of juveniles by other juveniles is more common, and cannibalism of juveniles by adults can be very common. Asymmetrical cannibalism has evolved because selection has favoured it where rewards, in terms of nutrition, reproductive advantage, sexual advantage or competitive advantage, exceed costs, in terms of conflict or potential loss of fitness.

Cannibalism is as common in marine vertebrates as it is in birds and dry-land vertebrates. Almost 200 years ago geologists were finding evidence of cannibalism in the petrified faeces of 200 million-year-old marine reptiles (Buckland, 1835), and today it is marine cannibalism that provides some of the most stunning examples of the benefits of cannibalism exceeding the costs. In 1948 intrauterine, or within-the-womb, cannibalism was discovered in the sand tiger shark, *Carcharias taurus*, also known as the grey nurse shark, where the largest and strongest embryos eat their weaker siblings in the process of adelphophagy (literally *consuming one's brother*). Sand tigers have two oviducts, and the first young in each oviduct to reach 6 cm swims to the uterus where it feeds on its siblings; a large part of the reason that it is commonly around 100 cm at birth. The major benefits from an evolutionary point of view are that surviving sand tiger young experience very rapid growth, are very active predators at birth, and often have a considerable size advantage over other predators. The pike-like freshwater game-fish the walleye has provided examples of cannibals within cannibals within cannibals, as larger walleyes were found to have eaten smaller walleyes, which had eaten still smaller walleyes, for at least a four-fold cycle. Cannibalism in marine mammals is now well documented. Cannibalism has been seen among grey seals in Canada and elephant seals in Argentina, but even though sea lions have been studied since at least de Bougainville's voyages in the 1760s and Johann Forster's voyages in the 1770s – the latter's studies mentioned by Darwin in *Descent of Man* – it was only as recently as 1999 that cannibalism was first recorded in sea lions, when twenty-four cases were seen in just twelve weeks in one colony of New Zealand sea lions.

In his classic 1966 work George Williams provides us with a wonderful example of the utter incongruity between human sentimentality and Dawkins' natural world "pitiless indifference". He recounts the attitudes of an audience being shown a film about elephant seals: "Amid the crowded but thriving family groups there was an occasional isolated pup, whose mother had deserted or been killed. These motherless young were manifestly starving and in acute distress. The human audience reacted with horror to the way these unfortunates were rejected by the hundreds of possible foster mothers all around them" (pp.188–9). Williams' point was to show the fallacy of good-of-the-species theorising – "It should have been abundantly clear to everyone present that the seals were designed to reproduce themselves, not their species" (p.189) – but the passage serves equally well to demonstrate the leap of faith it takes to suggest that the blind, pitiless indifference of natural selection could produce common human decency.

When the sociobiologist Sarah Hrdy was documenting the casual slaughter she witnessed in langur monkeys, she admits that it was her own tears that were among the problems she had to overcome. And Takayoshi Kano, leader of the bonobo research project at Wamba, recorded that when his colleague Mariko Hiraiwa-Hasegawa observed male chimps in the process of tearing an infant from its mother "Hasegawa momentarily forgot her position as a researcher and, brandishing a piece of wood, she intervened and confronted the males to rescue the mother and infant" (cited in De Waal 1997, p.119). Note the danger that Hasegawa was putting herself in here: one human female confronting multiple violent adult male chimpanzees each of which, Hasegawa would have been fully aware, more explosively powerful and faster than the average human adult male, because while we have more slow-twitch muscle fibres for endurance they have fast-twitch fibres for speed and power. While *every* adult langur or chimpanzee will tear infants of their own species to pieces without batting an eyelid, humans shed tears over the deaths of infants of *another* species, or run in to protect them against attacks by their conspecifics even at significant risk to life and limb. And this is supposed to be a fundamentally new evolutionary programme that has evolved once in all the billions of years of evolution, and once in billions of species? For reasons we will come on to it cannot be the case that individual-level or gene-level natural selection has come up with a unique and antithetical genetic strategy for humankind. DNA neither knows nor cares. DNA just is.

Natural selection is about *sacrifice* for those that carry your genes, not what we would understand as *love*. A mother may fight savagely to protect her offspring, but when she knows the game is lost her behaviour changes immediately. Weak offspring are often killed if this is the most efficient strategy. Mother chimpanzees mate contentedly with their infant's killers. And no grief, of course, since one gene vehicle is likely to be as good as another, and just as much of a biological tool. Smaller mammals, with less access to reliable sources of food, and worn down by a long period of having to suckle, will kill and eat their own offspring rather than allow them to fall into a predator's hands. This is because a healthy mother will get a chance to mate again next season, so it is time to build herself up rather than waste energy fighting the inevitable. Why risk serious harm to yourself when the product is replaceable? In nature, infants are important, but you can have others next season, so they are only worth fighting for up to a point. The point when the costs outweigh the benefits.

VERY SORRY, BUT THERE ARE NO EXCEPTIONS TO THIS RULE ...

"October 3, 1989: ... Meanwhile, *Lukaja* handed the infant to the alpha male *Ntologi*, who dragged, tossed, and slapped it against the ground. *Ntologi* climbed a tree with the infant in his mouth. He waved it in the air, and finally killed it by biting it on the face. … Conspicuous competition for meat and meat-sharing was observed as usual. Three adult males and an adult female obtained meat from *Ntologi*. Two adult females, two juvenile females, a juvenile male, and an infant recovered scraps from the ground or were given scraps. At 13:00, *Ntologi* was still holding the skin of the carcass."

– **Hamai** *et al.*, "New records of within-group infanticide
and cannibalism in wild chimpanzees", *Primates* (1992, p.152)

One of the problems with trying to discuss the implications for humanity from natural world studies is that many academics still see such research as a personal affront. Frans de Waal is one of the world's leading primatologists, albeit specialising in captive rather than field data, and de Waal has acknowledged that chimpanzees live in "a world without compassion" (1996, p.83). But like many working outside biological evolution itself de Waal continues to stubbornly resist a gene-selectionist explanation of natural world behaviour.

Richard Dawkins writes: "The medieval bestiaries continued an earlier tradition of hijacking nature as a source of moral tales" (1998, p.210). Dawkins lambastes the "spate of authors" today reacting indignantly to the idea that nature is genetically selfish, singling out de Waal, author of the tellingly-titled *Good Natured*. "De Waal … is distressed at what he mistakenly sees as a neo-Darwinian tendency to emphasise the 'nastiness of our apish past'. Some of those who share his romantic fancy have recently become fond of the pygmy chimpanzee or bonobo as a yet more benign role model" (p.211). Ethologists studying animal infanticide have also noted that "De Waal tends to dwell on the niceties of animal societies – 'Survival of the kindest' (1998). … There is still fundamentalistic resistance in the scientific community to the idea that animals act selfishly – particularly when it comes to infanticide" (Sommer 2000, p.13). Volker Sommer was himself writing the introduction – revealingly entitled "The Holy Wars About Infanticide. Which Side Are You On? And Why?" – to van Schaik and Janson's edited collection of recent animal infanticide reports.

Rightly or wrongly, Hrdy's groundbreaking paper had asserted that so much of the resistance to reports of primate cannibalism and infanticide seemed linked to the group-selectionist paradigm. "Because of the overriding conviction that primates behave as they do for the good of their group, the early naturalists' descriptions were dismissed as 'anecdotal, often bizarre, certainly not typical behavior'" (1977, p.41). And De Waal, like many group- and multilevel- selectionists, does seem hostile to genic selection because of his mistaken assumptions about what it must imply for human behaviour, and his corresponding need to have morality at the genetic level. Citing both Huxley and George Williams, he explains: "in this view, human kindness is not really part of the larger scheme of nature: it is ... a cultural counterforce[4]. ... Needless to say, this view is extraordinarily pessimistic, enough to give goose bumps to anyone with faith in the depth of our moral sense" (1996, p.2). De Waal's open hostility to gene-selectionism is apparent both when he describes as "monumental confusion" the position of Bill Hamilton, "the discoverer of kin selection, [who] has written that 'the animal in our nature cannot be regarded as a fit custodian for the values of civilized man'" (pp.15–16), and when he says of an understanding that explains evolved altruism

---

4   De Waal actually writes here "either a cultural counterforce or a dumb mistake of Mother Nature", but I have neglected the latter in the main text because what De Waal is suggesting of genic selection is not what is on offer. Gene and individual selection are both offering an amoral ape with the "dumb mistake" (if you like) of a brain so large it became subject to the hopes, fears and insights that manipulative – here ironically in the good, meaning crucial, sense – psychological systems like religions can work off. The amoral genetic coding is still there, but capable of being (at least partly) offset. What sociobiology, evolutionary psychology and group-selectionism all want at the very least is an adaptational "mistake", or by-product, that created an ape decent at the *genetic* level.

entirely through selection at the level of the gene: "a more cynical outlook is hard to come by" (p.14).

But cynicism has nothing to do with it. George Williams did not develop gene selection explanation because he was trying to be cynical, any more than Darwin developed individual selection explanation to be cynical. Nastiness could evolve as easily if selection was at the level of the individual as it would at the level of the gene; it is only group selection that could theoretically have broken this cycle, and hence the "faith" – this is de Waal's term above – so many tend to put into group selection, and their seeming blindness to its mathematical and theoretical flaws. It is only right to note at this point that some group-selectionists (e.g. Sober and D.S. Wilson, 1998) draw attention to the early work of Robert Boyd and Peter Richerson which suggests, as did Darwin, an answer in *cultural* (and not genetic) group selection. But Boyd and Richerson's work effectively overlays cultural group selection onto the immorality at the biological level of genic-selectionism, and multilevel-selectionists like Elliott Sober fail to recognise this key distinction.

Returning to the earlier point, though, when George Williams wrote the foreword to the author's 2003 book on human evolution, the bonobo was regularly being touted as a paradigm for human biological development. "Certain primatologists like to draw attention to the relatively peaceful nature of bonobos, that they 'make love, not war'. Some suggest that bonobos might be better models for early man (if one can overlook the fact that bonobos regularly indulge in sex in every possible combination … and have no exclusive sexual orientation). There are some facts about bonobos that should, however, be considered" (Miles 2003, p.69). That book noted that Craig Stanford had used the pages of *Current Anthropology* to point out that the number of field observation hours on bonobos was a small fraction of the hours spent field observing chimpanzees, due to bonobo temperament, the impenetrable forests they inhabit, and regional instability. Stanford (1998) had also noted that half of all encounters between bonobo communities do still result in aggression of some sort, and that observer bias, including the overemphasis on captive, rather than field, observation, may be misleading the public and scientists alike. While infanticide and lethal intercommunity aggression are both common in chimps, they are still restricted in time. Furthermore, natural selection will tend to come up with a counter-strategy where possible; if males are going to kill unrelated infants, females will tend to have been selected to steer clear of males for the period when infanticide can advance oestrus. Similarly, intercommunity conflicts are predictable but tend to be short-lived. Consequently chimpanzees had to be observed for more than fifteen years before lethal intercommunity aggression was finally witnessed, even in de Waal's exemplar of a species living in "a world without compassion".

Many of Stanford's points had been well taken by other bonobo researchers, especially the field researchers. Katharine Milton reminded her colleagues that: "we do not have to look far into the past to recall how, as more field data emerged, the sunny image of the playful, fruit-eating chimpanzee at Gombe was gradually revealed to have a darker side" (1998, p.412). Takayoshi Kano, head of the bonobo project at Wamba, noted that lethal bonobo intercommunity aggression might indeed one day be witnessed, citing his own observation of "a severe laceration" on one young adult that got separated from his main party for a few days (1998, p.410). And even de Waal was quick to point out (1998) that he himself had said that infanticide may yet be witnessed in bonobos when more study has been undertaken. De Waal recalls that "science has erred before with a range of so-called peaceable species, from gorillas to dolphins. ... Generally, such idealizations mean that something highly significant has been overlooked or, worse, covered up" (1997, p.84). Such hedging of bets seemed wise. Noting that infanticide by males is most advantageous where lactation is long relative to gestation, van Noordwijk and van Schaik (2000) had predicted that all great apes are vulnerable to infanticide, even though, whilst well recorded in gorillas and chimpanzees, infanticide had not then been witnessed in wild orang-utans or bonobos. Frequency of expected attacks, however, is largely a function of the counter-strategies females have evolved. Female orang-utans are semi-solitary. Thus while female orangs are exposed to male attacks – including frequent documented rape – whilst actively receptive to sexual encounters, after giving birth mothers with infants rarely associate with conspecifics. Frequency of infanticidal attacks is thus expected to be low but not zero.

It is over a decade and a half since George Williams wrote that foreword, and in that period the image of the bonobo has begun to change. Infanticide has still not yet been confidently witnessed in wild orang-utans or bonobos, and some researchers have argued that orang females form special bonds with protector males to guard against infanticide. Others have suggested that concealed ovulation, deliberate paternity confusion, and behaviour including ranging, may provide reduced benefits from infanticide, fewer opportunities, or just less chance of observation. But in 2009 David Dellatore and colleagues reported two incidences of female orang-utans eating their recently deceased infants (Dellatore *et al.*, 2009). At the same time, the primatologist Andrew Fowler at the Max Planck Institute for Evolutionary Anthropology in Leipzig noted that it "had been suggested in the past that bonobos might feel more sympathy for victims, which is why they didn't hunt monkeys", but that image had been shattered in 2009 when scientists discovered that bonobos do indeed kill and eat monkeys. And in 2010 Fowler and Gottfried Hohmann witnessed an example of a bonobo mother consuming, along with most other apes in her group, the body of her recently deceased 2.5-year-old infant (Fowler and Hohmann, 2010). As the BBC put it, Fowler and

Hohmann's observation "does further challenge a widely perceived notion that bonobos are an especially 'peaceful' ape species" (Walker, 2010), and Fowler stressed again how few long-term studies of bonobos there have been. In 2016 Nahoko Tokuyama of Kyoto University and colleagues reported, after having caught on video, similar bonobo maternal cannibalism (Tokuyama *et al.* 2017). This occurred at two sites in the Democratic Republic of the Congo, and involved mothers contentedly eating their dead offspring and sharing the carcasses with others including juveniles and infants; watch the video produced by Melissa Hogenboom (2016) from Tokuyama's graphic footage and available at the BBC Earth website.

To argue that bonobos are relatively peaceful, and perhaps therefore even proto-moral, is to misunderstand the mechanism of gene-selectionism. There is no morality in nature. Like orang-utans, the reason that bonobos rarely, if ever, commit infanticide is purely because they do not get the opportunity. Bonobo groups are largely female-dominated, whereas chimpanzees are overtly male-dominated. In bonobos, females get to set the rules. One rule they set was sex. De Waal comments that what the female bonobos are doing might be construed as an anti-infanticidal strategy. "They have managed to make paternity so ambiguous that there is little to fear. Bonobo males have no way of knowing which offspring are theirs and which not" (1997, p.122). Male chimps, de Waal notes, have a tendency to kill identified unrelated infants, so it is no wonder that chimp females stay away from large gatherings of their species for years after having given birth. No such worries for female bonobos, however, because a male bonobo who knew his offspring "would have to be a genius"; "if one had to design a social system in which fatherhood remained obscure, one could scarcely do a better job than nature did with bonobo society" (pp.120–1). Furthermore, notes de Waal, since bonobo females tend to be dominant, attacking them or their offspring would be a risky business. Most likely if a male were to be perceived as a threat to any infant, females would band together in defence.

Chimpanzees are already acknowledged to live in "a world without compassion", yet bonobos also live in this gene-selectionist world without compassion, and bonobo behaviour can be every bit as vicious as chimpanzee behaviour. Primatologists have been intrigued by the high rate of physical abnormalities in the male bonobos at Wamba. As Amy Parish told de Waal in interview, this could have something to do with the females. Females in captivity establish dominance over male bonobos by overt aggression. At one zoo, noted Parish, the females occasionally held down the male and attacked him, and had bitten off parts of his fingers and toes. At another zoo the alpha female had a similar relationship with her adult male: "It is assumed that she once bit his penis almost in half", Parish reported (De Waal 1997, p.115).

In bonobo groups the whole strategy of infanticide by males becomes counterproductive, because males can never be sure they are not killing their own offspring. But anyone who wishes to argue that such constrained behaviour demonstrates proto-morality or a "good nature" would have to conclude that a man-eating shark in a secure aquarium is similarly "good natured" simply because it had not yet found an opportunity to devour its keeper. "A more cynical outlook is hard to come by," writes de Waal. But gene-selectionism is not cynical, at least not when in the hands of Williams and Maynard Smith; it is simply evolutionary theory applied without fear or favour, just as Darwin did with individual selection. And there are, there can be, no exceptions to the rules.

At least as early as 1989 George Williams had been predicting that cannibalism would be recorded in all great apes, and indeed that it could be expected in all animals except strict vegetarians. Due to his illness Williams never became aware that cannibalism had finally been recorded in bonobos, as Fowler and Hohmann's report did not appear until 2010. With cannibalism recorded in chimps and orang-utans, and Dian Fossey having apparently found gorilla remains in the faeces of other gorillas in the 1970s, and notwithstanding that gorillas stick mainly if not strictly to a vegetarian diet, bonobo cannibalism seems to round off the great ape set. Williams had made a *genetic* prediction about cannibalism based on his and Maynard Smith's updating of Darwin's theory, and two decades later field researchers would prove his prediction correct in regard to our closest *genetic* kin.

NATURA NON FACIT SALTUM ...

Nature does not make a leap. *Natura non facit saltum*. The Latin expression quoted by Darwin in the sixth chapter of *Origin* was from Linnaeus' classic 1751 work on taxonomy. Saltation theories are theories that rely on macromutation, or a sudden large beneficial jump that is consequently incorporated into the gene pool of a species. Saltationism is a neo-Darwinian heresy. And yet evolutionary psychology's claims are not simply implicitly group-selectionist involving processes impossible under Darwinian inheritance, they are also saltationist. EP's suggestions would fundamentally have to rewrite natural selection's genetic code, being the immorality detailed above, the world without compassion of our closest kin. Evolutionary psychologists accept that up until 100,000 or so years ago our ancestors were selfish apes. So, if the evolutionary psychologists were to be right, what would have to be the implications for that last genetic change?

> "On the theory of natural selection we can clearly understand the full meaning of that old canon in natural history, 'Natura non facit saltum'".
>
> – **Charles Darwin**, *Origin of Species* (p.233)

All primates, all mammals, all vertebrates, all animals, are born programmed through an identical behavioural code, the code Richard Dawkins terms "pitiless indifference", the code George Williams calls "gross immorality" (1988, p.385), and "evil [but] also abysmally stupid" (1996, p.213). This codes for species-wide patterns of cannibalism, infanticide (and the voluntary mating with those that have killed your infant), rape, levels of lethal violence against same-species members many thousands of times higher than rates found in even the worst American cities, and indifference to the suffering of non-kin. Patterns not that *some* within a species are coded for, but that *all* within a species are coded for. Such conclusions followed from numerous studies. This code is not restricted to a few murderous genes; gross immorality is the programme of natural selection. This is a programme that has been favoured by selection over hundreds of millions of years because it works extremely efficiently from an evolutionary point of view. Utter selfishness and indifference to others' suffering (where they can be of no use to you, or are not closely related to you) is a message coded into the entire natural world behavioural genotype, it is not something tacked on a few million years ago. It has been the guiding force behind evolution for almost four billion years, and it dominates all behavioural coding. Blind, pitiless indifference is not simply a characteristic of natural selection; blind, pitiless indifference *is* natural selection.

Nature never starts again, and can only build on what has gone before. In his contribution to Orion Books' Science Masters series, *Plan & Purpose in Nature*, George Williams introduces us to what biologists call phylogenetic constraint, or phylogenetic inertia. "Evolution never designs anything from scratch. It can only tinker with whatever happens to be already there, saving those slight modifications that provide immediate benefits, culling those that cause harm. Much of anatomical human nature derives not from anything currently desirable but from adaptive changes made in the early history of the vertebrates" (1996, p.175). We have two pairs of limbs, says Williams, not for functional reasons but for purely historical ones. "The first lungfish that crawled from the water and pushed its way through the mud did so with the help of two pairs of appendages" (p.177). Degeneration, too, is an historical drama, though one usually played out at a different speed. Snakes are limbless – though some do have claw-like hind limb remnants – as their limbs were gradually selected to get smaller over time. Snakes have also lost eardrums and moveable eyelids, but gained vertebrae. In general degeneration can be enormously faster than generation. It required millions of years to make vertebrate eyes, but only thousands of years to lose them in caves.

And as historical constraints exist with regard to anatomy, so they exist with regard to behaviour, for similar reasons. Each part of the anatomy, and each basic natural world behaviour, is coded for by numerous genes and linked to other parts of the anatomy and other behaviours. By changing one factor it may have vast implications for many other factors, and nature has no foresight. Nature progresses by the efficient selection of purely random mutation. Nature has to work within the limitations given by the fact that existing features are already coded, and decoding is therefore greatly constrained. You cannot simply ignore what has gone before, or pretend it does not matter. Nature has taken millions of years to code for the set of behaviours in primates. While you can tinker with these behaviours, and add to them, and remove certain behaviours gradually over time, you cannot rip up the rulebook and start again.

The anthropologist Jared Diamond famously described humans as the third chimpanzee in his book *The Rise and Fall of the Third Chimpanzee*. Humans share around 99% of their DNA with both the common chimpanzee (*Pan troglodytes*) and the bonobo (*Pan paniscus*), once called the pygmy chimp. We split off from a common ancestor with the chimpanzee and the bonobo some six to eight million years ago. The point of the first part of Diamond's book was to show – using the work of the molecular biologists Charles Sibley and Jon Ahlquist whose studies have since been reconfirmed by many others – that human beings are actually more closely related (genetically) to both species of *Pan* than both species of *Pan* are to the other apes. As Diamond noted, the common ancestor to the chimp, the bonobo and the human split off from the ancestor to today's gorilla, the next nearest ape, more than a million years before the common ancestor to chimps, bonobos and humans split. In consequence, we and the chimp and the bonobo all share just less than 98% of our DNA with the gorilla. And the genetic distance separating humans from bonobos or chimps (less than 1.5%) is actually less than the genetic distance between the common gibbon and the siamang gibbon, who were found by Sibley and Ahlquist to have a 2.15% variance. The human/chimp relationship is usually given as just under 99% when calculating using single nucleotide substitutions, and although this method has been standard when comparing human/chimp DNA, it can be slightly misleading. For example, in September 2002 Roy Britten reported that the human/chimp relationship falls to perhaps 95% when one also includes indels, insertions and deletions of DNA found in one species but not the other. There is some dispute about the significance of such findings, but since indels exist across other species boundaries it almost certainly does not change the observation that humans are more closely related to both species of *Pan* than both species of *Pan* are to the other apes. Our DNA is remarkably close to all other apes, and the idea that this one and a half per cent difference – this difference gained in the small evolutionary period since we split from our common ancestor – can fundamentally rewrite the rules of evolved behaviour is just wrong.

But the problem is worse than that. As Diamond goes on to explain, although we split from a common ancestor with the chimpanzees some six plus million years ago "for most of the time since then, we have remained little more than glorified chimpanzees in the ways we have made our living" (1991, p.27). Our ancestors remained little more than glorified chimpanzees – with all that that should imply – until a couple of hundred thousand years ago. And these glorified chimpanzees were genetically even closer to us until, in the last instance, "perhaps they shared 99.9% of their genes with us. ... The missing ingredient may have been a change in only 0.1% of our genes" (p.46). There is no evidence that these glorified chimpanzees, several distinct species of *Australopithecus*, *Homo habilis*, *Homo erectus*, maybe *Homo heidelbergensis*, and the only slightly more advanced archaic *Homo sapiens*, managed to break from the pattern of pitiless indifference, the "world without compassion", that runs throughout natural selection.

These ancestors, finally only maybe 0.1% away from modern man in their genetic makeup – such a tiny variance that this same 0.1% is the genetic distance between two modern human beings selected at random – were still coded for cannibalism and infanticide. And evolutionary psychologists accept this, which is why they postulate that morality emerged from immorality some 100,000 years ago in that last genetic blip which produced modern *Homo sapiens*. Yet, even ignoring the non-existence of such a selecting mechanism, it seems an evolutionary impossibility that we could have retained 99.9% of a chimp's DNA, glorified or otherwise, yet expect that final infinitesimal 0.1% to have been the locus of the drive for selfishness as old as life itself. Instead, for Diamond, as for almost all biologists who have thought deeply about this question, something *extra* was added in that last 0.1% change.

We didn't *lose* anything, and certainly not a four-billion-year pattern for extreme selfishness, we *gained* something. We gained a susceptibility to culture with the emergence of the capacity for spoken complex language, although this susceptibility also required a very large and densely connected brain which had itself taken millions of years to evolve. Evolutionary geneticists have long known that this tiny change could have easily added the necessary genes, and that both speech and brain complexity may depend on very few new genes. The reasonable view is that we received something extra in that last 0.1% shift. Just compare this view with the evolutionary psychology alternative that nature backtracked through the human genome, deleting or inhibiting genes for the great majority of animal behaviours while substituting genes for a vast number of new human behaviours.

Mutations with large effects, or macromutations, do occur, and where they produce a radical difference in the visible characteristics shown by an organism such is termed a "monster". But macromutations cannot contribute to evolution because they will be eliminated by natural selection. The great majority of mutations are deleterious to offspring, and are consequently removed by selection. Existing organisms are by definition reasonably well adapted to their historic environment, and any random mutation is a game of Russian roulette with a very small likelihood of an empty chamber. While the aftermath of a mutation is dependent on the gene affected and the nature of the mutation, natural selection's game of tinkering with genetic material can be not only ultimately hazardous, but immediately lethal. There are perhaps 20,000 protein-coding genes in the human genome, which is very similar to a mouse, and arranged along twenty-three pairs of chromosomes. There are over 3 billion base pairs of nucleotides in a human being, the basic units of nucleic acid molecules found in the genes, although only a small percentage of these may be functional. Yet a mutation that causes the loss of just three nucleotides on a single gene on chromosome seven is the most common cause of cystic fibrosis, an illness where thick mucus builds up in the lungs and can cause life-threatening infections. So even tiny mutations are a risky business in nature, and the more mutations that occur, the higher the risk of problems.

But occasionally a mutation does occur which is not damaging to offspring and also gives an actual advantage over others. Even a beneficial mutation will probably be lost by chance, but, given the frequency of small mutations within large populations, such a beneficial mutation will reappear and will sooner or later begin to be favoured by selection and ultimately incorporated into the gene pool of the species. But modern biology rejects the notion that nature can work through huge leaps in organism design, or that you can throw away much of what goes before. As Dawkins puts it, "The greater the number of simultaneous improvements we consider, the more improbable is their simultaneous occurrence" (1986a, p.234). Most complex characteristics under genetic control are, and have to be, polygenic, governed by the combined interaction of a number of genes. So if you argue that in that last genetic spurt man inherited genetic coding for all sorts of new moral and behavioural attributes you are positing the chance addition of multiple new (working) gene complexes.

> "Darwin was a passionate anti-saltationist, and this led him to stress, over and over again, the extreme gradualness of the evolutionary changes that he was proposing."
>
> – **Richard Dawkins,** *The Blind Watchmaker* (p.248)

Changing brain size several times since departing from that common ancestor with the chimp, or modifying neural connection densities, well here you are only adding in stages to what already exists, just tinkering with what is already there in a very straightforward, albeit time-consuming, way. In contrast, evolutionary psychology's theories would require entirely new fully wired-up behavioural mechanisms, even the foundations of which could not conceivably have existed in our ancestors, and the removal of existing and largely antithetical behavioural coding. We are thus into the realm of astronomical statistical improbability.

WHEN SIZE DOES MATTER ...

It has long been recognised that the speed of cultural change undermines attempts to explain human societies and their behaviour in biological terms. As John Maynard Smith put it, "human societies change far too rapidly for the differences between them to be accounted for by genetic differences between their members" (1992, p.82). Or as Richard Dawkins notes: "Many human societies are indeed monogamous. In our own society, parental investment by both parents is large and not obviously unbalanced. … On the other hand, some human societies are promiscuous, and many are harem-based. What this astonishing variety suggests is that man's way of life is largely determined by culture rather than by genes" (1989, p.164). So the arguments of those trying to justify human behaviour in genetic and adaptationist terms "do not begin to square up to the formidable challenge of explaining culture, cultural evolution, and the immense differences between human cultures around the world" (p.191). Yet while this is well understood, what is less well appreciated is how and why natural selection constrains group sizes.

As Frans de Waal writes: "What is most amazing is that our species is able to survive in cities at all, and how relatively *rare* violence is" (1996, p.195). Chimps can live only in groups of up to one hundred or so individuals, and bonobos tend to live in similar or slightly smaller groups. Yet humans live side by side with non-kin in cities and nations of millions, group sizes unknown outside the immense kin groups of the social insects. The philosopher of science Elliott Sober and the biologist David Sloan Wilson are no friends of selfish gene theory. Yet, like the leading selfish gene theorists, they too openly admit the incongruity of humans living in cities. Human groups have, like social insect colonies, "been interpreted as superorganisms for centuries", say Sober and Wilson in their book *Unto Others*, but biologists need some explanation for "why humans are ultrasocial" (1998, p.158). D.S. Wilson is still one of the most influential levels-of-selection theorists within what is known as the multilevel selection (MLS) tradition. Sober and Wilson find their answers to human cohesion in genetic group selection; as they put it: "At the behavioral level, it is likely that much of what people have evolved to do is *for the benefit of the group*" (p.194; emphasis theirs). Similarly Martin Nowak – who wrote the 2010 paper with Ed Wilson attacking Hamiltonian kin selection and placing eusociality under multilevel selection and mutations prescribing the persistence of the group – calls humans "SuperCooperators" (2011, with Roger Highfield). Gene-selectionists have no such easy outlet however.

> "But natural selection ... implies concurrently a complete disregard for any values, either of individuals or of groups, which do not serve competitive breeding. This being so, the animal in our nature cannot be regarded as a fit custodian for the values of humanity."
>
> – **Bill Hamilton**, "Selection of selfish and altruistic behaviour in some extreme models" (1971a, p.219)

Altruism in nature can be explained through the two main mechanisms known as reciprocal altruism and kin selection, both ideas in different ways touched upon by Darwin. While somewhat prefigured by a 1955 paper by Maynard Smith's mentor, the geneticist J.B.S. Haldane, it was William Hamilton who first firmly drew the biological community's attention to inclusive fitness and the importance of kin selection in his seminal two-part paper in 1964. "Hamilton's Rule" as developed in that paper was applicable to all species by virtue of their relatedness, but the paper is partly remembered for the way it was applied to the genetical asymmetry of haplodiploid Hymenoptera (which includes ants, bees and wasps, but not termites). Mammals, being diploid, have a double set of chromosomes, one from each parent. In haplodiploid

Hymenoptera, diploid females develop from fertilised eggs and have a double set of chromosomes, one from each parent, while haploid males develop from unfertilised eggs and have only a single set of chromosomes from their mother to pass on. Sperm from a male are thus genetically identical. The coefficient of relatedness of mother to daughter has the normal value of 0.5. But the average relatedness between daughters from this male is 0.75, closer than it would be to any offspring they might conceivably have. Helping your siblings – who may number in the hundreds of thousands – can become of overriding genetic importance. Hamilton noted that family relationships in Hymenoptera are potentially very favourable to the evolution of reproductive altruism.

Another route very favourable to the evolution of reproductive altruism is inbreeding because relatedness can rise above the value of 0.5 that normally applies under outbreeding. Thus, noted Hamilton, an individual should be more altruistic than usual to its immediate kin. Termites, for example, are not haplodiploid, but can indulge in cycles of intense inbreeding within colonies and outbreeding to found new colonies. Some termites however found new colonies with daughters from a queen produced by parthenogenesis; multiple identical clones, effectively, but thereby permitting a far greater number of offspring while avoiding the problems of inbreeding. There are subtle problems to seeking the origin of social insect eusociality in simplistic application of coefficients of relatedness, and the question of insect eusociality is therefore by no means settled. Nevertheless, modern biology generally seeks its answers to the origin and maintenance of extreme insect sociality within (and blending) a limited range of possibilities, from very close genetic relatedness, to pheromonal suppression of fertility, parasitic influence, resource dependency, and other ecological factors. Vast offspring production plus irreversible reproductive specialisation, morphologically delineated castes, and a high level of hard-wired behaviour may also enable social insects to achieve group sizes impossible within the non-human mammals.

Important to this last understanding is the naked mole-rat. The naked mole-rat is "arguably the closest that a mammal comes to behaving like social insects such as bees and termites, with large colonies and a behavioural and reproductive division of labour", write Bennett and Faulkes in *African Mole-Rats: Ecology and Eusociality* (2000, p.i). The Damaraland mole-rat is the other eusocial mole-rat, with non-reproductive offspring, yet colonies are tiny, with an average size of only twelve members, and a maximum size so far found of around forty members. Damaraland mole-rats have a strong inbreeding avoidance mechanism and have a relatedness coefficient of no higher than the normal 0.5 found in outbred first-degree relatives. In contrast, even more extreme eusociality is displayed by the naked mole-rat, where average colony size is around eighty, and colonies of up to 300 animals have been discovered. Intense inbreeding among naked mole-rats has led to average intra-colony relatedness of 0.81, the highest recorded for a natural mammalian population, and naked mole-rats protect against some of the problems of inbreeding through the discovery of an outbreeding disperser morph or form. Comparison between the two species and other mole-rat species has tempered the initial view that it is inbreeding that explains all in naked mole-rat eusociality (there is one breeding queen, one to three breeding males, and the rest sterile or reproductively suppressed workers). Though levels of relatedness are always an important factor, ecological factors are also thought to be critical. Also implicated is a harsh and unpredictable climate and location producing benefits from assisted living, plus the very high costs constraining dispersal, both in terms of creating a new subterranean environment from scratch and the low probability of finding alternative food and mates.

There are reasons for why social insects display their extraordinarily high degree of co-operation. There are also reasons for why naked mole-rats display their kin directed co-operative breeding. Yet these models are so very different from what occurs in *Homo sapiens*. There is no suggestion that unique genetic, or fertility, or parasitic, or ecological factors have played a role in human social development. Leading gene-selectionists understand that biology cannot explain human cohesion. As Maynard Smith says of altruism, biologists "have explanations – such as the fact that the altruist may share genes with the recipient of its altruism, and it is genes, not individuals, that matter in evolution – but they are ones that work only for altruistic behaviour among the members of small groups" (1992, p.119).

> "The laws of the animal world are ruthless. Plenty of parents kill their children, and plenty of children murder their sibs. ... The surplus young are a biological insurance policy, and when times look good their parents begrudge the cost of cover."
>
> – **Steve Jones**, *Almost Like a Whale:*
> The Origin of Species *Updated* (p.172)

Human cohesion cannot be explained biologically. Genetically, we should not be able to live in groups much larger than those of the other apes, groups of up to one hundred or so individuals. We should not be able to live in cities. Human groups have, like social insect colonies, "been interpreted as superorganisms for centuries", say Sober and D.S. Wilson (1998, p.158). The problem is explaining this biologically, or at least outside the explicit group-selectionism of Sober, Wilson (David S., and now Edward O.) and Nowak. Or the "implicitly group-selectionist", and faith-based, writings of Steven Pinker and the evolutionary psychologists.

6

"THAT OPPORTUNITY'S OPEN TO EVERYBODY ON THE PLANET"

> "But also, you know, I started life in a council house in Manchester. I've worked quite hard to get where I am today and I don't feel particularly hair-shirted about the fact that I've been quite successful. … And you know that opportunity's open to everybody on the planet."
>
> – **Jim Ratcliffe**, interviewed on the BBC's HARDtalk (Sackur, 2016)

In May 2018 the *Sunday Times* Rich List announced Jim Ratcliffe as the UK's new wealthiest person, with a fortune of £21.05 billion at that date. Ratcliffe is the founder, chairman and majority owner of the oil, gas and chemicals giant Ineos. Politically he appears to be only moderately right wing, though he is certainly no fan of trade unions. He moved Ineos's head office to Switzerland in April 2010 to avoid the company having to pay UK taxes, he does undertake charitable work though often linked to the geographic regions he has a financial interest in, and although he avoids the limelight he was an important and influential campaigner for Brexit. And in August 2018, only two months after he was knighted, it was reported that Ratcliffe was himself relocating to Monaco where he could avoid paying UK personal tax. Yet Sir Jim, the wealthiest single person in Britain by quite some margin as at May 2018 and still one of Britain's most respected businesspeople, truly seems to believe that "everybody on the planet" could have done what he did and become moneyed. And of course paying your fair share in taxes might seem less necessary when you think that everybody has all the same opportunities you had, and could have done what you did irrespective of their background and social circumstances. In interview Ratcliffe goes on to mention his admiration for America precisely because "America embraces" this understanding that everyone gets the same chances to be wealthy "much more warmly than we tend to do in the UK".

What the above indicates is how little real understanding of the world the one per cent often have. They lack appreciation of how – undeservedly – fortunate they were and are in life. They lack understanding of the absolute role luck plays in human life. And they lack understanding of how – undeservedly – unfortunate many others are in life, and that indeed many have not the same opportunity to succeed, have not just less opportunity to succeed, but have zero opportunity to succeed. Because no one else on the planet had the opportunities to do what Ratcliffe did, and Britain's former richest person is fundamentally ignorant on this point. No one else starting life in a council house in Manchester had the opportunity to build an industrial powerhouse, even if Ratcliffe has conveniently managed to persuade himself otherwise. It took a particular (undeserved) biology combined with a particular set of (undeserved) fortuitous environmental triggers, contacts, and life chances, to reach his singular outcome.

Now let's be generous to Ratcliffe and suggest that the above comment is hyperbole from a man who doesn't often give interviews, and that he does not mean to suggest that a child born into starvation and disease a hundred miles from the nearest doctor could have risen to become the billionaire founder of a chemicals giant. Let's take it that Ratcliffe really only meant to suggest that anyone born in a largely corruption-free Western economy with access to good and affordable medical care – though slightly less affordable after Ineos sheltered close to half a billion pounds from the UK tax authorities just a few years into the third millennium – and free primary and secondary education, had the same opportunities he did. But even then, this is complete tosh, and ignorant self-serving one per cent tosh at that. The belief that anybody could become president of the United States, or that everybody in a well-run American state or British city has the opportunities to succeed economically is wholly untrue. In a universe that reduces to just biology and environment many get not reduced opportunity to succeed, but zero opportunity to succeed, and seemingly particularly in Ratcliffe-hyped countries like America that actively play up to the myth of free will, and play down the importance of taxation-enabled environmental opportunity. The above is not meant to suggest that we should not listen very closely to Ratcliffe's views on global oil and chemicals imbalances, listen fairly closely to his position on global trade, and even give some thought to his views on unions. But it does suggest that we should almost completely ignore Ratcliffe's views on inequality, opportunity, and social justice as uneducated and ill-informed, and should probably largely discount his opinions on council housing and tax shelters.

Ratcliffe's particular brand of self-serving delusion is common among the one per cent. Even more seemingly liberal billionaires freely repeat this line that in the West unlimited opportunities are open to all. Jeff Bezos, founder of Amazon, was the world's richest person by quite some margin in this same month of May 2018 with a fortune, and before his divorce, of $130 billion according to *Forbes'* World's Billionaires list. When Bezos was persuaded by his brother to give the Baccalaureate Address at Princeton in 2010 it was entitled "We Are What We Choose", and that speech displayed a complete lack of awareness that success reduces not to free choice but to undeserved dumb luck. Yet Bezos is a supporter of gay marriage, and after purchasing the *Washington Post* received a great deal of credit for maintaining that paper's outstanding commitment to serious investigative journalism, and providing it with the resources to continue to do so. Although he has come under close scrutiny for Amazon's questionable employment practices and working conditions, Bezos is generally considered liberal in his social views. "Cleverness is a gift, kindness is a choice," stated Bezos in his address to Princeton students. But this is also complete rot; both cleverness and kindness are wholly the chance gifts – the undeserved chance gifts – of biology and/or environment.

Bezos may be liberal in his social views, but his character often appears to be driven by his firm libertarian belief that state intervention is generally wrong or at least unhelpful. Writing for the *New Yorker*, Charles Duhigg commented that, "'Jeff is a libertarian,' a close acquaintance, who has known Bezos for decades, told me. 'He's donated money to support gay marriage and donated to defeat taxes because that's his basic outlook – the government shouldn't be in our bedrooms or our pocketbooks.' One of Bezos's earliest public donations was to the Reason Foundation, a libertarian think tank and publisher". The article mentioned Amazon's implacable opposition, both through money and threats, to a unanimously passed 2018 Seattle City Council measure attempting to address a spiralling homelessness crisis – Seattle now has one of the largest population of homeless in the US – and the Council's eventual reluctant surrender with the comment that the battle was not winnable because the opposition had "unlimited resources". The *New Yorker* continued: "Bezos's close acquaintance agrees: 'There's an empathy gap there, something that makes it hard for him to see his obligations to other people. … the one time Amazon could have pitched in, on the homelessness tax, instead of taking the lead Jeff threatened to leave. It's how he sees the world'" (Duhigg, 2019).

The journal of the Reason Foundation, which confirms that Bezos has donated in the past, notes that the "soft media consensus" is that Bezos "is a quiet libertarian, though thankfully not the scary kind" (Welch, 2013). And it should be recognised that after all the publicity Amazon received for derailing the homelessness initiative, the company has somewhat changed course, as Duhigg points out. "Since then, it has given grants to advocates for the homeless, and it is creating a network of Montessori-inspired preschools in low-income communities." It should also be acknowledged that Bezos made a significant donation to struggling US food banks during the 2020 pandemic. Yet Bezos lets himself down intellectually by advancing the myth of free choice. And it can only be damaging for the world's richest people to appear to buttress their political and economic views with falsehoods. Perhaps Bezos will continue to be a quiet libertarian even were he to internalise the understanding that luck swallows everything in human life, but as he is not the scary kind of libertarian maybe it would moderate somewhat "how he sees the world". Because for Bezos to say "cleverness is a gift, kindness is a choice" is just as factually wrong and socially and economically misleading as for the philosopher Dan Dennett to state earlier that "luck plays a role but so does skill; we are not *just* lucky". Skill does not lie outside the undeserved lottery of biology and upbringing, and neither does kindness. In a world without freedom of choice luck swallows everything (G. Strawson, 1998). Everything. Cleverness and kindness. Ineptitude and skill. Homelessness and empathy gaps. *Everything*.

The myth of free will may particularly benefit the one per cent, but it is by no means restricted to them; we'll see later that at least eighty per cent of the UK public is similarly unenlightened. Because seeing through the myths we are raised with is not easy, particularly when many scientists and philosophers are actively trying to suppress certain knowledge. There's a section in one of my friend Richard Oerton's books where he recounts that when he was a young child in the 1940s riding home from school on the bus he used to look out the window and feel anger at the unemployed he saw just standing around. Why couldn't they be as diligent and successful as his hard-working father, he fumed? It took a lifetime as a defence lawyer, and many years reading and thinking, for Richard to work out why some people have not just fewer, but zero, opportunities to succeed in life. Richard would go on to spend decades fighting the myth of free will, but this only came after he was one of the very, very few UK lawyers willing to fight – eventually successfully of course – for the decriminalisation of homosexuality in Britain in the 1960s. Although himself heterosexual and happily married, Richard took significant risks with his career, and in the face of almost universal hostility from both leaders and rank and file within his profession. I once asked him to send me copies of some of the legal periodicals where he was writing and being answered, and his colleagues' views on homosexuality in the late 1950s and early 1960s, invoking mental illness and perversion, make nauseating reading today. And a number of those colleagues have gone on to hold senior positions in the British legal profession.

The point of citing Ratcliffe and Bezos, and even a ten-year-old Richard Oerton, is to show just how toxic is this myth of free will, particularly to the socially and economically less fortunate. It tends to lead to a deserving poor versus undeserving poor view of the world, or Sir Jim Ratcliffe's taxes-are-largely-unnecessary-as-everyone-gets-the-same-opportunities-in-life attitude, when those without opportunities would benefit significantly from an end to this most insidious of myths. Because Ratcliffe is undoubtedly correct: Americans have bought into the free will myth more than Britons, but Britons have been indoctrinated into this myth more than the average Continental Western European. And there can now be little doubt that the more a nation promotes the myth of free will, the more socially and economically divided that nation tends to be. My colleague Bruce Waller is somewhat unusual among philosophers in that he is a philosopher interested in psychology, culture and statistics. And as Waller has written: "there is a deep *cultural* connection between strong belief in [free will and] moral responsibility and grossly excessive prison populations, extremes of poverty and wealth, absence of genuine opportunity for large segments of the culture, and inadequate protection of the innocent". Strong cultural allegiance to free will and moral responsibility, says Waller, is linked with "gross disparity between rich and poor, weaker commitment to equal opportunity, and a meager support system for the least fortunate" (2015, p.208).

In fact the myth may be more toxic even than that. Because when you find yourself low down on the economic scale, and you hear the one per cent telling you that "everybody on the planet" could have started in a council house yet still become a billionaire, it tends to drive your thought process in a very specific direction. When Herman Cain, the late pizza multi-millionaire and one-time front-runner for the 2012 Republican presidential nomination, says that "if you don't have a job and you're not rich, blame yourself" (Pearlstein 2011), human thinking will go in quite predictable ways. If society is hiding the fact that there is no freedom of choice and that undeserved dumb luck provides the only relevant moral distinction between rich and poor, the only relevant moral distinction between a beggar and a Ratcliffe, and all you are hearing from those at the top is that with effort you could have been a billionaire or at least a millionaire, and that you can only blame yourself for not being so, human nature presents two options. If you are not informed enough to see through the self-serving cant of Britain's richest man – and even of Silicon Valley's liberal billionaires – you can either agree with Ratcliffe and Cain that you had all the opportunities you needed to succeed and that you failed to take advantage of them, or else you can agree with Ratcliffe and Cain that you had all the opportunities you needed to succeed but that *someone else stopped you taking advantage of them*. And human nature makes it very likely that most will choose the latter over the former. Many who are lectured to by Ratcliffe or Cain will look for someone to blame for the fact that they started in a council house but never ended up as a billionaire or even a millionaire. Jews, Muslims, gypsies, blacks, Hispanics, Latinos, freemasons, immigrants, emigrants, George Soros, Bill Gates, the European Union, vaccinating doctors, experts, homosexuals, transsexuals, bisexuals, atheists, liberals, feminists: please insert here your global conspiracy or scapegoat of choice.

Without the myth of free will we lose our blindness to the role of luck in human life, as the influential free will apologist Thomas Nagel recognised in his philosophical treatise *Mortal Questions*, and within the section entitled "Moral Luck". When one discounts for "factors beyond one's control", Nagel wrote, for temperament and for elements which "are the product of antecedent circumstances", the area not subject to moral luck "seems to shrink under this scrutiny to an extensionless point" (1979, p.35). Yes, because in a world without freedom of choice, luck swallows everything. Cleverness and kindness. Ineptitude and skill. Homelessness and empathy. Diligence and indolence. Queen's Birthday Honours and Monaco tax shelters. Everything. *E-v-e-r-y-thing*.

THE "DESERVING" AND THE "UNDESERVING" POOR

Thomas Halper showed in a 1973 *Polity* essay that attitudes to poverty – including our corresponding compassion towards the poor or lack thereof – have always depended upon our views of personal merit and choice in one's position, but Halper's most worrying conclusion comes when he describes how the main reason for the great longevity and influence of the notorious distinction of the deserving from the undeserving poor "was its profound legitimating power" (1973, p.76). When some are identified as deserving their station through choice rather than luck or accident it becomes not only an excuse not to do anything to help them but, perhaps even more malignantly, it is given as proof that such a society *is* just. The conceit of free choice not only takes away any moral impetus to assist the less fortunate, as their lowly station is no longer seen as misfortune, but the myth then acts to legitimise the whole social order from the very bottom to the very top. The social historian Steve Hindle likewise argues (2004) that the pre-nineteenth-century growth in compassion for at least some of the poor appears to have been matched by the growing reliance on the belief that choice produces the varied stations of poverty. In other words there was now a clear division of the poor into those who are poor through their own choice and continue to deserve no sympathy and the new recognition of those who are poor through no choice of their own and so deserve sympathy, with the latter recognition at the same time serving to validate contempt for the former group. And Robert Haggard (2000) actually suggests that the development of the early British welfare state was only possible due to a declining belief in poverty through choice, and the recognition of just how many are at the bottom of the social order because of nothing more than misfortune.

In more recent years the recognition of a substantial deserving poor has declined again, and in June 2009 the Joseph Rowntree Foundation published research showing that around 83% of Britons think that "virtually everyone" remains in poverty in Britain not as the result of social misfortune or biological handicap but through choice (Bamfield & Horton 2009, p.23). 69% agreed, another 14% were undecided but did not disagree, and only 14% actually disagreed. Because of their belief in the fairness of "deserved inequalities" such respondents were discovered to have become almost completely unconcerned with the idea of promoting greater equality, while at the same time asserting that Britain was a beacon of fairness that offered opportunity for all. According to the JRF report there was a "clear sense" across all the groups surveyed that an individual's situation "is largely of his or her own making". Anyone can make it "if they really try", the great majority of participants asserted (pp.23–4). Around the same time, the 26th British Social Attitudes Report, produced in 2010 by the National Centre for Social Research, also found that there had been a fall in those supporting any form of wealth redistribution, from 51% in 1994 to 38% in 2010: sympathy was now limited to those who did not choose to live in poverty. Citing this second report, BBC Radio 4's *Analysis* interviewed politicians and commentators to highlight a tendency within the welfare debates to distinguish between those who are poor through bad luck and those who are poor "because of personal choices" (Bowlby, 2010). Free will may just be the primary excuse that many use to legitimise a contempt for the poor which would exist independently of their professed belief in free will, but free will assertion nonetheless provides the ethical fig leaf for such contempt that would be far harder to rationalise (and therefore tolerate) without the myth of free will. The myth of free will doesn't just excuse indifference to poverty. It creates and maintains much of that poverty in the first place.

The influential American Pew Research Center has concluded that successive Pew Global Attitudes polls "find that at every income level, Americans are far more likely than Europeans to believe that individuals, not society, are responsible for their own failures, economic and otherwise" (Allen & Dimock, 2007). Returning to Haggard's point that the development of the British welfare state required a somewhat declining belief in poverty through choice, then by inference it is at least plausible that the United States lacks a working welfare state in large part because of an even more strongly inculcated belief in the existence of free choice than in Britain. Mink and O'Connor's encyclopaedia of the historical, political, and social background to poverty in America tells us that mainstream public discourse since the early nineteenth century has made the distinction between the deserving poor and the undeserving; has raised the issue of choice, worth and merit. Moreover, the book notes that both women and racial minorities have been substantially excluded from the ranks of the deserving poor (2004, p.226), while the growth in the US of the idea of the undeserving poor coincided with the period of mass immigration of those of non-WASP stock. It is not just adults who are targeted under the free will conceit. The US *Encyclopedia of Children and Childhood in History and Society* includes an entry by social historian Peggy Shifflett asserting that, among other things, the distinction between the deserving poor and the undeserving poor has even been applied to the population of homeless children in the States, estimated to range from 500,000 to more than two million (2008). Early twentieth-century runaways – who were viewed, Shifflett tells us, as having freely chosen to leave their homes – were generally categorised as the undeserving, while she cites studies suggesting that more recent attitudes have not been significantly more tolerant.

In 2009 Jasmine Carey surveyed over 250 undergraduates and found that those who believe in unrestrained free will were significantly more likely to believe in a just world for themselves and others, with "just world" here defined solely as the tendency "to believe that people deserve the things that happen to them" (2009, p.8). As Carey noted, "the responsibility of free will is necessary for belief in a just world" (p.20). Even those who are trying to defend the free will conceit have provided evidence for the malignity of the myth. The free will libertarian and social psychologist Roy Baumeister, writing with Andrew Vonasch, unconsciously demonstrated by experiment the discriminatory effects on the poor: "The narrative of the deserving versus undeserving poor is a staunch perennial feature of public debates about welfare, but its only relationship to free will beliefs is that those with higher free will beliefs feel more sympathetic to those who really are trying to lift themselves by their bootstraps" (2013, p.224). Yet if you feel more sympathy towards those trying to lift themselves you are by definition less sympathetic towards those not trying to lift themselves out. Such people are using a *myth*, a *fiction*, to differentiate between the two groups in favour of one and, almost by definition, to the detriment of the other. "People with higher beliefs in free will were more likely to say that 'personal choice' is a cause of poverty [and] people with high belief in free will … actually felt more sympathy towards the person working hard to try to get out of poverty" (p.224). Again, such people are feeling more sympathy towards one group based on an incorrect belief that the other group's members could actually do something about their situation when, in a universe without free choice, they can do literally nothing without assistance. Some have even suggested that blame and a corresponding belief in freedom of choice have, at least in America, been used to move the debate beyond a distinction between the deserving and the undeserving poor and into the territory of whether we ever need feel compassion for the poor. Monica Potts, who writes on poverty and opportunity for *The American Prospect*, says that the "political and policy discourse about the poor in the United States has centered, to a considerable extent, on whether and how the people who can't make it into the middle class are to blame for their own plight … It's as if the political debate … has calcified, and we have only two choices: 'You should feel sorry for the poor' or 'You shouldn't'" (2014, pp.103–4).

Free will appears to be the legitimating excuse that is used to ignore the plight of the most unfortunate. Under the free will conceit the world is not now examined to see if it is just, but instead is simply assumed to be just. Henry Ward Beecher, the

American nineteenth-century minister, wrote that no man in the United States suffers from poverty "unless it is more than his fault, unless it is his sin", while the early nineteenth-century English politician Edward Bulwer-Lytton wrote that in other countries poverty was seen as a misfortune "but that for Englishmen it was viewed as a crime". Under the mindset epitomised by Beecher and Bulwer-Lytton the existence of poverty is used as proof of a failure of free choice. Referencing the research of Thomas Halper again, some churchgoers have traditionally argued that there are no worthy poor as a just God would not have consigned them to such a horrible fate "if they did not deserve it" (1973, p.75). The poor and unlucky can never win at this shell game because, thanks to the conceit of free will, the *existence* of poverty becomes the *legitimisation* of such poverty. As desert morally requires free will, the existence of a segment of society struggling at the bottom is given as proof of free will: they wouldn't be struggling if they did not deserve to be.

> "One can put the point by saying that the way you are is, ultimately, in every last detail, a matter of luck – good or bad. ... In the end, luck swallows everything. ... No punishment or reward is ever ultimately just."
>
> – **Galen Strawson**, philosopher (1998a, s.4-6; 1994, p.16)

Personal initiative, diligence and character are all down to luck, but so is everything else, because luck swallows everything in human life. As the Oxford philosopher Neil Levy put it in *Hard Luck: How Luck Undermines Free Will and Moral Responsibility*, Dennett is just plain wrong to argue that luck averages out in human life, because luck "tends to ramify" (2011, p.199), both the bad and the good. "Chance events that are genuinely lucky and that actually compensate for constitutive luck are rare and extraordinary." If you start off with a poor biological – or environmental – hand it will largely follow you, particularly in countries like America and Britain that make a fetish out of the self-made-man myth. Dennett writes that "everyone comes out more or less in the same league" (1984, p.96), but this is absolute hogwash, and mean-spirited hogwash at that; undeserved dumb luck gives some vast opportunities in life and others absolutely zero opportunities. Dennett's suggestion is that the differences we are born with or to, such as innate intelligence, physical beauty, skin colour or wealth, and are then raised with such as education and family connections, confer "such a relatively small initial advantage" as to "count for nothing" (1984, p.95), and that "many of the differences that survive are, in any event, of negligible importance" (2003, p.274). But this is both intellectually false and morally obnoxious. The differences, advantages and disadvantages, turn out not to be small and not to count for nothing; in a world that reduces to biology and environment they count for everything.

In his book *The Success Equation* the investment strategist Michael Mauboussin tells us about what sociologists call the Matthew effect of accumulated, or cumulative, advantage. It is called the Matthew effect because of what is known as the Parable of the Talents in Matthew 25: *for to every one who has will more be given, and he will have abundance; but from him who has not, even what he has will be taken away*. From a financial success point of view, Mauboussin writes: "the Matthew effect explains how two people can start in nearly the same place and end up worlds apart. In these kinds of systems, initial conditions matter. And as time goes on, they matter more and more" (2012, p.118). Or luck tends to ramify, as Levy noted. In his 2016 book *Success and Luck: Good Fortune and the Myth of Meritocracy* the economist and *New York Times* columnist Robert Frank catalogues the utter coincidences that have led to the success of some of the world's wealthiest people, including Bill Gates. A more poignant example, though, is the late Steve Jobs. Jobs, a temperamental and deeply insecure child –

the "central trauma" of his life "was being given up for adoption" (Goodell, 2011) – credited surviving school because a fourth-grade teacher literally bribed him into learning, and built his self-confidence. And Jobs only met Steve Wozniak, the technical brains behind what they co-founded as Apple, because his parents moved the family to help his education, and a neighbour introduced them. Frank notes that the rich continually underestimate the role of undeserved dumb luck in their own success, and discusses the economic harm this does to society at large, mentioning studies that show that just getting people to recognise the role of luck in their own success makes them more likely to be charitable. The theoretical physicist Alessandro Pluchino and colleagues at the University of Catania have tried to model the contribution of talent against random luck, and have noted that "the model shows that, actually, randomness plays a fundamental role in selecting the most successful individuals" (2018).

Citing Mauboussin, the financial blogger Nick Maggiulli also gives us a number of examples of the Matthew effect in operation. When the world's most successful horror writer Stephen King published some of his later horror novels anonymously under the pen-name Richard Bachman they certainly weren't ignored, but they were selling only in the tens of thousands. Then a book store clerk noticed the similarity in writing styles, confronted King who confessed and agreed to an interview, and the books were re-released and sold in their millions. Maggiulli notes that a similar effect happened when J.K. Rowling published under the name Robert Galbraith, albeit this example is somewhat less instructive as she was now publishing in a very different genre of adult crime thriller. As Maggiulli notes, the Matthew effect "explains how King and Rowling sell millions while Bachman and Galbraith don't, despite being of similar quality" (2018). And such an example "reveals a harsh truth about success and social status – winners keep winning ... those who start with an advantage relative to others can retain that advantage over long periods of time". Maggiulli incorporates a mathematical simulation in his blog to show how small initial random advantages can have huge cumulative and long-lasting effects. "The purpose of this simulation is to demonstrate how important starting conditions are when determining long term outcomes. ... We like to think in America that most things come down to hard work, but a few lucky (or unlucky) breaks early on can have lasting effects over decades." Touchingly, Maggiulli admits that he has had far more luck in his life than most, but Maggiulli and Mauboussin both still underplay their hand. Maggiulli concludes that there is a need for you and me to recognise "luck as a primary determinant in your life", while Mauboussin's book is subtitled *Untangling Skill and Luck in Business, Sports, and Investing*. Yet luck is not "a primary determinant" to success in life, it is the only determinant to success, and we cannot "untangle" skill and luck, as skill is just another form of undeserved biological plus environmental luck.

Neil Levy (2011) makes the further observation that standard justifications for free will by both conservatives and liberals create what he calls a "double dose of injustice" and unfairness. Far from having evolved to be the fair and the just ape, most of us, conservative and liberal, are the doubly unfair ape, the doubly unjust ape. First there is the poor developmental luck many have to suffer. But free will justification then adds a *second* dose of injustice, Levy writes, to that first dose of indifference. This is the unfairness of claiming that the person was somehow responsible for their first dose of unfairness, or at the very least that blame and suffering are their just deserts. And free will apologists double dip on reward, in that not only are they lucky enough to benefit from great good fortune but, as with Gary Watson, will usually seek to claim that such good fortune was somehow due them. The predominant system, says Levy, amplifies good luck for the more fortunate, and amplifies bad luck for the less fortunate, while both denying that it is doing any such thing and making us all complicit in the unfairness and the injustice.

THE STRANGE POLITICS OF THE FREE WILL MYTH

> "There is not a person on earth who chose his genome, or the country of his birth, or the political and economic conditions that prevailed at moments crucial to his progress. And yet, living in America, one gets the distinct sense that if certain conservatives were asked why they weren't born with club feet or orphaned before the age of five, they would not hesitate to take credit for these accomplishments."
>
> – **Sam Harris**, *Free Will* (pp.61–2)

It is often claimed by liberals that the political right is particularly focused on identifying, even scapegoating, the undeserving poor. Conservatives, writes the neuroscientist and liberal anti-free will polemicist Sam Harris, have made a "religious fetish" (2011, p.47) of self-creation and rugged individualism. Many seem to have absolutely no awareness of how lucky one must be to succeed at anything in life, he comments, whereas the disparities in human luck are both morally relevant and harrowing to contemplate. But how even-handed is Harris's accusation that conservatives have made a fetish of self-creation and rugged individualism, while liberals have not?

There was certainly a punitive view of the poor from American conservative figures like Ronald Reagan, and social theorist Robert Goodin is clear in his belief that the New Right criticism of welfare provision drew almost exclusively on ethical notions of moral desert and on personal choice (1988, p.279). Similarly, it is the American neocon Gertrude Himmelfarb (e.g. 1984) who is most often credited with reintroducing into Western political discourse the earlier division of the deserving poor from the undeserving. "'Deserving' and 'undeserving' – these terms epitomize the difference between the Victorians and ourselves. The Victorians spoke the language of morality" (Himmelfarb, 1995). Margaret Thatcher was a great influence on Himmelfarb, and Baroness Thatcher herself saw morality towards the poor in terms of their supposed freedom of choice, as was attested to by the veteran BBC political interviewer John Humphrys (2006) who had spoken to her about her beliefs.

Furthermore, the myth of free will is built into the very moral philosophy of the hard right. In October 1994 the paleoconservative Charles Murray was dubbed "America's Most Dangerous Conservative" by the *New York Times Magazine*. Murray, co-author of *The Bell Curve*, has for thirty years been Rupert Murdoch's favourite political philosopher, and Murdoch's newspapers helped relaunch Murray's career, promoting his views into widespread circulation since the 1980s. Murray related in interview how Murdoch once sent a private jet to fly him to Aspen (DeParle, 1994), and Murray is the only author Murdoch admits to re-reading. Rupert Murdoch apparently passed Murray's books on to Donald Trump's future son-in-law and senior adviser Jared Kushner, reportedly helping to influence Kushner's rightward shift politically (Graves, 2017). Yet Murray's world view and right-wing apologism is largely built on the illusion of free will. Because in America, writes Murray, "the options are always open. Opportunity is endless" (1984, p.234). And Murray's metaphysical world view of course informs his social policy. Murray is known for arguing that the welfare system should be abolished because it doesn't work, that a welfare system is anyway unnecessary as everyone gets the same opportunities in America, and that because everyone gets the same opportunities calling for the end to welfare is not lacking in empathy ("there is in this stance no lack of compassion but a presumption of respect" – 1984, p.234). It is Murray's book *Losing Ground: American Social Policy 1950–1980* that is credited by the hard right American Enterprise Institute (AEI) as being the intellectual foundation for the 1996 PRWORA welfare reform and Work Opportunity Act, a cornerstone of the Republican Party's Contract with America. To quote one of Murray's colleagues at the AEI, Christopher DeMuth, Murray's analysis: "meant that social engineering, like physical engineering, faced hard natural limits, and also that the modern quest for equality was, in important respects, self-defeating" (2009).

Yet while Harris is right that conservatives – from Ratcliffe and Thatcher, to Himmelfarb and Murray – have made a religious fetish of self-creation and rugged individualism, and that the myth of free will is built into the very ideology of the hard right, he overplays his hand, because the liberal-left has often been similarly deluded. The British Labour Prime Minister Tony Blair and his Chancellor Gordon Brown saw the poor in terms of deserving versus undeserving. Commentators have noted that Gordon Brown, himself to become prime minister, was significantly influenced by Himmelfarb, whose writings he kept to hand and admired greatly; it was Himmelfarb's "unashamed moralism" regarding the poor that appealed to Brown (Vallely, 2007). Blair and Brown took the British left with them, with opinion polls suggesting that Labour Party voters began to make a sharper distinction between the deserving and undeserving poor from the late 1990s. Yet in so doing Blair and Brown were arguably only taking the Labour Party back to its roots, as from the late nineteenth century the working class has had an automatic tendency to make a distinction between those it saw as deserving and those it saw as undeserving. Meanwhile, the British intellectual left has mirrored this return to Labour's originating tendency with, for example, Will Hutton, a key figure within the highbrow left given his early cataloguing of Britain's growing social divide, encouraging the left to "re-moralise" on the issue of poverty. Hutton says that the political left needs to learn to say to some people: "you're in the situation you're in because of personal choices, yes we disapprove and we don't like it" (interviewed in Bowlby, 2010). In his book *Them and Us* Hutton writes of his desire to drag the left much further into debates about the division of society and about the limiting of opportunity for some along the lines of desert, or what he likes to call "deservingness" (2010).

And it is liberal intellectuals who have made an absolute fetish of self-creation, or at the very least of the self-creation myth. It is the militant atheist Dan Dennett who argues that the differences we are born with and raised with "count for nothing" (1984, p.95), and writes that "I must look like a spin doctor to those who are unconvinced by my carefully marshalled analyses" (2012b, p.20). It is the Canadian philosopher and four times social democratic parliamentary candidate Charles Taylor who writes that "self-resolution in a strong sense ... is within limits always up to us" (1985, p.42). It is the Californian humanist Gary Watson who writes that "the force of the example does not depend on a belief in the *inevitability* of the upshot. ... The thought is not 'It had to be!'" (2004, p.243). It is the progressive John Martin Fischer who tells us he "is not troubled by" issues of moral luck, winners' justice, and absence of opportunity; "why be disturbed by" such concerns? (2007, pp.69–70). And it is the liberal thinker Saul Smilansky who writes of "the moral necessity of belief in the justness of deeply unjust practices" (2000, p. 279).

Of course there have been major liberal philosophers who have openly recognised the overwhelming role of undeserved dumb luck in human life. John Rawls introduced the ideas of natural lotteries and social fortune in *A Theory of Justice*. "Even the willingness to make an effort, to try, and so to be deserving in the ordinary sense is itself dependent upon happy family and social circumstances ... we may want to adopt a principle which recognizes this fact and also mitigates the arbitrary effects of the natural lottery" (1971, p.64). Hence for Rawls, public institutions could be configured to help offset undeserved (good and) bad luck. But, *pace* Harris, frequently it has seemed to be iconoclastic thinkers on the right who are more exercised about lack of opportunity than are many on the liberal-left. No American politician more decisively rejected the conceit of free will than the Republican Abraham Lincoln, and it has been suggested that it was Lincoln's rejection of the myth of free will which partly informed his virtues and his love of freedom: virtues of tolerance, forgiveness, and justice. "Let us judge not that we be not judged", Lincoln wrote, "with malice toward none; with charity for all" (Guelzo 1997, pp.78–9). Lincoln is representative of the more moderate and traditional right-wing attitudes which are fully capable of accepting that equality of opportunity – a long-standing call from the right – firstly requires a rejection of the myth of freedom of choice. However, even more provocative conservatives have been startlingly advanced in their thinking, and perhaps none as surprising as the Nobel Prize-winning economist the late Milton Friedman.

Friedman, often seen as both Margaret Thatcher's and Ronald Reagan's intellectual inspiration, is still a hate figure to much of the liberal-left. A few years before his death in 2006 Friedman was interviewed by Matthew Miller of the *Boston Globe*. Miller noted that early in his career Friedman "wanted very much to prove – mathematically – that luck isn't as important in human affairs" as we instinctively presume, actually publishing this view in a 1953 paper. But Miller went on to report that Friedman had now completely reversed his world view: "Friedman chuckled as he recalled the article. … 'I think that luck plays an enormous role', he went on. 'My wife and I entitled our memoirs, *Two Lucky People*. Society may want to do something about luck. Indeed the whole argument for egalitarianism is to do something about luck. About saying, *Well, it's not people's fault that a person is born blind, it's pure chance. Why should he suffer?* That's a valid sentiment'" (Miller, 2003).

Although even at this more advanced and admirable stage of his thinking, Friedman failed to appreciate that in a world without free will, logically, luck swallows everything. As per Strawson's comment above, we have the luck – good or bad – in being born the way we are, and then the luck – good or bad – in what comes along to shape us. Undeserved dumb luck does not play Friedman's "enormous role" in success or failure, it plays a 100% role in success or failure. Friedman hadn't quite realised that you cannot get beyond the luck formula, and in the interview he did display a real lack of awareness ("not all differences are attributable to luck") that all abilities must by necessity be down to luck. After all, name one ability, or disability, that is not down to luck. Logical mind? Biology and education; both down to undeserved dumb luck. Absence of dyslexia? Biological luck. Perseverance? Some biological luck but also good character training. Skill? Similar. An acquaintance with Euclidean geometry? A good education on the back of 2,000 years of Western history which valued useful knowledge; deterministic good environmental fortune, albeit it helps not to have innate number blindness. But Friedman did at least openly realise and recognise that "personal initiative and character" are down to nothing more than undeserved luck, and as against so many on the liberal-left, from Hutton and Blair to Dennett and Watson.

And of course this has huge implications for public policy. "This awareness of luck's role … is what led Friedman to stress the importance of providing equal opportunity via education. … Friedman also told me that it inspired his call for the provision of a decent minimum to the disadvantaged, ideally via private charity, but if government was to be involved, via cash grants" (Miller, 2003). Again, there was a weakness to Friedman's thought, in that he hadn't realised that in a world without free will, and a world driven by luck, we can never have equal opportunity, even if we can at least work towards materially less absence of opportunity. And given Friedman's – somewhat ideological, though also somewhat reasonable – suspicion of government inefficiency, his call for charity still accorded with his much better-known views, though his obvious compassion towards the less fortunate also marks him out from many on the right, plus from many of the opposite political persuasion.

Miller finished his interview by noting how so few of Friedman's "acolytes on the *Wall Street Journal* editorial page" have "imbibed the decency of their mentor", but we should also be mindful of how few on the liberal-left have seemingly imbibed such decency, in a world where undeserved dumb luck swallows everything. Because, as Neil Levy reminds us, judging by past and present experience we are not – at least biologically – the decent ape, we are the doubly unfair ape; we are the "double dose" of unfairness ape. Firstly unwilling to be fair, but then further incapable of even fairly defining the concept of fairness. So *of course* human sociobiology defined us as the decent animal; human sociobiology never had a workable and unbiased definition of *in*decency in the first place. Of course evolutionary psychology names us as the moral animal; evolutionary psychology never had a viable and impartial definition of *im*morality from the outset.

"WE ARE LOOKING INTO AN ABYSS"

Some thinkers, such as Darwin and Spinoza, suggested that humans mistakenly believe we have free choice because we are not conscious of the determined nature of our desires. Darwin and Spinoza were in effect arguing that we don't know our own minds, an eminently sensible suggestion given that, as the theoretical physicist Leonard Mlodinow writes (2012), the brain receives over ten million bits of information each second from various sensory systems, but the conscious mind can handle only up to about fifty bits per second. The unconscious does the heavy lifting and consciousness seems to be a deliberately simplified model of the world to stop us drowning in data. In contrast David Hume suggested that it was the experience of indecision that made us think we have free will. And more recently Seth Lloyd, a physicist and mathematician at the renowned Santa Fe Institute, has suggested (2012) that it is perhaps the intrinsic computational unpredictability of the decision-making process that gives us the impression that we are freely choosing. Whichever suggestion or suggestions one leans towards, the last forty years of cognitive psychology have been a growing realisation of just how poor our brains are at understanding the real world. The psychologist Daniel Kahneman won the Nobel Prize in economics by showing that the basis of modern economic theory had been wrong to think of agents as rational and with stable preferences. Kahneman and his long-time co-author Amos Tversky showed, in a series of papers over many decades, that experts place far too much faith in their intuitions, and that our thinking can be easily fooled and manipulated by both internal and external factors.

Cognitive theorists are only too aware now that our minds play tricks on us: we invent reality within our minds, with our brains making up all the missing pieces. Neuroscientists call the explanations our minds invent after the event confabulations, a form of "honest lying", because the individual is unaware that the information is false. Experiments show that eyewitnesses remember far less than they themselves insist upon, because many of their recollections have been filled in or invented by their brains. And neuroscience is showing the very feeling of intention to be an illusion created by the brain. The most famous experiments throwing doubt on classical conceptions of free will were performed by Benjamin Libet in the early 1980s. Libet got volunteers to watch a clock, move their wrists, and report at what time on the clock they chose to move. At the same time Libet measured electrical activity over their brains, and found that the neural preparation to move preceded the volunteers' conscious awareness of the intention to move by over 300 milliseconds.

So there was a spike of brain activity 0.3 seconds before the volunteers chose to move their wrists, or to put it another way the volunteers' brains prepared to move before the volunteers consciously decided to move. Libet's work has now been verified, modernised and extended by numerous other neuroscientists such as John-Dylan Haynes, Itzhak Fried and Patrick Haggard, while Haynes co-authored a 2008 study issued by the Max Planck Institute which showed that entire seconds before we are aware of making a decision our brains have already made the decision. In 2019 neuroscientists in Australia published a study whereby they were able to predict voluntary imagery decisions or choices of participants from their decoded brain activity fully 11 seconds before people were consciously aware of making such decisions (Koenig-Robert & Pearson, 2019). But while some of the errors in the free will debates are understandable, others are less easy to excuse.

> "When we consider whether free will is an illusion or reality, we are looking into an abyss."
>
> – **Dan Dennett**, American philosopher (2008, p.249)

Determinism means that every action in the quasiclassical universe has a cause. In contrast, fatalism is a resignation to events which suggests that as everything is determined it is pointless to act because of a belief that no matter what one does one's future will not change. The philosopher Derek Parfit argues that even a thinker of the quality of Kant mixed up something as logically distinct as determinism and fatalism. Kant made this mistake, Parfit asserts, when he implied that if determinism is true there would be no point in our trying to decide what we ought to do, that we would have to be *passive*, waiting to see what sort of decisions we shall be caused to make. "That is not so. Even if determinism is true, we can be *active*, by trying to make and to act upon good decisions", writes Parfit (2011, p.262). Almost 2,500 years ago the Stoics called fatalism the "lazy" or "idle" argument because it spawned inactivity, and showed that it was nonsense to argue that action will never have any effect. Cicero says that Chrysippus criticised the fatalist argument by demonstrating that determinism left plenty of room for taking action, such as calling a doctor. Chrysippus showed that you will get better *by* calling the doctor; it is just that the act of calling the doctor is itself also part of the chain of cause and effect. Determinism is delinked from fatalism. Actions and efforts still have effects and change the outcome from what it would have been if the effort had not been made, but the outcome can still be defined in terms of prior causes. Yet mistaking determinism for fatalism exists across the academic writing on free will, although it is perhaps concentrated these days within the psychology literature. And one of the recurring themes of this book has been the mistakes within various branches of psychology, and particularly North American psychology. Be that evolutionary psychology, social psychology, or behavioural genetics. Because, as we shall see later, even behavioural genetics is a sub-branch of psychology, a soft science, and not a hard science at all.

Roy Baumeister and Kathleen Vohs are influential North American social psychologists who claim that believers in free will, and disbelievers in determinism, are more pro-social, less aggressive and less selfish, and more likely to work hard, but their analysis is undermined through the confusion of determinism and fatalism, and through having apparently led test subjects into the same confusion, as the author has previously shown (2013, 2013a). For example, Baumeister and Vohs make the error themselves: "a deterministic view ... suggests that efforts do not matter" (Stillman, Baumeister, Vohs *et al.* 2010, p.44), and Baumeister has inadvertently led his participants into the error: "apparently disbelief in free will subtly reduces people's willingness to expend that energy" (Baumeister *et al.* 2009, p.267). The philosopher

Bruce Waller has likewise noted of this North American social psychology research, which has "drawn significant attention from … the popular media" – and indeed has been lauded in influential publications from *Nature* and *New Scientist* to *The Economist* – that "the researchers primed their experimental group not toward belief in determinism, but rather in the direction of a diminished sense of self-efficacy, to acceptance of helplessness" (2011, pp.279–82).

Over the last decade a number of papers have now been published in North American social psychology asserting both the putative pro-social benefits of belief in free choice and the possible dangers of disclosing doubts about the existence of free choice. Roy Baumeister has suggested that belief in free will reduces aggression and promotes selflessness (Baumeister, Masicampo, & DeWall, 2009). Kathleen Vohs, Jonathan Schooler, and Azim Shariff have argued that disbelief in free will encourages cheating and undermines moral behaviour (Shariff, Schooler, & Vohs, 2008; Vohs & Schooler, 2008). Tyler Stillman, Baumeister and Vohs have asserted that believers in free will make better employees (Stillman *et al.*, 2010). And Stillman and Baumeister argue that belief in free will facilitates learning from emotional experiences, while disbelief in free will reduces learning, amusingly at the same time seeming to link belief in determinism and "psychopathy" (2010). Yet these papers appear to be built on some major misunderstandings, and going far beyond just mistaking determinism for fatalism.

Every US and Canadian social psychologist named above, and a multitude of unnamed co-authors, appears to be a libertarian. Roy Baumeister noted in the *British Journal of Social Psychology* that: "for the record, our view is that it is the duty of scientists to tell the truth, regardless of what it is. If it were proven that there is no free will, then scientists and others should go ahead and say so. But it is not proven" (Vonasch & Baumeister, 2013). But as pointed out in reply to both Baumeister and the psychologist John Bargh, logic *has* proven that there is no free will, and as a result less than 14% of philosophers surveyed today even think free choice the remotest possibility, with fewer than 8% fully happy with the idea. The four most commented upon theoretical developments in the last few decades of the free will debates – illusionism, modern reactive-attitudinism, semi-compatibilism, and the nuanced libertarianism of Robert Kane that argues for a form of self-creation but not in a way that allows for the ability to have done otherwise – "help to reinforce the understanding that belief in libertarian free will is now the exception not the norm at the academic (non-lay) level" (Miles 2013a, p.233).

And the methodological errors in this North American social psychology tradition – work that Dan Dennett has nevertheless described as "pioneering" (2012a) – seem to go further, and may be built into the very fabric of the language being used. There is a branch of philosophy termed experimental philosophy, a hybrid of philosophy and the methods of psychology, that investigates folk psychology, or lay beliefs, including those around free will. Shaun Nichols is the most high-profile of those who wish to show that the masses have libertarian sensibilities, while Eddy Nahmias is probably the most visible of those who wish to try to prove the masses have compatibilist tendencies. But even Nahmias has to admit that his own studies have appeared to show that between two-thirds and three-quarters of the public appear to believe that at any given moment people can choose to do otherwise. In one scenario well over two-thirds thought so, and in another "76% of participants responding that both Fred and Barney could have done otherwise" (Nahmias *et al.* 2005, p.570). And this is possibly an underestimate of belief in freedom of choice, because as Sam Harris points out even "Nahmias and his coauthors repeatedly worry that their experimental subjects didn't really understand the implications of determinism" (2014).

The leading experimental philosophers from across the traditions agree that it is unmistakably easy to unintentionally mislead participants when it comes to free will responses, and remarkably difficult to interpret what participants' responses imply for their understanding of the questions being asked. North American social psychology nevertheless seems somewhat unmindful of what experimental philosophy sees as the need for such slow and cautious interpretation, notwithstanding that social psychology would appear prone to accidentally leading participants astray. The author had to chide the doyen of this tradition, Roy Baumeister, for appearing "to have a slightly too flexible approach to defining free will" (2013a, p.232), with the thought that if the experimenter cannot keep track of his definitions what hope is there for his participants?

And while Bruce Waller (e.g. 2011) had suggested methodological problems, others actually went on to try to replicate the results of some of the above papers, but largely without success. One example is the cognitive psychologist Rolf Zwaan and his team at Erasmus University Rotterdam. Quoting from Zwaan's blog: "What might account for the stark differences between our findings and those of [Vohs and Schooler]?" He continues: "How about the subjects in the original study? V&S used … *30 undergraduates* … that's all it says in the paper. Kathleen Vohs informed us via email that the subjects were undergraduates at the University of Utah. Specifically, they were *smart, devoted adults about half of whom were active in the Mormon Church*. One would think that it is not too trivial to mention in the paper. After all, free will is not unimportant to Mormons" (2013). But Zwaan's team may have been overtaken by events. In 2015 social psychology was rocked when the Center for Open Science-led "Reproducibility Project", a collaboration of 270 contributing authors trying to repeat almost one hundred published experimental and correlational studies – ninety-eight papers and one hundred replication attempts, as in two cases there was duplication of testing by separate teams – failed to verify many of those key social psychology papers. As that *Nature* headline put it in August 2015, "Over Half of Psychology Studies Fail Reproducibility Test". Or as the *New York Times* reported, of the ninety-eight published psychology studies, one of the studies that "did not check out" when retested was a paper on the dangers of challenging the myth of free will, the paper apparently cited "the most" of any of the studies. So why might this have been a study that did not hold up when retested? "One possible reason, the authors suggest, had to do with how subjects' opinions about free will were manipulated" (Carey & Roston, 2015).

We will not take up again the widespread problem with *p*-values and misunderstanding simple statistical significance within psychology, as we mentioned this in detail in an earlier chapter, except to say that while many are concentrating on reproducibility and statistical (in)significance, of perhaps equal concern should be study design. Does it even matter if a study can actually be reproduced if the study is misleading in its very formulation? In the section on mistaking determinism for fatalism Waller noted above that "the researchers primed their experimental group not toward belief in determinism, but rather in the direction of a diminished sense of self-efficacy, to acceptance of helplessness". I do not believe the researchers would have done this intentionally, but if you so misunderstand the absence of relationship between determinism and fatalism – a non-relationship first recognised within philosophy two and a half thousand years ago – that you mislead your participants into a connection that should not be made, there should perhaps be questions over social psychology's involvement in such investigation rather than, say, experimental philosophy's involvement. Remember that these studies have been influential, with their findings reported uncritically by publications from *New Scientist* to *The Economist*, but studies drawing social, economic and political conclusions should always be more carefully reviewed.

Turning away from methodology there is also a significant unacknowledged ontological problem with the Canadian and US social psychology research. The tradition appears almost wholly oblivious to the problem of moral luck – and by extension Richard Double's criticism of the "moral hardness" of libertarian free choice apologists – a key confounding factor in any attempt to claim ethical benefits arising from the free will conceit. For all the criticism of thinkers like Dennett, Watson, Smilansky, and Fischer, each of these theorists is nevertheless acutely aware of the problem of moral luck and is trying to somehow reconcile or answer that problem, even if their answer is, like Smilansky and Dennett, to direct attention elsewhere and even close down discussion. Their work may be wrong both intellectually and ethically, but because it at least tries to reconcile the problem of moral luck it is not automatically self-negating in the way the work of (for example) Baumeister, Schooler, and Vohs can be argued to be.

7

"I TOO WOULD LIKE TO BE A FALLEN SOLDIER"

"As a teenager in Israel, I too was initially captivated by the nationalist promise ... and in between flag waving and poem recitations, I naturally thought to myself that when I grow up I too would like to be a fallen soldier."

— **Yuval Noah Harari**, *21 Lessons for the 21st Century* (pp.274–5)

There has been much talk about disruptive technologies, digital disruptors, and disruptive business models, which are supposed to be changing the very economics of society. The Oxford College of Marketing writes that "digital disruption is a transformation that is caused by emerging digital technologies and business models". But while we have certainly seen emerging digital technologies, there has as yet been little evidence of emerging business models. Far from these emergent technologies driving society forward into the bright new twenty-first century, much of the direction of travel is back to the old economic models of the early twentieth century, most of the nineteenth century, and even parts of the fifteenth century.

These supposedly disruptive business models have largely seen the replacement of, or at least the superseding of, one group of Ivy League white males by another group of Ivy League white males. The main thing that was stand-out about the new Ivy Leaguers was their relative youth, although to be absolutely correct I guess we should say replaced by IvyPlus white males. Although Mark Zuckerberg and Eduardo Saverin attended Harvard, and Jeff Bezos attended Princeton, Google's Sergey Brin and Larry Page attended Stanford, and Stanford is part of the eleven-school IvyPlus Exchange, not the eight-school Ivy League. And what these "disruptor" businesses have done is concentrate wealth and power in the hands of a privileged white elite, while manipulating and impoverishing people of colour and poor whites. Which is exactly the same business model that corporate America was running at the founding of the IvyPlus colleges.

Meanwhile, data aggregation and usage by Facebook and Google, and other platforms like Twitter, has often been algorithmically optimised to engage and manipulate those of lower education, and generally of lower socio-economic position. And while there has of course been social disruption, this has largely turned the clock back, and seen the return of an earlier, less secure, more divided and nativist, America. Turning the clock back is scarcely showing us something new and emergent. And the early Facebook, Google and Twitter models deliberately sought this, though Facebook's most of all. Facebook revenues are driven by advertising, which relies on eyeballs, which are or at least were grown through an optimised policy of manipulating emotions, dividing groups, and leaving particularly less educated people feeling more and more scared and angry. Albeit this business model was first used by American talk radio, American cable news, and political campaigning after Richard Nixon. And like Big Tobacco, Facebook pushes an addictive drug, and is marketed in strikingly similar ways to how tobacco has traditionally been sold. Like tobacco, Facebook can have serious health issues for a significant proportion of the population, although mental health over physical health this time, with similar market failure in the form of large costs to be absorbed by the rest of us.

We did see some positive sides to social media during the 2020 global pandemic, and an earlier backlash had already forced the giants of social media to invest heavily in platforms less open to third-party manipulation. Yet digital disruptors from Facebook and Apple to Google either have or may have abused market power, monopolistic positions, and even their own employees and customers in ways that are remarkably similar to the predatory capitalism of the late nineteenth and early twentieth centuries, and before America brought in employment, anti-trust and competition legislation to protect staff, consumers and smaller businesses in a pre-digital age. Facebook allowed Cambridge Analytica access to data from tens of millions of its customers without their proper consent, and had to cut ties with one PR firm after effectively admitting attempts to falsely smear its critics. Facebook itself is run on an invasive and cult-like managerial orientation and has in the past adopted the seeming business model of ignoring regulation intended to protect its customers' (including children's) privacy, and instead choosing to absorb huge fines which are seen as the lesser cost. Google was fined $5 billion for abusing the market dominance of its Android phone operating system to force the pre-installation of Google apps, and voluntarily offered to build a censored search engine for the Chinese state, being the secret and now abandoned Project Dragonfly, though Microsoft has been providing China with a censored search engine since 2009. Google has had a disturbing internal culture, with instances of sexual abuse and racism reportedly tolerated until staff themselves resisted, staff who instead of being praised were often targeted for management retaliation. Uber was founded with an infamous management culture, and had to pay $245 million in settlements relating to the technology behind self-driving cars. And Apple, one of the lesser offenders perhaps because it is closer to a normal technology business rather than a bro-culture college venture, acts with monopolistic power with regard to its highly profitable App Store, even if it is still to be decided if this is actually abusive monopoly power.

Meantime, disruptor businesses from the union-busting Amazon and Uber to Deliveroo and Netflix have helped push down wages and leave many less socially and economically secure, and new technology has allowed the rise of the gig economy and fresh and improved forms of worker exploitation, with some further consequences during the 2020 pandemic. Using perhaps a lesser known example, Netflix and Amazon Prime have helped drive a significant reduction in both payments and contractual security for jobbing actors or rather, no surprise, for all but the top actors. None of this is anything new; this is just another form of early twentieth-century unfettered and largely unregulated free-market turbo-capitalism, and one that is very often being directed by, or at least honed by, executives trained at Harvard Business School, Goldman Sachs and McKinsey's, and funded and structured through the same venture capitalists and tax lawyers that helped build previous American financial empires.

And the effect of digital disruption on newspapers has returned not just to the nineteenth century, it has resurrected business models seen in the fifteenth century. Derek Thompson noted in *The Atlantic* that in the early nineteenth century American newspapers relied on patrons, particularly political parties. This was known as the "party press" era, and editors were paid by one party to publish vicious attacks on rivals. Journalism of this era was "hyper-political and deeply biased", Thompson writes (2018), but it did engage and galvanise, and may even have significantly pushed up voting rates. Advertising killed the party press model and freed newspapers from patronage, but this also led to a "neutered, detached style of reporting" to avoid offending the biggest advertisers such as department stores. With the death of the advertising-supported newspaper model as available spend gets hoovered up by Google and Facebook – noting that at the time of writing Facebook is facing a major advertising boycott, although representing only a tiny fraction of Facebook's revenue – we have seen the revival of patronage, but at the moment with a largely hands-off ownership style. Jeff Bezos bought the *Washington Post*, and Laurene Powell Jobs, widow of Steve, purchased a majority share in the very journal Thompson was writing in. Thompson refers to "a Medici-esque sponsorship model", thus harking back to a fifteenth-century business framework, and other big-name publications taken over by billionaire patrons include *Time* and *Fortune*, although some billionaires have had changes of mind. "Chris Hughes junked *The New Republic* when losses eclipsed his idealism", and Thompson mentions Phil Anschutz in 2018 closing the neocon bible, the *Weekly Standard*, due to its losses, notwithstanding Rupert Murdoch had apparently been happy to lose over $1 million a year when running it to 2009. Silicon Valley has certainly disrupted the newspaper business, but by providing an older business model, not a newer one. "We've accelerated backward, as if in a time machine", Thompson concludes, even if the coronavirus further speeded up Silicon Valley's dislocation of the newspaper sector, including forcing into liquidation the 179-year-old *Jewish Chronicle*, though it has since been rescued.

The point being that, with all due respect to The Oxford College of Marketing, born-to-wealth Harvard fraternity lads like Zuckerberg and Saverin wouldn't know an "emerging ... business model" if it came up and shook their hands. "We've accelerated backward." *But there is a real emerging business model on the horizon, involving its own disruptive tech.* It combines revolutions in neuroscience, advances in evolutionary biology, and maverick philosophers running "Logic 2.0". This technology will disrupt our thinking about morality, justice, fairness and the nature of social and economic opportunity; it will disrupt our thinking about sexuality, about people and their gods, and even about what it means to be human. Darwin's wager, and the modern advances in philosophical thinking, are a fundamental disruption to the reasoning that has gone on for 3,000 years and that has structured, and stratified, the very societies around us. And the IvyPlus rich and privileged are not part of this revolution, are not driving this revolution, and will not benefit from this revolution. Far from further entrenching privilege, power and wealth, *this* emerging business model would naturally force a more equal distribution of power and resources. Indeed, a fairer distribution of resources now appears to be a fundamental requirement for morality and justice.

A century ago philosophers were running Logic 1.0, running a script that kept crashing or returning error messages. Most philosophers at that stage believed in the possibility of free choice, even though such a belief has always been wholly illogical; what we could call Kant and others' logic of illogic. The last fifty years or so has seen philosophers updating their understanding of the world, as that majority belief in free choice morphed into an understanding that free choice is an impossibility, but an impossibility the public must continue to believe in. This we can call Logic 1.1; a merging of the new and the old, a merging of rationality with the ancient idea of the Philosopher King. Philosophers are the keepers of dangerous knowledge, this conceit goes, smarter, more fragrant, and better than the rest of you, and ideally placed to decide who should know what. As Saul Smilansky puts it condescendingly, you the public are "fragile plants" who need to be "defended from the chill of the ultimate perspective" (2011, p.436). But thanks to maverick philosophers like Derk Pereboom, Richard Double and Bruce Waller, we now have Logic 2.0, a blending of rational thought and the key understanding that democracy and morality are only safe when supposedly dangerous knowledge is taken out of the hands of the intellectual elites and made public.

And both Darwin's wager and Logic 2.0 force us to embrace far more disruption, and ask deep and uncomfortable questions that our species has hidden from for thousands of years. Questions such as: *Are some countries simply incompatible with morality and justice?* And: *Is my own country compatible with morality and justice?* Or: *Are some religions fundamentally immoral?* Then moving on to the granddaddy of all questions: *Am I myself even capable of morality, justice and fair play?*

We will hereafter be primarily concentrating on democracies – countries like India, Israel and the United States – because with democracies there is no hiding place. If a democracy is immoral it is because most of its people are fundamentally immoral, or at least amoral. Most people may be defined by that "double dose of unfairness", but as Darwin realised, so can entire democratic countries. Similarly incapable of being fair or just, and further incapable of even fairly defining fair play and justice. With autocracies there will always be the tendency for apologists to argue that an immoral autocracy or theocracy is immoral because of those in power, even though this often is not the case, and the immorality of the state seemingly reflects the deeper immorality, or amorality, of its underlying people. Iraq remains a brutal, dangerous country that was destabilised by many decades of self-interested Western interference, but is it still brutal largely despite its people or largely because of its people? There was a horrifying suggestion made that when a few years ago the rapists and slavers of the Islamic State were throwing homosexuals to their deaths off buildings in Iraq, they were doing this less to terrorise the immediate population than to buy favour and ingratiate themselves with enthusiastic rural Iraqi locals.

It was Plato who first wrote of the foundation myth that underlies, defines and controls states. Plato's call for a single coherent foundation myth, *gennaion ti hen pseudomenous*, is sometimes translated as noble fiction or pious falsehood. Both democracies and non-democracies have such foundation myths, often linked to religion and nationalism, and whether a state can ever be moral depends to a large extent on how toxic (to itself and others) its originating myth is, plus how integral to the state the myth becomes. Some countries and peoples impose the cost, while others have had to bear the cost, of deadly foundation myths. The 1994 Rwandan genocide has a number of causes, but the seeds were sown in the early twentieth century when brutal colonists from the Belgian state helped promulgate a myth that the more "European-looking" Tutsis were biologically superior to Hutus, and on the back of this favoured the minority Tutsis in their dealings. Hutu resentment inevitably followed, along with Hutu scapegoating of Tutsis after the Belgians were forced by the international community to grant independence, and the final outcome was genocide.

But toxic foundation myths can sometimes be controlled or rolled back to allow states to live harmoniously within the modern world. During the Second Sino-Japanese War, a deeply toxic myth of Japanese natural superiority led to many atrocities, including the Nanjing Massacre, which started in December 1937 and saw the torture, rape and murder of tens of thousands of Chinese women and small children. After Japan's surrender in 1945, and even ahead of the war crimes trials, there was concerted effort by the Allies to change the Japanese national myth. Shintoism was dismantled as a state religion, and the Emperor was forced to publicly renounce his divine status, in order to remove the supposed mandate of heaven and pave the way for constitutional government and democracy. The education system was overhauled, as was the economy, power was decentralised, and the teaching of ethics firmly removed from state hands.

It was a somewhat similar situation in Germany after the Second World War, a democracy that had fallen, fallen actually very easily, to demagogues. Denazification (*Entnazifizierung*) was the initiative to rid both Austria and Germany of the politics, culture and social structure of Nazism, though the original programme was modified due to difficulties on the ground, while some parts were rolled back after the start of the Cold War. The process was different in each zone, the American, British, French and Soviet sectors, but for the American and British zones a rugged democracy was a core intent. Within the American zone in particular re-education was a key theme. Literature that was Nazi or militaristic was confiscated, leading to the banning of school textbooks and even poetry books, and artists were restricted in the new art they could create. In the French zone three-quarters of teachers were removed at first, because teachers had been turned into propagandists under the Nazis, although practical considerations forced most to be rehired. And the Allies' Psychological Warfare Division was tasked with creating a sense of collective responsibility within Germany for war crimes, including the Holocaust. There is debate about how successful all these programmes were even in what would become West Germany, with some creating a backlash or not achieving the ends aimed at. However, due to concerted external effort both Japan and Germany today have very different foundation myths from the toxic biological superiority myths that dominated both countries in the 1930s.

FOUNDATION MYTHS, OR WHY "I TOO WOULD LIKE TO BE A FALLEN SOLDIER"

But let us return to the modern democracies, which offer us the perfect canvas upon which to assess human morality. India is the world's largest democracy, but the caste system, where status is defined by birth, is central to India's story of itself. Like the myths of 1930s Japan and Germany, or the Belgians' differentiation between Tutsis and Hutus, the Indian caste system is at heart another biological superiority myth. And although not restricted to Hindus, as castes were eagerly taken up by Muslims, Christians, Sikhs and Jains, the system originated in Hinduism. It may have existed for over 3,000 years, although some scholars believe that caste justifications were inserted later into the foundational texts of Hinduism, and it is now widely held that the Hindu creator god, sometimes called Brahma, originated the system.

The higher castes were held to have higher intellects. In particular the highest of the four castes, the Brahmins or priests, were said to originate from Brahma's head, from the source of his intellect, while the lowest caste, the Shudras (Sudras) or servants and peasants, were said to originate from his feet. Dalits, the out-of-castes, the Untouchables, are even lower than Shudras under this classification system, not originating from Brahma's body at all, and historically seen as unworthy to enter religious and social life. Dalits therefore perform the most degrading jobs, including latrine cleaning and being forced to work with the carcasses of holy animals, and are regularly verbally and physically assaulted for having to work with the carcasses of said animals.

This is a foundation myth in every sense, and Harvard's Sarah Cotterill and colleagues have found evidence that it is the Hindu belief in karma, also here called *sanchita*, that acts as a supposed justification of caste discrimination. The ideology of *sanchita* karma "suggests" to believers that high castes and the well-off are justly reaping the rewards for good deeds in previous lives, while low castes and the poorly off are "justly" paying for past wrongdoing. Low castes, including low caste children, are told to endure their hardships without complaint, as such acceptance is the only way to move to a higher caste in the next life. "It suggests that Karmic beliefs provided a unique mechanism for those possessing stable, pre-existing preferences for the conventional and unequal to legitimize their opposition to policies that would counter these preferences" (2014, p.108).

Since 1950 overt caste discrimination has officially been banned and quotas imposed, but discrimination and violence against low castes continues largely unchecked. The BBC (2018; "Caste Hatred in India") reports that in 2016 alone more than 40,000 crimes were recorded against Dalits and lower castes, according to official statistics, although such crimes are believed to be vastly under-reported. Some high castes, and particularly right-wing Hindu nationalists who have been in the ascendant since the original election of Narendra Modi in 2014, argue that caste discrimination no longer really exists in India, or at least not in cities. Some, surprise surprise, even call for an end to quotas, though foreign observers note that the violence against low castes is especially common among right-wing nationalists offended at the thought of low castes trying to improve their economic standing, even if not their social standing. The economist Smriti Sharma has found that crimes against low caste Indians rise as lower castes manage to reduce the economic gap with higher castes. "We interpret this as the upper castes responding to changes in threat perception created by changes in the relative positions between the two groups", she writes (2015, p.220). This is high castes wanting to protect their privileged position in society, and Sharma highlights this "perverse consequence of inter-caste equality".

While the argument that caste discrimination no longer exists goes against all the evidence, which is of entrenched discrimination even in the largest cities, India may one day see the need, and the opportunity, to move beyond the caste system. Hinduism has already seen many people converting away to other religions or no religion, and so they can be rid of the karma and Brahma influences. Furthermore, India, with its "Silicon Valley" cities, wishes to be seen as a modern economy and a modern democracy, and if the benefits of loosening the system come to be viewed by higher castes and nationalist politicians as outweighing the costs, we may one day see the end to this toxic biological superiority myth. The point being that this myth is not necessarily foundational to the modern Indian state, and with rising GDP, the need to integrate more fully into the world economy, and political will, Indian higher castes may stop viciously defending their place in the sun. Many states have gone through similar growing pains, forced to renounce serfdom, give working class men the vote, give women the vote, and at least partially dismantle segregationist social and voting systems, and India may one day join them. Because the point here is that unless a foundation myth is part of the very DNA of its people, it can be modified, as happened in Japan and Germany. But while we can have a small sense of optimism that the Indian caste system could one day be torn down, notwithstanding it will take decades of sustained external and internal pressure to force such an enormous cultural change, there is less optimism regarding our next democracy, Israel.

Israel appears to have a foundation myth that is in ways even more toxic than the Indian caste system, yet that will be far harder to end than the similar "chosen people" myths of 1930s Japan and Germany. The global publishing sensation and *Sapiens'* author Yuval Noah Harari is an Israeli teaching at the Hebrew University of Jerusalem, and Harari highlights the partisan propaganda of Jewish Israeli primary and secondary school historical education, the viciousness of the nationalist project, and yet the difficulty for any Israeli to escape the unceasing one-sided storytelling of the state. Despite his obvious intelligence and questioning character, Harari admits that he fell for the relentless propaganda of the state education system for many years: "As a teenager in Israel, I too was initially captivated by the nationalist promise to become part of something bigger than myself. I wanted to believe that if I gave my life to the nation, I would live for ever in the nation. ... I naturally thought to myself that when I grow up I too would like to be a fallen soldier" (2018, pp.274–5).

Although he doesn't say it, preferring to intellectualise his ultimate rejection of militant Jewish nationalism ("if I am dead, how would I know these kids were really reciting poems in my honour?"), it may well have been Harari's growing awareness of his homosexuality that eventually saved him from the endless state propaganda and group-think of his peers. As a teenager in school dreaming of becoming a fallen soldier, he must have realised the incongruity that the Israeli military he idolised proscribed his very sexuality, only accepting open homosexuals when Harari was almost out of his teens. How long does the infatuation with an institution last when that very institution rejects, mocks, and undermines you; how long before the disillusionment sets in? Israel is far more sexuality tolerant than any of its immediate neighbours, but to this day Israeli politics continues to treat LGBT people as second-class Jews, for example with a right-wing coalition voting down in July 2018 attempts to extend surrogacy rights to gay men. Oppressed and disregarded minorities, aware through bitter experience of how easy it is to twist knowledge and slant truth, have a greater tendency to learn to be sceptical of the information flowing around them, and Harari is the first to point out the utter lack of compromise that makes up the Israeli foundation myth. As he puts it, "One of the major obstacles for any peace treaty between Israelis and Palestinians is that Israelis are unwilling to divide the city of Jerusalem. They argue that this city is 'the eternal capital of the Jewish people' – and surely you cannot compromise on something eternal. What are a few dead people compared to eternity?" (p.274). But it is impossible to imagine Israel's existence without Jewish geographic nationalism. "If I believe in the Zionist story," writes Harari, "I conclude that my life's mission is to advance the interests of the Jewish nation ... by fighting to regain lost Jewish territory" (p.272).

The Israeli foundation myth is the idea of killing and dying for land, with a righteousness to that killing built around the notorious conceit of "a land without a people for a people without a land". While the latter contention was true, the former has always been wholly false. There is no "lost Jewish territory" for Israeli nationalists to fight to regain. The land Harari is referring to, the land to be "regained" by primary and secondary schoolchildren, and including existing settlements in East Jerusalem, is illegal under international law according to the UN Security Council, the UN General Assembly, and the International Court of Justice. The Fourth Geneva Convention of 1949 requires occupying powers not to move their own populations into the territory being occupied. Yet the real problem is far deeper, and far more intractable, than this, because it is not just expansionist settler land that is being taken from Palestinians with the assistance of the Jewish military. The original state of Israel was carved out of someone else's land without their permission and with killing and vast suffering, although Israel's foundation myth cannot ever afford to admit to this history. Even putting to one side the Occupied Territories, Israel itself incorporates major land areas including Acre and Ramle that in 1947 even the American-dominated UN had no intention of taking from the Arabs.

"Fighting to regain lost Jewish territory ... What are a few dead people compared to eternity? ... I too would like to be a fallen soldier." Under the Jewish Israeli foundation myth it becomes imperative to take land illegally ("lost Jewish territory"), to be indifferent to killing in taking that land ("what are a few dead people?"), and to die without ever having thought beyond what your school teachers told you ("I naturally ... would like to be a fallen soldier"). *Steal. Kill. Die.* I'm sorry if the above offends you, but this human conceit that we broke the four-billion-year pattern of life to evolve to be moral at the genetic level not only bears no relation to evolutionary logic at the level of the individual, it bears no relation to behaviour within leading Western democracies. We did not evolve to be the moral animal, the fair animal. We are,

remember, the "double dose of unfairness" animal, the doubly unfair animal that doesn't need fair, it just needs Dennett's "fair enough", it just needs Dennett's winners' fairness. Unwilling to be fair, but then further incapable of even fairly defining the concept of fairness. We steal the land you are settled on, then we change our very language to rationalise our stealing of your land. Your land was always our land, and your land was never your land, it was territory "lost" to us, it was ours for "eternity". All foundation myths reinvent reality, by definition. Karma, *sanchita*, legitimises discrimination against low castes through the creation of a cruel alternative reality where low castes are said to be paying for their past wrongdoing, and high castes are believed to be reaping the rewards of their past goodness. And it is worth highlighting that the *sanchita* karmic foundation myth is the Eastern equivalent – morally, practically, and intellectually – of the Western foundation myth of free choice. Each inflicts that double dose of unfairness by both making the more fortunate blind to the struggles of the less fortunate and then seeking to make the less fortunate wholly responsible for their lesser fortune in life. So we may one day have the strange inversion that Eastern intellectuals come to view the free will deceit with the same level of bemused horror as Western intellectuals currently view the *sanchita* deceit.

As Darwin said, it is culture, the best of culture, that civilises us, that makes us moral. So we need to fight for the best cultures, and that means allowing no hiding place to the offending cultures, even be that democracies like India, Israel, the United Kingdom, or the United States. These are democracies, and when they fail to show morality it is most of their citizens who lack morality. And what has to date made morality so extraordinarily rare within human societies is that even someone of Harari's obvious empathy, thoughtfulness and intelligence admits he so easily fell victim to a hyper-partisan foundation myth built on a reinvention of history.

The state of Israel perfectly embodies the nonsense of behavioural genetics failing to understand that definitions of morality, justice and fair play have – at least to date – been almost wholly a cultural construct. Stealing and killing for money is a crime in Israel, but stealing and killing for land is a virtue in Israel. Stealing and killing for money is unfair and unjust in Israel, but stealing and killing for land is perfectly fair and just in Israel. The state of Israel incarnates the profound ignorance of the evolutionary psychology claim that we broke the billion-year pattern of natural selection to be moral at the genetic level. Morality and a sense of justice can never be the preserve of behavioural genetics or evolutionary psychology because culture, not genetics and not evolution, has always defined these concepts. What, we are the moral animal, except for a billion high or higher caste Indians? We are the moral animal, except for the six million Israelis running off a steal-kill-die foundation myth? Some attributes, like impulsivity, may or may not be judged to have a sizeable genetic component, and particularly where we can see variations in such behaviour across the non-human world but, again, it will be culture that will largely determine whether such a characteristic is seen as a vice or a virtue. Impetuosity in young people leading to flagrant testing of cultural norms will be seen as a vice in Israel, but the impetuous soldier who is always the first to get in the face of ungrateful Palestinians who do not give the Jewish military its due respect will be the pride of his unit.

All countries and peoples tend to have foundation myths, often involving deities, and they are not always a bad thing, or overly powerful. But the democracy of Israel becomes a textbook study in ethics in that it seems to have a foundation myth that is so integral to the state's existence, and yet so toxic and separated from historical reality, that it has created a country that would appear to be permanently divorced from common concepts of morality, justice and fair play. Indeed, the state of Israel turns the idea of common morality on its head, and highlights the "disruption" that comes with Darwin's wager and running Logic 2.0. Judaism, its first half millennium aside, has shown itself to be as fine as any religion on the planet, and much finer than many. Yet unlike most other countries the Jewish Israeli foundation myth seems too divorced from historical reality to even suggest that it can ever be toned down. Japan and Germany were cured of their early twentieth-century foundation myths of biological superiority as the myths led them into wars they lost, allowing those they had turned on to restructure their schools, their civil societies, their arts and culture, and their economies. But there seems to be nothing on the horizon that can undo this similar Israeli "what are a few dead people compared to ..." mindset.

The Israel–Palestinian conflict is essentially irreconcilable, because the very existence of Israel requires the mental suppression of historical knowledge about the unfairness of how that land was obtained in the first place. Not only can the clock not be wound back – and it cannot be without triggering alternative injustices – it effectively cannot be wound forward either. Fairness and justice are impossible in this conflict, even if an unhappy compromise, such as an increasingly unlikely two-state solution, could ever be negotiated. Japan got the chance to join the community of moral progressive democracies after its cultural poison was deliberately drawn from the system. Logically, there seems to be no such hope for Israel. "I naturally thought to myself that when I grow up I too would like to be a fallen soldier." When even the smartest in the land admit to having fallen for such relentless militaristic brainwashing, and were likely saved largely by their growing outsider status, we can only despair.

For completeness and impartiality it must be mentioned that while the Palestinians, including Israeli Palestinians, bear the daily brunt of this ever-militant Israeli foundation myth, in the unlikely situation that the Palestinian people were one day to get their own separate country, the odds are probably very, very slim that that new country would ever evolve into anything other than another brutal and amoral Middle Eastern failed state. And Israel itself faces very real and very frightening security threats, surrounded as it is by barbaric medieval regimes (perhaps Jordan is the single exception) and barely sane militant groups. While these are not arguments against eminently valid Palestinian grievances, they are a practical assessment of the impossibility of ever achieving justice or fairness in the region. It seems impossible to find a moral route out of the impasse. Israel must continue to exist, at least in its pre-settlements form, but its existence can never be fair, even in its pre-settlements form.

This chapter is examining how toxic foundation myths can prevent even complex democracies being moral. So what of the United States itself? Can the democracy of the USA ever be moral, fair and just? Well, the USA would have to end its uncritical support for violent Israeli nationalism, which otherwise drags the US back down to the same poisonous benchmark. America is the primary third-party legitimiser of the militant Israeli steal-kill-die foundation myth, so for the foreseeable period the United States' moral future is in the hands of the state of Israel, and the outlook therefore isn't good at all. But even putting the toxic relationship with Israel to one side, there appear to be other significant entrenched obstacles within the US to be overcome. First, there is the overwhelming race problem, which goes far deeper than just militarised and out-of-control police departments. Economic, educational, employment and social stratification are an ongoing, day-in-day-out legacy of early twentieth-century segregationist policies like neighbourhood "redlining". For someone living outside the US it is often difficult to appreciate the fault line that complexion-based racism plays in that country, and in particular the almost pathological animus towards black Americans held by so much of white America. Yes, America elected a black president. But an America that would ever try to provide a level playing field and give equal opportunity to American Hispanics, Latinos and blacks? That would be a much bigger ask of white America, Democrat as much as Republican.

The tragedy of America is that a country built on looking forward to success will never be moral or just until it learns to look backwards to failure, but coming to terms with its past is not something America is good at, in the Northern states almost as much as the Southern states. Of course it is not just America that is poor at looking backwards. We mentioned earlier the post-Second World War advances within Japan and Germany, but only Germany has really come to terms with its history. It is still highly divisive within Japan to draw attention to the atrocities committed by the imperial Japanese army in the 1930s and early 1940s, such as the enslavement and forced prostitution of women and girls in occupied territories. In contrast, the German people have worked tirelessly to question themselves and acknowledge where they came from, albeit this really started in earnest from the 1960s. Only by facing the past can you overcome it, in German *Vergangenheitsbewältigung*, and it is a lesson that Japan, and in particular the United States, still has to learn. Second, morality also means coming to terms with the fact that luck swallows everything in human life, but as we shall see in a later chapter, this necessary recognition would seem to fly counter to an (unalterable?) streak of cruelty and small-mindedness within the American character, as well as counter to a foundational belief in America's pre-existing virtue – and how can you explain virtue to a people already convinced of their own virtue? – and manifest destiny to dictate to others. So, no, we should now be highly pessimistic that America will ever be a moral, fair or just society.

And all democracies will have to fight to be moral, as all democracies are under strain at the moment. Hate crimes have gone through the roof in many Western countries, from America and Britain to Austria and Poland, sometimes to levels not seen since the Second World War, leaving some to wonder if we aren't reliving the horrors of the 1930s. In Spain hate crimes almost quintupled by 2016 and in less than a decade. Prior to the global shutdown and closing of borders newspapers had been regularly reporting that attacks on Poles in Britain had spiked enormously, partly following the 2016 Brexit vote, but also after the 2008 financial crisis, and academic papers have been written on this new xenophobia and violence (e.g. Rzepnikowska, 2018). Hungary was singled out in 2018 by the United Nations Human Rights Committee for the widespread hate speech of Viktor Orban's government and the state media scapegoating of Roma, Muslims and refugees, while in 2017 the European Court of Human Rights found that the Hungarian police, and later the judicial system, had turned a blind eye while hate crimes were committed against the Roma. Meanwhile Poland itself has seen the huge growth of its own viciously racist political parties, as have Italy, Switzerland, Austria, Germany, and even those supposedly tolerant Scandinavian or Nordic countries from Finland and Sweden to Denmark. Russia, by the way, is not a functioning democracy, and the Economic Intelligence Unit has labelled it as an authoritarian state since 2011, so there is no need to catalogue here its vast tolerance for hate crime. Open bigotry – mainly against immigrants, ethnic groups, religious groups from Muslims to Jews, and homosexuals, but also with a rise in hostility towards the mentally and physically handicapped – is now seen by many in the West as acceptable, even publicly tolerated, whereas in previous years people at least sensed the need to hide their discrimination and hate. Some have referred to a Trump Effect behind the rise, others to a Brexit Effect, but these were both symptoms as much as causes. Hate and division are being stoked across the world, but were being stoked long before the Brexit vote or the presidency of Donald Trump, and even before the existence of Rupert Murdoch's Fox News.

"SHLILAT HA'GALUT, OR THE NEGATION OF THE DIASPORA"

> "How could faith in 'the Holiness of God' have arisen amid the death, famine, and wars of Semitic tribes? No, Charles insisted, the religious instinct had evolved with society. The primitive Jewish God, whose atrocities had 'lit up hell-fires in Christendom,' could be nothing but a barbaric tyrant."
>
> – **Desmond & Moore**, *Darwin*, (p.377)

The American hard right, for example at the American Enterprise Institute, has regularly looked to make capital by claiming that Islam is an unusually brutal religion, but actually it is not. Islam does have particular problems in the modern world, however. There are no true Islamic democracies, and most Islamic states are deeply authoritarian. Northern Cyprus is perhaps the closest a nominally Islamic country comes to free elections, even if with a degree of corruption, but Northern Cyprus only gets the prize here because it is a secular state. Although Northern Cyprus's secular status may not last given the rise of intolerant and politicised Islamic religion within Erdogan's Turkey, Northern Cyprus's protector. But this lack of democracy is not the main Islamic difficulty when it comes to the future of the moral animal. The word *Islam* is derived from the Arabic root *istaslama* which means submission (to God), surrender, giving in, and obedience without question, while the word *Muslim* come from the same root and means "one who surrenders". The key problem here is that morality and justice can now only come through the opposite of obedience without question – as a post-teenage Yuval Noah

Harari would attest – can only come through open, questioning, revisionist debate that admits to the errors of the past and to the possibility of doubt. Fundamentalist religion – be that Muslim, Christian, Jewish, Shinto or Hindu – is both an intellectual and a moral cancer, though to be even-handed it should be noted that militant atheism can also bear some of the same closed-minded hallmarks as religious fundamentalism.

Submission to a belief system, *any belief system*, any religious or nationalistic foundation myth, makes morality and justice close to impossible, unless that belief system just so happens to have hit upon justice and fairness, and most uncompromising belief systems have an exceptionally poor track record in this area. Morality is not natural to humans, and morality needs to be inculcated in the melting pot of culture, with all the evidence being that it takes questioning, evaluative, liberal institutions to even begin to instil morality, justice and a sense of fairness. And this will be the key challenge to moral Islam going forward. However, as regards the wider American hard right argument that Islam is an unusually brutal religion, the plain truth is that when it comes to primal savagery and bestiality the works of Islam cannot hold a candle to the five books of Moses, the *Pentateuch*.

"The Israelites took captive all the women of Midian and their children. ... 'Why have you kept all the women alive?' demanded Moses. ... 'Now kill every male child, as well as every woman who has been involved intimately with a man. However, all the young girls who have not been involved intimately with a man, you may keep alive for yourselves'" (*Numbers* 31:9–18). In addition to the Midianites, the *Book of Deuteronomy* tells us that the followers of Moses exterminated the Hittites, the Amorites, the Canaanites, the Perizzites, the Hivites, the Jebusites, and the Girgashites. Genocide, infanticide, slavery, the rape of slaves, the rape and then killing of children, arson, theft; the *Pentateuch* brags about them all. Oh, and there is the vindictive hamstringing of enemy horses (*Joshua* 11:9).

Now some may try to argue that we have no historical records of the period, and that this should be viewed as "locker-room banter", as one American president notoriously excused his caught-on-tape bragging about sexually assaulting women. But even if true, just bragging about genocide, infanticide, slavery and the rape of children firmly rules out such religious founding fathers from ever being representatives of evolutionary psychology's putative "moral animal". Furthermore, the followers of Moses were religious extremists who considered themselves not bound by even the inchoate moral codes of the day, and we have tragic evidence from Islamic State that such religious extremists, when they do not feel constrained by their neighbours' standards of behaviour, quickly descend into exactly this sort of slavery and genocide. ISIL's inhuman rape, enslavement and sexual trafficking of Yazidi and Christian girls as young as nine is shocking beyond words to modern sensibilities, but mirrors exactly the behaviour bragged about in the *Pentateuch*, so we can reasonably suspect *Deuteronomy* involved far more than just "locker-room banter". The companions of Moses were an ISIL of their day; religious fanatics who truly believed their god both excused and celebrated slavery, genocide, infanticide and child rape.

But what is the point of raising this? The point is exactly the one Darwin understood; everything that is good about Judaism came through the Diaspora of the Jews, not from the early scripts of Judaism with their "banter" about child rape and sex trafficking. And a further point not to be missed by the alt-right and the American Enterprise Institute is that if Judaism, not Islam, wins the award for aboriginal bestiality, then Christianity, including the foundations of American Christianity, must logically come runner-up, as Christianity is the only other religion that incorporates the *Pentateuch* word-for-word into its biblical canon, even if as a junior partner to the New Testament. Judaism is the greatest moral experiment in human history, because it has demonstrated both the zenith and the nadir of human ethical behaviour. The German philosopher Jürgen Habermas has written that "Universalistic egalitarianism, from which sprang the ideals of freedom and a collective life in solidarity, the autonomous conduct of life and emancipation, the individual morality of conscience, human rights and democracy, is the direct legacy of the Judaic ethic of justice and the Christian ethic of love. This legacy, substantially unchanged, has been the object of continual critical reappropriation and reinterpretation" (Calhoun *et al.* 2013, p.144). And Habermas is largely right, because Judaism did first give humanity the ethic of justice. Only it was not the *Pentateuch* that gave us this ethic, it was the subsequent Judaism that grew out of the Diaspora. "No, Charles insisted, the religious instinct had evolved with society."

A brutal and largely irrational Semitic religion that saw no crime in slavery, infanticide, genocide and the rape of children would become in exile the most morally and intellectually advanced system of thought on the planet. An anti-intellectual culture that gave us the murderous and narrow-minded bigotry of the *Pentateuch* would grow to place knowledge, understanding and education at the centre of both intellectual and ethical life. Many of the greatest minds in history grew from what was once diseased soil. From the brave and brilliant Baruch Spinoza – the philosopher and *de facto* radical anti-theist who indulged in supposed "evil opinions" and "abominable heresies" and was therefore excommunicated in 1656 by his Talmud Torah congregation in Amsterdam, meaning no one was allowed to communicate with him, stay with him under the same roof, or come within four cubits (about six feet) of his vicinity – to scientists and mathematicians including Einstein, Rosalind Franklin, Oppenheimer, Richard Feynman, Emmy Noether, Niels Bohr, Lise Meitner, John von Neumann, and amongst the twenty-nine per cent of the academic Nobel Prize-winners in the second half of the twentieth century. And not forgetting social scientists and philosophers like Freud, Durkheim,

Wittgenstein, Freddie Ayer, Karl Popper and Isaiah Berlin. But all these great Jewish thinkers, and all the important moral and intellectual legacies of Judaism, spring from the Jewish Diaspora, and not from the originating texts of Judaism.

Darwin was right. Culture, not biology, makes us human, but it makes us human in all our forms, from the nadir to the zenith and back again. From the steal-rape-enslave ethic of the early followers of Moses, to the renunciation of this ethic and the celebration of intellectual thought half a millennium later, and back again to the steal-kill-die ethic of militant Israeli nationalism. Because we are the products not just of the earliest foundation myths, but of the reinterpretation of those foundation myths over time. Cultural appropriation is a hot button topic for self-indulgently angry radical leftist teenagers, but cultures have always appropriated, and if they had not there would be very little civilised behaviour. And all of the greatest gifts of Judaism came from the Diaspora of the Jews; all came from Jews learning about brutality, theft and discrimination at first hand. All came from Jews living and working amongst other people, seeing many as human for the first time, and fundamentally reinterpreting their holy works. Because when you are living and working among other people, you cannot hold onto your original foundation myth of theft, slavery, rape and pillage. Something has to give. And the consequence is that had the Diaspora not happened, Judaism would probably have remained nothing more than a brutal Semitic religion. There would have been no Jewish ethic of justice, and no Jewish Enlightenment without the Diaspora. In a very real sense the Diaspora was Judaism's long-awaited "messiah"; the Diaspora was the saviour – the moral and intellectual deliverer – of the Jews.

But although it is the Diaspora that gave the world all the valuable facets of Judaism, Diaspora Jews are frequently held in disregard by Israeli Jews. When the state of Israel was established in 1948 the expectation was that Jewish communities in the Diaspora would by and large relocate to Israel. "When they didn't," writes the Israeli journalist Joshua Mitnick, "this posed a challenge to the Israeli-Diaspora relationship" (2018). Native Israelis viewed Jewish existence outside of the Land of Israel as "doomed and abnormal", says Mitnick, and "this attitude of placing no value on the Diaspora communities came to be known as *shlilat ha'galut*, or the negation of the Diaspora". The attitude became infused into Israeli education about Jewish history and modern-day Jewish life, "making it the dominant prism through which Israeli society looked outward for decades after the founding of the State".

Disregard if not condescension still seems to mark much of the Israeli attitude towards Diaspora Jews. Jewish Israelis (not Arab Israelis) were polled online and in Hebrew in November 2017 under the UJA-Federation Jewish Connectivity Research Project. The results, published in January 2018, showed that on the question of to what extent the government should take into account the views of US Jewish leaders when building settlements in the Occupied Territories, sixty-seven per cent who responded replied either "not much" or "hardly at all"; sixty-nine per cent similarly thought the government should be deaf to the views of US Jewish leaders over its treatment of Israeli Arabs. And yet the behaviour of the Israeli state has very real effects on Diaspora Jews, real effects the Israeli state cares little to nothing about. In a 2015 Ipsos Mori survey, *The Attitudes of British Jews Towards Israel*, sixty-eight per cent of British Jewish people admitted to having a "sense of despair" whenever a new settlement expansion is approved.

And just consider that sixty-nine per cent of Israeli Jews polled who think the government should be deaf to the views of US Jewish leaders over its treatment of Israeli Arabs. Yet Palestinian Israelis account for a fifth of the state's population but have deliberately worse access to education and healthcare, face vastly more intimidation from the security services, and have a much harder time leasing land from the state, although things have got worse since the 2018 nation state law where Israel gave Jews an exclusive right to national self-determination. The Israeli liberal-left tries to argue that this segregation is new, and is the result of those on the hard right who have dominated much of recent Israeli politics, including the quite shameless Benjamin Netanyahu, Israel's longest serving prime minister. But Harari admits he fell for the nationalist steal-kill-die mindset years before the extreme right took power with their open promotion of settlement building, and on the back of this steal-kill-die nationalism a social policy of segregation has existed within Israel for well over half a century. The ongoing settlements are thus in one sense an irrelevant sideshow.

How do evolutionary psychologists have the chutzpah to suggest that Darwin "lets us down", and that natural selection instead broke a four-billion-year pattern to make humanity moral at the genetic level? What, we are the moral animal, except for the six million Israelis running on a steal-kill-die platform? We are the moral animal, except for the perhaps one billion Muslims, the two-thirds of all Muslims, who willingly "surrender" critical thought for obedience without question? We are the moral animal, except for the foundations of American Christianity, three-quarters of religious believers, and nine-tenths of humanist philosophers? Culture, not biology, and not human reason, fundamentally determines whether we turn out moral or not. Judaism started with the terrible handicap of being the most vicious religious code known to human history, but from this all-time ethical low Jews were given new promise through the Diaspora. The religious instinct "had evolved with society", as Darwin put it. It was the serendipity of the Diaspora that gave Judaism, and then the world, the concept of justice. It was the accident of the Diaspora that put us on the 3,000 year trek that would give us the chance to one day become the moral ape. From the depths of human depravity to the heights of human promise. But now some want to "negate" the Diaspora, negate the one thing that gave Judaism vast moral and intellectual worth. It is not "doomed and abnormal" Diaspora Jewry that is betraying Judaism, it is *shlilat ha'galut* Jewry that is betraying Judaism; it is those who want to roll back the enormous advances that the Diaspora brought to both Judaism and the world.

Many have criticised Noah Harari for writing cod philosophy, while Israel's longest-running newspaper, the liberal *Haaretz*, even calls him the "pet ideologist of the liberal elites" (Gutwein, 2018), producing work that makes these elites, and particularly the Silicon Valley elites, feel optimistic about their future role in the world. Harari was apparently giving talks at Google before his first book even came out, and his sales only took off after both Mark Zuckerberg and Bill Gates enthusiastically endorsed his writing. Harari has since been wined and dined by the top people at Google's parent company, Twitter and Netflix, and it is probably fair to say that when you are the toast of Silicon Valley, and when you are on first-name terms with Mark Zuckerberg, you are no threat to the one per cent. Harari is, though, at least attempting to synthesise some of the new knowledge, including the realisation that humans have no freedom of choice, but Harari the writer is still less interesting than Harari the man: an intelligent gay meditating vegan medievalist living on a farming co-operative and horrified by the cruelty of factory farming once fell hook, line and sinker for the *steal-kill-die* foundation myth of the state he was raised in. Violently aggressive propaganda he only finally escaped probably thanks to his awareness of his own growing outsider status.

"Fighting to regain lost Jewish territory … What are a few dead people compared to eternity? … I too would like to be a fallen soldier." For 3,000 years humankind has not been the moral animal, in part because we rarely had either the intelligence or the incentive to ask the important questions, at least until we were forced to look more closely through our own experiences of bigotry and injustice, be

that Harari or the histories of Diaspora Jewry. We now have that incentive to look more closely, because if we don't start asking the meaningful questions, our chance to be the moral animal, our chance to become far and away the most unique creature that can possibly exist in the universe, may soon have passed for all time. If we want to become the moral animal we need to up our game, running Logic 2.0, incorporating revolutions in neuroscience and advances in evolutionary biology. Maybe even coaching Goldman Sachs and the Silicon Valley fraternity crowd on disruptive business models.

8

QUANTUM MYSTICISM, AND MOSCOW AMBULANCES

"This kind of thing is frightening to me, because it often gives me the feeling that the very concept of objective truth is fading out of the world."

– **George Orwell**, *Homage to Catalonia* (in Hitchens 2002, p.30)

The non-existence of free choice – and thus the existence of what is called the problem of moral luck – is a question in logic, rather than argument or contingent experimentation. If we live in a deterministic universe, a universe of cause and effect, then we act as we do because of the biology we inherit and the environment we are raised within. Our character, our choices, become the direct result of the pure luck of that biology and upbringing, and there would be no freedom of choice, no ability to have done otherwise. But even were we subject to indeterministic effects, the quantum world of potentially uncaused actions, there could be no freedom of choice, because indeterminism means the perfectly random occurrence of actions that would be emerging from outside of causation or character. Freedom of choice cannot exist in a deterministic universe, an indeterministic universe, or any combination of the two, and 86% of philosophers now grudgingly accept that free choice is a logical impossibility (Dennett, 2014). But the non-existence of free choice – and thus the overriding problem of moral luck – may well be the only moral enquiry that sits within a logical framework. Hence it is almost impossible to overstate how important recognition of the problem of moral luck is, because it happens to be humankind's single objective moral understanding discovered to date, and may well be the lone objective moral perception our species will *ever* have access to.

Please take a moment to reflect on just how stunning an achievement this is. Although the last 4,000 years have seen multiple moral codes, both religious and secular, every one of them has been subjective, unproven, and unprovable. The inability to tie moral principles to hard fact or logic leaves us awash on a sea of ethical relativism, where codes can reflect only social, cultural and historical circumstances. For this reason, the attempt by philosophers to deny or hide the knowledge that "luck swallows everything" must surely rank amongst the greatest intellectual betrayals of all time, the most poisonous *trahison des clercs*. If philosophy should be about anything, it should surely be about trying to establish universal truths, because as Aristotle wrote in the very first sentence of his *Metaphysics*, "all men by nature desire to know". There is a long debate over whether philosophy should be about knowing the truth or sharing that truth, but there is no debate that philosophy should at least be about perceiving truth. So by hiding, *often even from themselves*, the only universal fact in ethics that we can establish, and one of the very few recognisable truths of the human condition, the vast majority of modern philosophers have betrayed everything philosophy is supposed to stand for.

All religious codes are subjective, and must rely on little more than faith and tradition. Theologians have sometimes tried to posit logical "proofs" of God's existence, such as the thirteenth-century Thomas Aquinas's Five Ways, being his five proofs or arguments. But even Aquinas admitted these were not proofs of the Christian God's existence, and simply assigned a degree of content to what he was calling God. Hence his Argument from First Cause says nothing other than that there was a principal cause to the universe. Aquinas wanted to call this God; we could as easily call this the Big Bang, or the ignition event of the Big Bang, with no further clarity or meaning. Writing around 1660, the French mathematician and polymath Blaise Pascal gave theology one of its most famous arguments in favour of belief in God, but Pascal's argument was a purely pragmatic one, and not an epistemic one. Pascal's Wager goes as follows: if reason and logic can tell us nothing about the existence of God (the position of the agnostic), and yet there is even the remotest chance that God exists, then it always pays to wager in favour of God. If you wager for God, you stand to gain an eternity of happiness if God exists, while you risk losing nothing if He does not. If, however, you wager against God, you stand to gain nothing if God does not exist, while you risk losing everything if He does exist. Wagering on God is always the best bet, argued Pascal. But we have no proof of God here; just shrewd self-interest, as Voltaire argued when noting that the Christian God for one should not be swayed by such a self-serving calculation. Diderot then pointed out that an imam could just as easily reason this way, so the Wager tells us nothing about godly characteristics or, therefore, the right moral code.

But the secular world has had just as many problems as the religious world in trying to provide an objective moral code. The fact that we are, genetically, apes means nothing morally, as this would just be the appeal to nature fallacy. That we have been called "the third chimpanzee" does not therefore suggest that we must indulge in the penchant for public masturbation of chimp one and chimp two. Furthermore, civilisation and settled mass existence have only been possible to the extent we have overcome our baser chimp nature, so we certainly cannot ground ethics and justice in primate, or even human, biological nature. In an attempt to find an objective moral code, what is called utilitarianism has been attractive to many traditions of humanist political philosophy since the Enlightenment because it seems to offer the hope of a coherent and systematic moral method; the promise of a system that does not owe allegiance to any particular preconceived belief, including religious belief, or depend on some contingent point of view. Utilitarianism founds all practical reasoning in the concept of utility, or maximising the happiness of the community: the greatest happiness of the greatest number. But there is no provable sense of justice or morality under utilitarianism. In a sense utilitarianism is a form of anti-justice. All personal injustice is defined away once justice becomes only the interest of the greatest number.

When philosophers and scientists were first attracted to utilitarianism it was seen as progressive and reform-minded but – notes the ethical philosopher, the late Bernard Williams – modern utilitarians are "surprisingly conformist" (1972, p.102). While theorists can try to draw distinctions between total utilitarianism and average utilitarianism, what is called totalism and averagism, both can have similarly repugnant conclusions, and both have been heavily criticised. According to the political philosopher Will Kymlicka, "utilitarianism could justify sacrificing the weak and unpopular members of the community for the benefit of the majority" (1990, p.45), because when your only yardstick is the "greater good" there are no wider moral concerns to keep you centred. Under utilitarianism, and in contrast to, for example, Kant's system of Christian-derived justice, people are effectively considered as a means to a more important end, and not as ends in themselves.

"Act only according to that maxim whereby you can at the same time will that it should become a universal law without contradiction", was the first formulation of Immanuel Kant's categorical imperative. Kant held that true principles of morality are not imposed on us because the moral law is a law that our rational nature gives to itself. The influential twentieth-century political philosopher John Rawls was a lifelong student of Kant, and within Rawls' *A Theory of Justice* is a section entitled "The Kantian interpretation of justice as fairness". Rawls is famous for introducing into philosophy the concept of behind-the-veil wagering; under Rawls' analysis a system could be fair if all players were forced to wager from behind the veil of ignorance, not knowing where they would start from. It is a lot easier to argue that there is no duty to be fair to the less fortunate when one is guaranteed as not being amongst their number; self-interest will push most to urge consideration of the less fortunate if there is a chance they may end up as part of the less fortunate. Hence the purpose of behind-the-veil thinking is to promote real consideration of all positions and points of view, given a lack of knowledge of where one will start out.

The practical problem, of course, with Kant's first formulation of the categorical imperative or Rawls' behind-the-veil wagering, is that neither is realistic, as they presuppose non-situated players. Humans never start out as non-situated, or from behind a veil of ignorance, so many will be unwilling to engage with Kant or Rawls in their wagers. Humans always start from different positions of knowledge and power, and therefore many are unlikely to consider fairness from all points of view, specifically in relation to considering fairness from the point of view of the less fortunate. Life's winners often have little incentive to buy into the fairness of behind-the-veil considerations, or even an ethic such as *Do unto others*, as they already know they start ahead. They already know that no one can do unto them as they can do unto others.

So neither theism nor humanism has been able to give us a universal objective moral understanding; one that is either provable or that rests on foundations that others cannot simply refuse to accept. Critics of Rawls, and there were many on both the right and left, could simply refuse to accept his argument as having universal applicability. Rawls and Kant both effectively appealed to the separateness of persons, to respect for persons, while political libertarians, utilitarians and Leninists would all argue this is either a false starting position or misses the point. But "luck swallows everything" is not an argument based around respect for individuals that some can refuse to connect with; it is simply the truth of the human condition as built into the fabric of the cosmos. And it is the only objective moral truth of the human condition that we are aware of, and probably will ever be aware of.

ANALYSIS VERSUS "TRUER" ANALYSIS

"Dawkins, then, is a determinist, and so is every scientist who studies behaviour, even if they don't know it. ... What he would deny is the existence of something called 'free will' as an additional cause of behaviour."

– **John Maynard Smith**, *Did Darwin Get It Right?* (1992, pp.109–10)

Richard Dawkins and every scientist who studies behaviour is a determinist even if they don't know it. And Dawkins certainly knows it. When he was asked in 2006 by John Brockman's influential science forum *Edge.org* for the most dangerous idea he could think of, Dawkins chose knowledge of the non-existence of free will, because "assigning blame and responsibility is an aspect of the useful fiction ... of short-cutting a truer analysis of what is going on in the world in which we have to live. My dangerous idea is that we shall eventually grow out of all this and even learn to laugh at it" (quoted in Dennett 2008, p.253). This particular

2006 *Edge.org* survey was supposed to draw a direct parallel with other scientific "discoveries that were considered socially, morally, or emotionally dangerous in their time".

The philosopher of science Dan Dennett was, however, furious when his friend Dawkins sent this dangerous idea in to Brockman. As Dennett put it later, "such heavyweight scientists" as Stephen Hawking and Albert Einstein, "and the evolutionary biologists Jerry Coyne and (when he's not thinking carefully) Richard Dawkins" are among the thinkers who see the ancient idea of free will as "not just confused but also a major obstacle to social reform" (2014). But in Dennett's view those listed above, including Hawking and Einstein, "need to do their homework if they want to engage with the best thought on the topic". By *best thought on the topic*, Dennett left his readers under no illusions that he believed this to be his thinking. And yet Dennett's contempt and open hostility often seems to work. Dennett reveals his satisfaction that Dawkins "later regretted sending and tried ... to retract" (2008, p.253) his *Edge.org* article, and Dawkins has never since had the courage to open his mouth on this topic. To call Dennett patronising when it comes to the free will myth would be an understatement; the neuroscientist Sam Harris (2014) accused Dennett of being disingenuous, and of being vain, of "prickliness and preening", after Harris crossed him. And Harris is apparently one of Dennett's friends.

It is of course worrying that Dawkins is willing to even draw a distinction between analysis and "truer" analysis. It is also somewhat hypocritical that a scientist can draw such a distinction without comment from other scientists, when the Trump White House was – rightly – excoriated when it decided to differentiate between facts and "alternative" facts. But why was Dawkins, a scientist, further willing to self-censor in the face of such hostility from Dennett, a philosopher? Why is Dawkins even friends with someone who appears to treat his views, his *scientific* views, with such disrespect ("need to do their homework")? When such views are anyway mainstream for the most senior evolutionists? After all, Darwin himself called free will a "general delusion" (Barrett *et al.* 1987, p.608), John Maynard Smith thought the only natural, physical or social scientists who believed in free will were those who "don't know" what is going on, while George Williams used to term free will "a stupid idea".

Jerry Coyne, the other heavyweight evolutionary biologist Dennett refers to above, reminds us (2013) that Dennett, in his paper "Erasmus: Sometimes a Spin Doctor is Right", wholeheartedly agrees with the fears of Desiderius Erasmus. Erasmus, you may remember, is the sixteenth-century Catholic theologian, or "spin doctor" according to Dennett, who wrote that the general public was too "weak", too "ignorant", and too "wicked" (1524, pp.11–12) to be trusted with the knowledge that there is no free will. According to Erasmus, only these non-academics' social and intellectual superiors were to be allowed to discuss such knowledge; "discourses among the educated", as Erasmus put it. Philosophy is not always about truth and knowledge; sometimes it is all about spin. We must turn a blind eye, cautions Dennett, and continue to assume the existence of free will "within limits we take care not to examine too closely" (1984, p.164). Or as the late Harvard psychologist Dan Wegner put it on the issue of free will: "sometimes how things seem is more important than what they are" (2002, p.341). Which are not sentiments you hear all that often in advanced academia.

But it is not just Dawkins who is willing to be bullied into self-censorship and silence by heavyweight liberal philosophers. A little over a decade ago Greg Graffin, a graduate student of my late friend the Cornell biologist Will Provine, contacted 272 leading biologists and asked for their responses to a number of metaphysical questions. It was originally called the *Cornell Evolution Project, a Survey of Evolution and Religious Belief* (see www.polypterus.org), and Graffin's list of 272 reads like a *Who's Who* of the great and the good of the last half century of evolutionary biology, from Francis Crick, James Watson, Ernst Mayr, John Maynard Smith – misfiled under "Smith, J.M." – and George C. Williams to Lynn Margulis, Richard Lewontin, Gerald Edelman, Richard Dawkins, and Ed Wilson. Provine told me that Graffin discovered that while fewer than five per cent of these scientists expressed belief in the existence of a creator god, fully eighty per cent expressed belief in the existence of free will. So what is going on here?

"Free will is not a scientific concept: it means 'not caused by anything,' and the scientific worldview can only seek causes. It is a moral concept – an idealization", says Steven Pinker in interview (Blume 1998, p.155). But if free will is not a scientific concept, what were 80% of sampled biologists playing at? They were being interviewed as *scientists* yet four-fifths were giving a *non-scientific* answer, a moral, idealised, or political answer according to your point of view. Just as worryingly, four-fifths were giving what "heavyweight" scientists from Darwin to Maynard Smith, from Hawking to Einstein, would consider a poorly understood, and poorly reasoned, non-scientific answer.

"WHY SHOULD WE TRUST THEM ON ANYTHING?"

> "If the great evolutionists still believe in the myth of free will, why should we trust them on anything?"
>
> – **astrophysicist** writing to **Will Provine**, 1 February 2008,
> after viewing biologists' responses to the *Cornell Evolution Project*

Now there are a handful of senior biologists who still believe in the possibility of actual free choice; believe in something that "is not a scientific concept". The Nobelist Gerald Edelman, plus E.O. Wilson, certainly held or hold this view. Edelman has written that, "If what I have said is correct, a human being has a degree of free will. That freedom is not radical, however, and it is curtailed by a number of internal and external events and constraints" (1992, p.170). Edelman has claimed that the strong psychological determinism proposed by Freud does not hold, that there is indeterminacy in natural selection, and that indeterminacy is greater in conscious systems. Most of what Edelman was writing here was complete nonsense at the time he wrote it. Though interestingly, well after Edelman wrote this, and largely since he died, a few scientists have begun (re)investigating what can potentially be regarded as a level of "indeterminacy in natural selection"; for example the physicist and excellent science communicator Jim Al-Khalili, who has produced a TED Talk on the subject.

What is called quantum biology, an area of investigation which practitioners openly admit may be wholly wrong and needs far more study, is about whether quantum processes take place within living cells. The idea began in the first quarter of the twentieth century, with the Nobel Prize-winner Erwin Schrodinger probably its most high-profile early advocate, but has lacked credibility mainly because of the principle of decoherence mentioned earlier, which has to date suggested that living systems are far too delicate to maintain the necessary quantum entanglement. But the idea is being raised again – Al-Khalili has since late 2017 been co-director of the new Centre for Quantum Biology at Surrey University – though like all things quantum, the area is tough to research or even set up experiments for. Yet one of the fascinating suggestions (which may, remember, be wholly wrong) is that without quantum processes chlorophyll energy conversion efficiency cannot be explained. This conversion process appears to be so efficient – close to 100%, a mind-blowingly efficient energy conversion factor for the natural, or even artificial and mechanical, worlds – that the energy transported through plant cells may be benefiting from quantum processes like superposition. Fascinating, but *absolutely nothing to do with free will,* as free will cannot exist under either determinism or indeterminism. Edelman's suggestion that indeterminacy in biology can ground free will shows a questionable blindness to the last fifty years of debate in the field.

And returning to Graffin's list of 272, apart from Edelman we also have Edward Wilson who has suggested, wholly incorrectly, that "the paradox of determinism and free will appears not only resolvable in theory, it might even be reduced in status to an empirical problem in physics and biology" (1978, p.77). For some unknown reason Steve Jones was not on the original contact list of 272, but Jones has always demonstrated a worrying attitude to belief in free will. His books (e.g. 1994) show that he is a firm believer in freedom of choice, and I remember an unfortunate appearance he made on BBC Radio 4's *In Our Time* in September 1999. Melvyn Bragg was hosting as always, and the science journalist Matt Ridley (now Viscount Ridley) was the second guest. Jones announced his belief in free choice, only to be advised that the man he had just referred to as his intellectual hero, Charles Darwin, called belief in free will a delusion of mediocre minds, at which point Jones had to admit that he did not actually know this. Jones is an excellent technical geneticist, but it is always painful when scientists demonstrate belief in the illogical, and Jones was speaking as a Darwinian without even having checked out what Darwin thought of the conceit of free will.

But belief in the possibility of actual free choice surely gets us at most to a few per cent of the more than half who responded to Graffin's questions, not 80%. So what of the rest? Like Dawkins, many biologists still prefer to dissemble over free will, and to make his distinction between facts and alternative facts. "Short-cutting a truer analysis of what is going on in the world" still works for many biologists. For the tenured and the comfortably off, the free will fraud is all too often still seen as Dawkins' "useful fiction" that shouldn't be investigated further, and certainly not at the risk of a sharp word from colleagues like Dennett. And returning to his theme that free will is not a scientific concept, the evolutionary psychologist Steven Pinker continues his analysis. "I believe that science and ethics are two self-contained systems played out among the same entities in the world, just as poker and bridge are different games played with the same fifty-two-card deck" (1997, p.55). But interestingly science and ethics are only two self-contained systems *some of the time* for Pinker, a social liberal but an economic conservative. Pinker does not shy from taking political positions even at the cost to his scholarship, and he is a guru to the New Optimists, a largely ideological grouping that includes Viscount Ridley and militates for the power of unfettered free markets in driving human history, and established before COVID-19 clearly necessitated vast state intervention, including the Fed's unprecedented backstop to the corporate bond market. Andrew Sullivan, the erudite conservative commentator and former editor of the *New Republic*, has noted that he's "a huge and longtime fan" of Pinker. Nevertheless, Sullivan added, it has to be admitted that Pinker "has a faltering grasp of politics, the cycle of regimes, the vicissitudes of history, the decadence of democracies, or the appeal of tyrants. His view of history is so relentlessly Whiggish it's almost a self-parody" (2018). Like a number of evolutionary theorists and media dons, Pinker seems to believe that science is only a self-contained system when it suits him, and only when the prejudice under analysis happens to be "a major obstacle" to economic reform.

Yet as with evolutionists and the natural scientists, so often with the physical scientists. In actuality, there appears to be an even higher incidence of physicists who believe in the possibility of free choice, and notwithstanding its logical impossibility. This may have something to do with the fact that physics has a history of attracting, even at very highest levels, those who have been drawn to the mystical. We have already mentioned the celebrated nineteenth-century mathematical physicist Sir William Thomson, later Lord Kelvin, and in 1871 Thomson was to directly link his hostility to Darwinian gradualism and his belief in the Christian "miracle" of free will. James Clerk Maxwell, contemporary of Kelvin and an evangelical Christian, would seek his freedom of the will where the human mind could push systems balanced on the edge of a knife, writing in essays and in correspondence with Francis Galton. And in the 1920s the influential but deeply spiritual British astrophysicist Arthur Eddington was arguing that both quantum theory and Einstein's theory of relativity grounded belief in free will. It was Eddington who was apparently the inspiration for Alan Turing, the legendary cryptologist and father of computing, to also seek to connect quantum theory with free will, with the computer scientist Scott Aaronson writing that Turing "devoured" Eddington's popular works (2016). Then in the 1930s it would be the Nobel Prize-winning physicist Arthur Compton who would argue that quantum fluctuations could ground a two-stage model of free will.

Quantum mechanics does have a history of attracting very senior physicists with a weakness for mysticism, and indeed this is sometimes referred to as quantum mysticism. In the *European Journal of Physics* Juan Marin catalogued the legends of quantum mechanics who had such a failing. Marin mentioned Wolfgang Pauli's well-known predilection for "lucid Platonic mysticism", but also that Heisenberg viewed Pauli as "more rational" (2009, p.810) than Niels Bohr because for Heisenberg only Pauli was willing to acknowledge that the science directed towards something "pre-rational or mystical". Pauli was a close collaborator with, and shared the same anti-rationalism as, the psychoanalyst, occultist, alchemist, and sometime parapsychologist Carl Jung. Marin additionally pointed out that Schrodinger said he would "welcome … back" (p.819) the Eastern mysticism of his youth, and in a further piece of research Marin has shown that Hermann Weyl was "immersed" in mysticism, that David Bohm wrote extensively on Eastern mysticism, and that Max Planck was a propagandist for "the objectivity" of Christianity (see Zyga, 2009).

Now whether quantum mechanics is indeterministic or wholly deterministic still seems to be completely up for grabs, but the astrophysicist Adam Becker's book *What is Real? The Unfinished Quest for the Meaning of Quantum Physics* is a blistering historical analysis of Niels Bohr's anti-rationalism, obscurantism, and underhand tactics in the propaganda war against Einstein and all non-indeterministic interpretations of the quantum realm. The philosopher and mathematician Hilary Putnam recalls (2015, p.68) hearing the Nobel Prize-winning physicist Murray Gell-Mann saying that "Bohr brainwashed a generation of physicists", and the suspicion must remain that parts of quantum mechanics are suffering from a penchant for philosophical idealism bordering on solipsism. The Hungarian mathematician Imre Lakatos notoriously wrote that Bohr had deliberately started "an anarchist cult of incomprehensible chaos" within quantum mechanics. "After 1925 Bohr and his associates introduced a new and unprecedented lowering of critical standards for scientific theories. This led to a defeat of reason within modern physics" (1978, p.60). Evolutionary biologists have betrayed human self-understanding by omission, philosophers have betrayed it by commission, so is it really beyond the realms of possibility that theoretical physics is currently suffering from similar self-imposed anti-rationalist conceits?

Physicists exploring the concept of free will does not have to mean much in itself. Aaronson, mentioned above, was writing in a 2016 homage to Alan Turing which also featured chapters by such great names as the mathematician Roger Penrose, but Aaronson was keen to argue that Turing was seeking only to find scope for freedom from determinism. Aaronson tells us that the whole point of his essay is that he thinks he now understands what

Turing was doing, before going on to suggest that the interesting question becomes whether there can be a strong kind of ultimately unquantifiable physical unpredictability – what is termed Knightian uncertainty, after the economist Frank Knight – as standard quantum models are still governed by ironclad, externally knowable statistical laws (a sorry and pathetic kind of free will, as Aaronson calls it). Aaronson is the first to admit that the Knightian freedom he tries to defend is fundamentally about ignorance with regard to initial conditions within a mechanistic world view, and is anyway highly speculative. And yet, crucially, Aaronson – and therefore by extension Turing – wants something *more*. Free will, meaning free choice, is itself largely outside the scope of science, Aaronson clearly tells us on a number of occasions. Fair enough, so what is he trying to do with his supposedly less sorry and less pathetic version of free will? His version of unpredictability, he tells us, does have a "vague" connection to actual free choice. This form of true unpredictability is a "necessary condition" for real free will, he says. So the question becomes, what are scientists like Aaronson, and by extension Turing, doing trying to connect physics to something not only largely outside the scope of science, but wholly outside of all human logic as well? Free choice is an illogical concept, and you cannot have a necessary condition to an illogical concept, because it is just a meaningless waste of time, and university funding.

Today we still have physicists jumping on the free will bandwagon with an ideological fervour. The quantum gravity theorist and bestselling science writer Paul Davies has called for the suppression of the growing intellectual recognition that there is no free will. Free will, suggested Davies in a 2004 essay commissioned for the journal *Foreign Policy*, may be "a fiction worth maintaining". Davies has called knowledge of the absence of free will one of the "world's most dangerous ideas", even as he accepts that such knowledge has "more than a grain of truth" to it

(2004, p.37). Interestingly, Davies is a *Templeton Prize for Progress Toward Research or Discoveries about Spiritual Realities* laureate, and a former member of the board of trustees of the Templeton Foundation. The Templeton Foundation is a conservative religious body that has given Florida State University $4.4 million to "investigate" free will, though such investigation appears somewhat self-serving from a conservative religious point of view. The Templeton Foundation has part-funded social psychology papers that warn of the dangers of disabusing the public when it comes to the existence of free will, and see the funding statements attached to Baumeister *et al.* (2009) and Stillman *et al.* (2010).

Returning to the physics of free will apologism we have other academics of world-class standing, including the astrophysicist Roger Penrose and the string theorist Brian Greene. Penrose, writing with the anaesthesiologist Stuart Hameroff (1995), has suggested – in work widely rejected and, anyway, incoherent – that cellular "microtubules" may be the source of human free will. Interestingly, Aaronson argues that his and Turing's version of free will is less extreme than Penrose's because it rejects all of Penrose's further speculations beyond simple Knightian uncertainty. And as Aaronson reminds us, work usually attributed to the MIT physicist Max Tegmark has demolished the idea of quantum coherence being maintained for timescales relevant to cognition within the hot, wet environment of the human brain, while microtubules display no particular sensitivity to the quantum nature of spacetime. Like the wider field of quantum biology, useful to know, but again absolutely nothing to do with free will, as free will cannot exist under either determinism or indeterminism, quantum coherence or quantum decoherence, and no matter how hot and wet, or cold and dry, the environment. Meanwhile, Brian Greene (he of John Brockman's $2m payday) has suggested that "it's at least possible" (2004, p.456) that free will might yet find a concrete realisation in physical law, because according to Greene multi-universe theory may be the solution to the paradox of free will. But not only is there no evidence for such an assertion, we will see in a later chapter that parallel universes, and alternative versions of "you", offer us absolutely no way out of the free will and moral luck (luck swallows everything) paradoxes.

Yet the potential problems within physics may actually go well beyond quantum mysticism and the above free will irrationalism. For over two decades now there have been serious concerns that modern physics may have gone off the rails. The first concerns were raised around string theory, particularly with two books in 2006 by American theoretical physicists, one by Lee Smolin, and the other by Peter Woit. *Not Even Wrong*, which is Woit's book, takes its title from a saying by Wolfgang Pauli, regularly used as a term of abuse in physics, and meaning something so poor it's little more than a silly idea. Woit highlighted the acerbic 1987 comment of the Nobel Prize-winner Richard Feynman that "string theorists don't make predictions, they make excuses", and the even earlier view of another Nobelist, Gerard t'Hooft, that string theory isn't a theory, and not even a model, it is in fact "just a hunch" (2006, pp.180–1). Woit revealed that Cambridge University Press had refused publication of his book, not on the grounds that it was wrong, but for being too controversial in undermining string theory and string theorists. CUP apparently "publishes many of the most well-known books on string theory" (p.228). Woit even mentions one Harvard physicist who suggested, in all apparent seriousness, that academics who criticise the funding of superstring theory "were terrorists who deserved to be eliminated by the United States military" (p.227). Yet the problems in physics seem to go beyond string theory, and Woit noted at one point that "these arguments are circular, and should best be interpreted as an argument that the fates of supersymmetry and string theory are linked" (2006, p.172).

Criticism continues to build, and some of the most trenchant recent work is that of the quantum gravity theorist and prolific blogger Sabine Hossenfelder. In *Lost in Math: How Beauty Leads Physics Astray* she summarises criticisms that she has been blogging about for a decade, attacking not just string theory, or even string theory plus supersymmetry, but also grand unification theory, large parts of the modelling of cosmological inflation theory, and multiverse theory. Indeed, the last she seems particularly scathing about, calling it "math fiction" and a fringe idea within a small part of the physics community notwithstanding one that has gained unwarranted popularity outside of physics. Hossenfelder believes the search for beauty and "naturalness" in physics has led to the much-commented-upon stagnation for two generations. The search for beauty is in effect an opposition to it-is-what-it-is "ugly", fine-tuned, or contrived, models and even though the successes of the Standard Model of particle physics are seemingly partly the result of ugliness and contrivance. The Large Hadron Collider did find the Higgs boson that was expected to be found, but has spectacularly failed to find the "new physics" that string theory and supersymmetry require, and that were predicted at LHC energy levels. Yet despite many decades now of seeming abject failure to produce results or evidence, fields such as string theory continue to dominate attention and grab much of the funding.

Most of us, the author included, will never come close to having the mathematical ability to judge the validity of the arguments for and against string theory, or to judge whether Smolin, Woit and Hossenfelder are correct, or whether string theorists and multiverse theorists like Brian Greene and Leonard Susskind are correct. But when we have seen that nine-tenths of our most highly trained logical thinkers have deliberately hidden from probably the only moral absolute that humankind will ever have access to, and that the world's most senior biologists have fumbled in their explanation of Darwin's own understanding of human evolution and handed the field to those not mathematically qualified to contribute, and finally that mysticism, obscurantism and wishful thinking drove early quantum theory, it is surely not beyond reasonable to suspect that there may be something similarly "ugly" behind the decades-long failure of large parts of theoretical physics.

MOSCOW AMBULANCES, THE MAFIA, AND THE WEAPONISATION OF MISINFORMATION

A couple of years ago I came across an article by, I think, a foreign diplomat who was leaving Moscow after many years in Russia. The saddest thing about the piece was his description of what happens when an ambulance turns on its siren in city traffic. Absolutely nothing. No one attempts to get out the way, because there is a very widespread belief in Russian cities that ambulance drivers are simply acting as private chauffeurs for wealthy Russians who want to get around quickly. Apologies to the author, but I cannot relocate his article, though I have been able to find similar comments in Ajay Goyal's work *Uncovering Russia*: "Moscow drivers, for their part, seldom give way to ambulances or rescue squads", Goyal wrote right back in 2003 (p.138). Goyal was founder of the influential 1998–2005 weekly newspaper the *Russia Journal*, and noted the all-pervasive corruption – both real and perceived – of the urban police and emergency services. And while his views can be suspected of being somewhat political as he was an uncompromising critic of powerful Russian oligarchs, who he called Russia's Robber Barons, he was an early supporter of President Putin and maintains a deep love of Russia.

The sorrow is that such a level of distrust undermines any real possibility of civil society, which is what ties it to one of the main themes of this book: truth and the direction of knowledge. The foreign diplomat in the Moscow story had mentioned the all-pervasive bribery, distrust of all civil servants, and substitution by the black economy. Whether those ambulance drivers are all, largely, or rarely corrupt is almost beside the point; once such cynicism has become widespread the result is effectively the death of civil society, and it's difficult to see how such a state easily returns from the brink. But failed states, "alternative" facts, and the weaponisation of misinformation, go hand in hand. The investigative journalist Alex Perry is a recognised expert on the Italian Mafia, particularly the 'Ndrangheta, the Calabrian Mafia that is thought to smuggle 70% of the cocaine in Europe and is possibly the most successful money launderer on the planet, being the money launderers' money launderer. But as Perry writes, the 'Ndrangheta largely survives because of misinformation. "The mob thrives on chaos. It likes chaos", says Perry in interview with *Slate*'s Isaac Chotiner (2018). There "is a hole at the heart of Italy, where there should be a center and established certainty and facts. There's a vacuum". Perry recounts the example of a notorious bomb attack in Rome in 1971. "To this day, nobody knows who did that, and there are both fascists and communists serving time for the same bomb attack. That's the real tragedy of Italy. Nobody knows what's true. And in that environment of distrust, the mob thrives. ... In that kind of atmosphere, where it's difficult to distinguish right and wrong, wrong can thrive." GI-TOC, the Global Initiative Against Transnational Organized Crime, released a report in late March 2020, "Crime and Contagion: The Impact of a Pandemic on Organized Crime", that analysed how mobsters were exploiting the chaos and uncertainty surrounding the coronavirus disaster, from selling worthless or non-existent equipment and medical cures to trading in disinformation.

Which brings us to what has been called reality apathy. The technologist Aviv Ovadya was one of the first to see the dangers to democracy of social media, arguing almost from the start that it was algorithmically optimised to reward information that was both misleading and polarising. As *Buzzfeed* put it: "he predicted the 2016 Fake News crisis" (Warzel, 2018). The danger was made worse as the tech industry effectively had, at least at that stage, no real checks and balances to stop the abuse. There is, says Ovadya, a "critical threshold" when the abuse ultimately comes to threaten the credibility of fact itself. Ovadya mentioned such risks as spam emails, enhanced by artificial learning, getting so good at mimicking your friends and colleagues that people no longer trust anything hitting their inbox. Which takes us back to Moscow ambulances; in a sense it no longer matters whether ambulance drivers are rarely, largely or overwhelmingly on the take, because what Ovadya terms reality apathy has set in. Muscovites have now given up on both reality and their emergency services, even if they will themselves be the likely long-term losers.

It's easy to think that democracies are relatively robust and can't be undermined effortlessly. But authenticity, trust, and belief in the concept of fact and truth, are critical to democratic discourse. There is the proven power of tech to manipulate legislators, such as the one million fake bot accounts that flooded the FCC's open comments system to amplify the call to repeal net neutrality protections, with researchers concluding that the authenticity of the open comments system had been undermined and legitimate comment obscured (Warzel, 2018). And apparently President Trump has stopped saying that his pre-election comments about using his power to force himself on women were harmless banter, and now tries to suggest the tapes are hi-tech forgeries, a claim that may become increasingly easy for the unscrupulous as advances in reality-distortion software take hold. Although the tech industry is at least starting to fight back against misuse of their platforms, and Ovadya talks with partial optimism of checks and balances falling into place, plus tech solutions such as cryptographic verification of images and audio.

Donald Trump's undermining of "verifiable facts", and his declaration that journalists were "enemies of the people", was condemned by UN experts as deliberately undermining press freedom in America (BBC, 2018a). Trump's attacks on an independent judiciary and independent security apparatus served similar goals of eliminating checks and balances, and were assisted by the cynical billionaires who have deliberately created conspiracy pumps. For instance, Rupert Murdoch's Fox News has promoted "birtherism" and misinformation over Barack Obama's birthplace, called for the closing down of the investigation into Russian meddling in American democratic elections, has pushed the idea that the FBI put spies into the Trump camp, and suggested that Charlottesville protesters were actually actors. Broadcasters (but not newspapers) in Britain have to adhere to a code of "due impartiality", though of course they do not always get it right. For example, while judged not guilty of the same level of overt pro-war bias as their US counterparts, both the BBC and ITV are still trying to live down their broadcasting of sanitised propaganda passed to their credulous embedded reporters by the military during the Second Gulf War. But unlike ITV and the BBC, Fox News is primarily a grievance and conspiracy platform and not an independent news channel, and as such doesn't come close to passing the British due impartiality test, as the media regulator Ofcom effectively ruled in November 2017 when criticising Fox News content. Fox News was taken off the air in the UK, where it had been previously carried by Murdoch-dominated Sky.

But the conspiracy-pumping that Murdoch's Fox News does well, Russia does brilliantly. According to the Brookings Institution in Washington, General Philip Breedlove, Supreme Allied Commander in Europe, has described the Kremlin's tactical use of propaganda facilitating its invasion of Crimea as "the most amazing information warfare blitzkrieg we have ever seen in the history of information warfare" (Hill, 2017). Putin's weaponising of misinformation both at home and abroad is sometimes traced back to his former spin doctor, sometimes called his grand vizier, Vladislav Surkov. *The Economist* gave this view of

Surkov in May 2013: "Mr Surkov engineered a system of make-believe that worked devilishly well in the real world. Russia was a land of imitation political parties, stage-managed media and fake social movements, undergirded by the post-modern sense that nothing was genuine". Surkov "promoted cynicism along with consumption, telling the middle class not to trouble itself with politics", while others have accused Sarkov of being the key figure who turned Russia into a "managed democracy" or a "post-modern dictatorship". According to the Brookings Institution piece again, Peter Pomerantsev and Michael Weiss of the New York-based Institute of Modern Russia have "accurately described how the Kremlin sought 'not to convince or persuade, but to keep the viewer hooked and distracted, passive and paranoid, rather than agitated to action'". By exploiting existing societal fissures, including race, class, ethnicity and immigration status, the Kremlin has "successfully created political instability in Germany, Estonia, France, Ukraine, the Czech Republic, and elsewhere". As Pomerantsev himself wrote (2014) in an op-ed piece for the *New York Times*, "At the core of this strategy is the idea that there is no such thing as objective truth".

Sapiens' author Yuval Noah Harari makes the perfectly correct argument that humankind has always been a post-truth species, and that "fake news" started long before Facebook and Donald Trump. After all, democracies fell to mendacious demagogues long before Twitter was around. And Harari points out that Putin "can hardly hold a candle to Stalin" (2018, p.238), who convinced vast numbers on the left in the West that he hadn't really starved to death millions of his own people, either through incompetence or deliberate policy. In the Kremlin's paranoid and past-rewriting Russia it is once again dangerous to highlight Stalin's purges and incompetence; Putin embraces a self-serving national myth that all Russia's recent problems are externally created, and are not at all the fault of 100 years of gangsters and liars running the country.

"The truth is that truth was never high on the agenda of *Homo sapiens*. ... If you want power, at some point you will have to spread fictions", Harari writes (pp.238–41), and he is quite right. Yet although liberals have certainly made good use of Dawkins' "useful fictions", deliberate untruth does tend to be associated more frequently with authoritarians of either the left or the right.

Harari's point, well made as it is, underplays the greater risk post-truth poses today, and not just through the rise in technology that can bring post-truth into our homes and more easily create self-sustaining echo chambers. From the 'Ndrangheta to Vladimir Putin, from Fox News to Donald Trump's remaking of the modern Republican Party, the human project itself is now fundamentally imperilled when these players undermine the possibility of civil society, attack liberal democracy, or attack Western mainstream media. The above is not to say that Western mainstream media is without fault, and liberal elites have been guilty of ignorance and stunning high-handedness, including when it comes to accepting the difficulties also being faced by the white working class, but some countries, such as the UK, do at least impose legal duties of impartiality on their broadcasters – and on primary and secondary school teachers – if not on newspapers, and have helped to shut down conspiracy pumps like Fox News.

The Brookings think tank reminds us (Hill, 2017) that there are steps we can take to counter the threat from outside our democracies. We can take the propaganda fight to Russia, which we have not done so far. We can ban international TV stations that are nakedly hostile to liberal democracy, like the slavishly pro-Kremlin RT (which used to be called Russia Today). RT is a large-scale disinformation and conspiracy platform that puts even Fox News in the shade, and which in July 2019 was heavily fined by the UK media regulator for serious and repeated failures of the due impartiality code. Similarly, there are steps we can take to counter the threat from within democracy. At least across political think tanks we need to recognise and reward bipartisan analysis and behaviour. We need to start drawing our philosophical class much more widely; if philosophy is to move on it is no longer appropriate for Anglo-American philosophy to be dominated by privileged white folk who find it difficult to empathise with life's less fortunate. And neither philosophers nor scientists should be making a distinction between analysis and "truer" analysis, or talking about useful fictions, faith, spin and masquerade.

9

THE DEATH OF SCIENTIFIC RACISM

"It's true that slavery is an evil, but it is an extremely lovable evil."
— **Leo Tolstoy** (quoted in Hruska 2007, p.627)

One of the immediate effects of Darwin's better-than-evens wager for the human animal is that it would seemingly kill the "science" part of racial science once and for all. Race science, sometimes called race realism, or scientific racism, and even human biodiversity (this last by the alt-right), is currently resurgent, though it has remained not far below the surface since the late 1960s. While there is an element driving race science that is purely related to bigotry and race hatred, racial science as an "intellectual" discipline continues to draw on a much more influential strand that is, or at least professes to be, largely about economic justice in origin and argument. It is this economic-apologism strand to race science that has recently attracted even high-profile liberal apologists. But it is also this economic-apologism strand that now seems to be mortally threatened.

Most race science since World War Two has progressed under the banner of IQ research. In his 1977 article "Unnatural Science" Sir Peter Medawar, the biologist and Nobel Prize-winner, notes both the extent to which some scientists will go in order to prove a pet prejudice, and the poverty of understanding of this complex issue even among IQ researchers. Medawar begins by discussing the notorious case of Sir Cyril Burt, the British educational psychologist, twins researcher and professor at UCL. As Medawar notes, it was a team of investigative journalists at the *Sunday Times*, led by the paper's medical correspondent Dr Oliver Gillie, who began an investigation which ultimately "questioned the probity of Burt's entire work" (1977, p.17), and concluded that many of those who had supposedly supplied Burt with data did not, in fact, exist. The investigations followed earlier criticisms of inconsistencies in the data by the left-wing geneticist Leon Kamin. Burt's work, which had concluded that there was such a thing as general, not specific, intelligence and that general intelligence was largely fixed by age eleven, was one of the main driving forces behind the eleven-plus examination in Britain. This was an examination that effectively determined children's positions in life on the basis of a single test taken at age eleven. But why did Burt act deviously, asks Medawar. "Villainy is not explanation enough: Burt probably thought of himself as the evangel of a Great New Truth" (p.17). As Medawar points out, the really important question is whether or not it is possible to attach exact percentage figures to the contributions of nature and nurture. "In my opinion it is *not* possible to do so, for reasons that seem to be beyond the comprehension of IQ psychologists, though they were made clear enough by JBS Haldane and Lancelot Hogben on more than one occasion, and have been made clear since by a number of the world's foremost geneticists" (p.14). The reason, he says, "which *is*, admittedly, a difficult one to grasp", is that the contribution of nature is a function of nurture and the contribution of nurture is a function of nature, the one varying in dependence on the other, "so that a statement that might be true in one context of environment and upbringing would not necessarily be true in another".

Notwithstanding Medawar's scepticism, IQ research is today the mainstay of race science. One of those deeply influenced by Cyril Burt was Arthur Jensen, who in effect brought IQ research and race science together in the late 1960s. Jensen, who died in 2012, was the American psychologist at Berkeley who really began the modern argument that different races have different average intelligences. Jensen claimed that the social differences between black Americans and white Americans were largely rooted in genetics, and Jensen's arguments were then used to oppose American welfare provision for both black children and poor whites, including opposition to the 1960s Head Start health, education and nutrition programmes. This was effectively the beginning of the economic-apologism tradition that continues to dominate the academic arguments fuelling the arguably more acceptable face of modern racial science and scientific racism.

In 1994 Charles Murray co-authored the book *The Bell Curve*. To quote Murray's colleagues at the right-wing American Enterprise Institute (AEI): "The book's capital sin was not its discussion of differences in average intelligence among racial and other groups, but rather its demonstration of the reality, durability, and pervasive social consequences of differences in intelligence among individuals. That was, indeed, dangerous. It meant that social engineering, like physical engineering, faced hard natural limits, and also that the modern quest for equality was, in important respects, self-defeating" (DeMuth, 2009). Following *The Bell Curve*, and the vicious reception it received from the great majority of biologists, racial science went quiet for a decade. But in the mid Noughties three anthropologists touted, and eventually published, a paper that even parts of the liberal media could get behind. "The Natural History of Ashkenazi Intelligence" argued that "the unique demography and sociology of Ashkenazim in medieval Europe selected for intelligence" (Cochran *et al.*, 2006). *The Economist* noted that the thesis had its strong points and was an example of "one of those hypotheses that dare not speak its name", before reminding us that Gregory Cochran is the "iconoclast" who had previously "suggested that homosexuality is caused by an infection" (2005).

Homosexuality as an infection? Really? Yet we witness regular homosexuality and bisexuality – primatologists prefer the term ambisexuality – in the natural world without any need to postulate infection as a cause. As George Williams (1988, p.395) commented: "homosexual behavior is common in a wide variety of vertebrates (Beach 1978), and perhaps homosexual preference (Weinrich 1980)". Before positing homosexuality as an infection we should perhaps take more note of how common bisexual behaviour is in nature, and that such behaviour is species-wide. There are a number of suggested reasons, some fanciful, some very well evidenced, for homosexual behaviour in vertebrates, ranging from group cohesion, conflict resolution and bonding, through to practice. One of the most amusing and illuminating examples is bonobo behaviour.

Our closest living relatives are the chimp and the bonobo, the latter found only in the DRC. Bonobos use sex as a primary method of maintaining their small group bonds. Bonobos tend to live in groups of only a few dozen, while chimps can live in slightly larger groups. Whereas chimps maintain intra-group bonds by mutual grooming, bonobos also add lots of sexual play. As Dawkins put it in *Unweaving the Rainbow*: "They seem to copulate in all possible combinations at every conceivable opportunity. Where we might shake hands, they copulate" (1998, p.211). Age and sex do not matter to bonobos; youngsters copulate together, males perform sexual services on males, and females gratify other females. Copulation is so common and ritualised that half the time partners are hardly paying attention. Yet I know of no primatologist who has suggested that such bonobo behaviour – behaviour in our closest natural world relative – is caused by an infection.

And yet Cochran's latest evolutionary argument was greeted with excitement by many even on the liberal-left. The *New York Times*, in an article by the now-controversial Nicholas Wade, reported Harvard's Steven Pinker as saying: "It would be hard to overstate how politically incorrect this paper is", and that it was "certainly a thorough and well-argued paper, not one that can easily be dismissed outright" (Wade, 2005). Pinker went on to write his own long article on the lessons from Ashkenazi Jews in the *New Republic* the following year (2006). And Murray's colleagues at the AEI were keen to add their two cents. Lazar Berman assessed the Cochran argument alongside others trying to give an evolutionary rationale for high Jewish IQ and mental performance. Jews make up 0.2% of the world's population but reportedly won 29% of the academic Nobel Prizes in the second half of the twentieth century. Berman noted that Murray had himself postulated a theory that it was all to do with the particular rules imposed by Jewish fathers: "the less intelligent would drift off to join other groups, leaving behind a more intelligent core" (2011).

Yet for Berman and the AEI, the point of this IQ debate was clear. If IQ distribution between groups is down to evolution and genes "this fact has social significance because IQ (as measured by IQ tests) is the best predictor we have of success in academic subjects and most jobs". In other words, this is race science driven by warm-hearted and honest social justice and economic justice concern, and Berman put the evidence for environmental rationales rather than evolutionary explanations as "weak", a racial conclusion he noted as supported by Steven Pinker. "The hereditary hypothesis must play a significant role", argued Berman, and any other conclusion was "political correctness" trying to restrict academic debate. Because, as Murray had always argued, "there is in this stance no lack of compassion but a presumption of respect", and tearing down welfare was not selfishness by the undeservingly privileged and more fortunate but rather economic common sense driven by profound respect for the poor. Welfare, Murray had always pointed out, will not benefit many within those groups, including those ethnic groups, with naturally lower average IQ.

Modern racial science has now moved across to include the alt-right, although it grew out of the work of Burt, Jensen, and Murray. Gavin Evans (2018) noted in the *Guardian* that the alt-right sometimes goes beyond the evolution of intelligence and wishes to raise the spectre of other genetic racial differences, including violence and criminality. Evans suggests that the main figures in the alt-right racial science camp are Stefan Molyneux and Nicholas Wade, the latter the one-time *NYT* science correspondent but now a major booster of biological racial differences. Molyneux is an alt-right podcaster, and Evans quotes Wade telling Molyneux that he was also countering economic injustice ("'wasted foreign aid' for African countries") and that attacks on his 2014 book were "purely political", but Evans also reports that Charles Murray had been a recent guest on the Molyneux podcast. Yet in many ways racial science is becoming more and more mainstream. Andrew Sullivan is a witty and well-read conservative commentator and former editor of the *New Republic*, but is no fan of the alt-right or even the modern Republican Party. While this may be partly self-preservation as Sullivan is openly gay, and some on the alt-right dislike homosexual conservatives almost as much as they detest heterosexual liberals, Sullivan has always been seen as socially relatively liberal, if economically on the radical right. And this didn't stop him being one of the most influential proselytisers of *The Bell Curve* in the mid 1990s. Importantly Sullivan is another example of those who are boosting racial science because of what we have called the economic-apologism argument first started by Jensen and Murray, rather than through any observable racial animus.

As Sullivan put it on his own blog when in argument with a commentator in the *Atlantic* over the evidence behind Murray and others' proclamations of average Jewish intellectual superiority and innate average black intellectual inferiority: "notice that my sole interest in this is either to counter what would be an injustice (affirmative action) or pure curiosity" (2011). It is interesting to see that it is the *Atlantic* here combating race-hype. It is to that journal's credit that it continues to maintain open web access to some of its darker publications, as back in the early twentieth century the *Atlantic* was sometimes at the forefront of the deeply ideological American eugenics movement. This is Vernon Kellogg, Stanford evolutionary biologist and son of the Kansas Attorney General, writing in the *Atlantic* in 1913: "Submit the whole population to a stress of living that results in a certain mortality, and this selection by death may well be advantageous to the race. It may weed out the weak, the biologically incompetent, the stupid, or the depraved. It may be a purification by fire".

So note Sullivan's argument that the *intellectual*, rather than emotional, race science debate ("sole interest") is about, firstly, the truth ("pure curiosity") and, secondly, economic fairness ("counter … an injustice"), in that welfare, and affirmative action, is argued to be largely wasted on some ethnicities because biology has, Sullivan believes, set limits on certain groups. Another example of how mainstream the race science arguments are becoming is shown by the militant atheist and poster-boy liberal Sam Harris welcoming Charles Murray into his life. In April 2017 Harris used his own podcast to defend both *The Bell Curve* and Charles Murray as pioneers of intellectual openness. Interviewing Murray, Harris was also told that the main use of the work "came in countering policies, such as affirmative action in education and employment" (Evans, 2018). Harris is worried about being seen as closed-minded, but while Harris and Sullivan are undoubtedly correct that there is a dangerous strand – "the chilling effect" – in both modern liberalism and Anglo-American liberal academia that comes worryingly close to censorship, Harris and Sullivan's support of the science behind *The Bell Curve* and Gregory Cochran's paper seems at best premature and at worst downright naive.

Some will always advance anti-intellectual race-hate arguments regarding black inferiority and there is nothing we can really do to end their agenda. However, much more pernicious and powerful than the race-hate arguments are the academic and economic race science arguments being proposed from Jensen and Murray to Pinker and Sullivan, and we seemingly can destroy these arguments by careful application of gene- and individual-selection Darwinian theory.

> "The infant was still alive. *Ntologi* began to bite on the fingers of its right hand. He struck the infant against a tree trunk, and also dragged it on the ground as he displayed. ... In total, ten adult females and eight adult males came to eat."
>
> – **Hamai** *et al.*, "New records of within-group infanticide
> and cannibalism in wild chimpanzees", *Primates* (1992, p.153)

Racial science, in the hands of Jensen, Murray, Pinker and Sullivan, is nominally built upon a quest for truth ("pure curiosity"; "well-argued") and economic efficiency and economic fair play ("success in ... most jobs"; "counter ... an injustice"). Racial science, *intellectual* racial science, is built on the sociobiological conceit that man is born a moral, decent and co-operative ape capable of living in vast social groups, and that "success in ... most jobs" is purely down to biology, with no environmental conditioning required on top. So if Darwin's wager is correct, it would destroy the conceit from Murray through to Sullivan. In Darwin's wager, culture, tax-funded culture, including education, ritual and strong institutions takes an ape and makes a human. Tax-funded culture builds each and every one of us, from someone on welfare to each of Murray, Harris, Pinker and Sullivan. "The history of civilization details the steps by which men have succeeded in building up an artificial world within the cosmos", as Darwin's bulldog, Thomas Huxley, put it (1894, p.141). Civilisation, including most of its jobs, and *all* of its intellectual jobs from fellow at the AEI to editor of the *New Republic*, is an *artificial* construct.

Sullivan tells us the point of listening to IQ research is "to counter what would be an injustice (affirmative action)", as affirmative action becomes an injustice for Sullivan if some through their innate biology cannot benefit from such spending, and thus waste taxpayers' money. But it was "affirmative action" that effectively *created* Andrew Sullivan, the former editor of the *New Republic*. It was affirmative action that created Jensen, Murray, and Pinker. In the case of Sullivan it was a combination of tax-funded and tax-exempt education in Britain that took a cannibal ape without compassion or the ability to live in groups larger than around one hundred, and through targeted application of the necessary resources – which is all affirmative action actually is – created a learned, intelligent, empathic ape capable of wit and insight, and of entertaining a room of many hundreds. And yet despite benefiting from the tax-funded and tax-shielded affirmative action spending that allowed him (and his parents, who then passed on to him the benefits of earlier state support) to take advantage of every single opportunity he has ever received, Sullivan, like so many on the economic radical right, will deny to the less fortunate even a lesser level of such support.

Under Darwin's better-than-evens wager for the human animal we are all born vicious, self-interested cannibalistic killers, incapable of co-existing in large groups. This sort of ape would be unable to successfully perform almost any human job. Murray told Harris that the use of his research came in "countering policies, such as affirmative action in education and employment, based on the premise that 'everybody is equal above the neck … whether it's men or women or whether it's ethnicities'" (Evans, 2018). But from a behavioural point of view we effectively *are* identical above the neck – identically incapable of being successful at almost any human job until cultural conditioning gets to work on us. Success in almost any job, and every job Murray, Sullivan and Pinker have held, comes from the cultural overwriting of Ntologi's genetic code. Welfare isn't unjust support of the naturally inferior; we are all naturally "inferior" until culture gets to work on us. Welfare is simply the way those with less initial opportunity access the cultural assistance that those with more opportunity have already wholly relied upon for their success, while both denying this truth and treating it as their birthright. And even if it happens to be the case that Sullivan required sixty economic "units" to get him from cannibal ape to journal editor, whereas someone else might require seventy economic units to get them from cannibal ape to a low-wage job, how can anyone logically suggest that the "right" cut-off for society is sixty units? Why not fifty-five units? And, who knows, if we'd cut off at fifty-five units maybe Sullivan himself would have ended up as our feral problem, to be chased after with a net? Though this question, and a future alt-right "sixty unit cut-off" movement, should not unduly concern us; human development is so messy it will always be next to impossible to realistically argue that it took sixty "units" with Sullivan, and more for someone else.

But, moving on, Darwin's wager can perhaps tell us somewhat less about the ultimate basis of IQ and the contribution of IQ than it can about other social attributes. I am highly sceptical of the IQ theories of Jensen, Murray, Sullivan and Pinker, but to be honest I'm not sure I place much more faith in many of those who write against them. IQ is a notoriously slippery field of study, for the reasons Medawar outlined earlier, because no genes have reliably been associated with normal intelligence in healthy adults while a network of many genes are likely to be involved in intelligence, and because environment can have such an impact on IQ that it becomes very difficult to pick apart the genetic component. This is then compounded by the problem we shall see later that those who undertake such study can be spectacularly credulous.

Studies show that the Ashkenazi are unusually intelligent on average. But that differential could easily be down to, say, one of the best-evidenced parts of this debate, what is known as the "Flynn effect". James R. Flynn was the first to recognise the extraordinarily quick leaps in IQ (which cannot be genetic, as evolution works over long periods) that occur as groups and societies develop in health, nutrition, education, parental literacy and lifestyle. The Ashkenazi are today above average in intelligence as tested by IQ scores, but as Gavin Evans pointed out "tests conducted in the first two decades of the 20th century routinely showed Ashkenazi Jewish Americans scoring below average" (2018). Evans comments that it was tests just a couple of decades later where "Jewish IQ scores *were* above average", and where the Flynn environmental effect is seen time and again: "The most rapid [change] has been among Kenyan children – a rise of 26.3 points in the 14 years between 1984 and 1998, according to one study".

Although it is possible that high intelligence might have quite a sizeable biological component, we should be sceptical that high intelligence is overly necessary for business and economic success anyway. Contacts, opportunity, confidence, tenacity, gravitas, height (seriously), accent, the temperament to make use of others' strengths, a willingness to skirt with immorality or even illegality, and luck, very often matter far more to business success or perceived success than acumen and intelligence. Notwithstanding his inheritance of vast wealth, Donald Trump entered the White House having sold himself as a superb businessman. Yet Trump is one of the very few businesspeople ever to lose money running casinos. Because "the house always wins". The house edge and controlled payouts mean it should be impossible not to make money owning a casino unless you are particularly inept in business. Due to casino card dealing rules even blackjack has a house advantage of around 0.5 to three per cent depending on player skill; it's around a flat five per cent for roulette, varies for craps depending on the bet but can get up to over fifteen per cent, and can be programmed to be just as high for slot machines depending on jurisdiction. Business success, and perceived success, often has more to do with confidence and the willingness to be manipulative than it does with overly high intelligence.

It's also surprising how often the mighty in business get re-evaluated. The financial crash of 2008 humbled every single titan on Wall Street, who completely failed to see coming something they were paid to watch out for. These titans made money when making money was easy, but left their institutions broken and insolvent and needing state bail-outs at exactly the time when what their shareholders needed was management with real skill and acumen. And it is interesting how often big businesses that are held up as paradigms of excellence fail as soon as the market moves on. Researchers at Xerox – admittedly, many of them bought in with past lives funded through the deep pockets of the US Defence Department – invented a number of the key ingredients of home and office computing in the mid 1970s, including the graphical user interface, the mouse, networked desktops, and word processing with a what-you-see-is-what-you-get interface. Despite their researchers being almost a decade ahead of the competition, a vast advantage in that fast-moving inchoate industry, Xerox is a case study in failing to realise the importance of what was coming along. Xerox, which had dominated global office hardware supply, was wedded to a model of leasing expensive and maintained equipment. It was caught flat-footed by a Japanese model of far cheaper and more durable design in office copiers, but even without this distraction it did not understand the need to develop a keep-it-relatively-cheap home and office computing model, or indeed any business model that did not involve leasing and vast corporate expense. And though General Electric's Jack Welch was touted for decades as America's legendary businessman, in classes taught at every business school up to Harvard, concerns are now growing that by largely surrounding himself with people who would not challenge him, Welch may have built up real problems for his successors.

IQ seems to have only a limited role in business and economic success, but we will never kill race science by counterarguments about the Flynn effect or the data sources, because IQ is such a slippery subject it deliberately shields both bad and good argument, and always will. Hence inveterate race haters will always be able to point to a study that claims this or that, and pooh-pooh counter studies. To engage racial science by examining the evidence around IQ is largely to have given up before you begin. To kill the less intellectual side to race science, the non-Andrew Sullivan side, we would need to make biology so costly for the race-baiters that they do not want to go near it. But Darwin's wager for the human animal has the potential to do just this. Can you really see the alt-right continuing to tout biological explanations of society once genetic orthodoxy incorporates the message that not only is homophobia unnatural but that we all carry cannibalism, and maybe even as an outside chance bisexuality, in our DNA?

"the animal in our nature cannot be regarded as a fit custodian for the values of civilized man".

– **W.D. Hamilton**, "Selection of selfish and altruistic behaviour in some extreme models" (1971, p.83)

Bill Hamilton, father of the theory of kin selection that would be crucial to cementing selection at the level of the gene, published two versions of this paper. In his collected papers it is published as "cannot be regarded as a fit custodian for the values of humanity", while when he first delivered the paper to the Smithsonian Institution in 1969, as published in 1971, it was "cannot be regarded as a fit custodian for the values of civilized man". Two versions, two interpretations. Does the animal in our nature stand separate from civilised behaviour, from only the good, or separate from humanity, with both its evil and its good? As Richard Dawkins put it at the start of our Chapter 5, genetics, evolutionary genetics, reduces to "no evil and no good, nothing but blind, pitiless indifference". Because so much human nastiness seems to be vindictive, and the polar opposite of natural world indifference. Thus an interesting question for scientists and philosophers to take forward, but somewhat irrelevant. Because all that matters here is that social Darwinism, behavioural genetics, and race science need the good in us to be natural, which it can never be.

BEHAVIOURAL GENETICS – A FINAL RECKONING

At the time of writing the latest pop behavioural genetics work causing a flurry is Robert Plomin's book *Blueprint: How DNA Makes Us Who We Are*. Plomin is an interesting character, because although he is in some ways a more extreme version of Charles Murray, and though Murray is relentlessly savaged by the liberal-left, Plomin is almost treated with deference by influential parts of the left. While Murray wears his politics on his sleeve, a friend to Rupert Murdoch and drawing his salary from the hard-right American Enterprise Institute, Plomin is more careful to appear non-political. He was interviewed at length for the *Guardian*'s Science section ("So It Is Nature Not Nurture After All?"), providing him with much-needed left-wing promotion for his new book. He was even thanked by the *Guardian* for his "thought-provoking" words and for explaining "the scientific facts" (Anthony, 2018).

Plomin is somewhat more extreme because while Murray actually admits a (small) role for environment, Plomin refuses to do even this. Yes, says Plomin, there are effects from nature, and there are effects from nurture, but even the effects from nurture *are genetically influenced*. The important environmental effects "are mostly random", he explained to the *Guardian*, "which means that we cannot do much about them". Some, suggests Plomin, are born to rise to the top of society but many are born to sink to the bottom, and apparently "we cannot do much about" this. Plomin then touches on the economic argument used by Murray and the AEI. Yes, says Plomin, many might of course conclude that taxes should not be spent on those who are destined to bring the least advantages and the greatest costs to our economy. But, he lectures, while recognising this lack of added value surely we must "bring children who didn't draw good genetic cards at conception up to minimal levels of literacy and numeracy"? After all, even nature's bottle-washers and parking valets need to be able to return our change, and store our car keys correctly.

What on earth can we make of the *Guardian*'s almost obsequious review of Plomin's work ("'I'm holding my breath,' he says, smiling")? We should perhaps recall that the intellectual left has historically had almost as much of an attachment to both behavioural genetics and eugenics as has the hard right, while the traditional left has always made a distinction between the deserving poor and the undeserving poor. Perhaps Plomin's message is just giving the well-educated left the excuse it needs to disengage with apparent honour from those struggling at the bottom. We battled nobly for the less fortunate, the *Guardian* can now argue, but finally had to surrender in the face of what are, apparently, "the scientific facts". But what can we say about Plomin's actual work? Plomin is representative of the great majority who write from within behavioural genetics. Yes, there are behavioural geneticists – like James Flynn already mentioned, and Eric Turkheimer –

who are much more sceptical of the evidence that Plomin and others like to quote. However, the belief that nature is much more important than nurture in social position, and even that "we cannot do much about" the people at the bottom of society, continues to dominate the behavioural genetics industry. The *Guardian's* interview touched on three key areas: intelligence, morality and empathy. We've already considered IQ, so let us turn to morality and empathy.

Homosexuality is perfectly natural, and we know this because it is all around us in the natural world. *Homosexuality* cannot be unnatural, because it is a common part of the natural world, but *homophobia*, and prejudice against homosexuals and bisexuals, is unnatural and entirely cultural in origin. Attitudes towards bisexuals, or what we might term ambisexuals, have been much less studied than have attitudes towards homosexuals, but what studies exist suggest that attitudes towards ambisexuals mirror attitudes towards homosexuals, and that ambisexuals experience a similar degree of discrimination, violence and hostility. One 1997 study of American undergraduates even found more hostility towards bisexuals than towards homosexual men and women. Yet bisexuality is natural. It is not only that cultures have existed that openly practised (male) homosexuality and bisexuality, and where a number of the ancient Greek city-states raised male–male love to one of the finest of the virtues. Spartan military prowess and morale, for example, is widely regarded as having been built upon or at least strengthened by homosexuality, including the bond between male lovers fighting together. But it is also that homophobia does not exist in nature. Ambisexuality is perfectly normal in the natural world, and homosexuality is often used for group bonding. Non-humans do not get worked up about it. Chimpanzees, given the chance, would not troll other chimps on Facebook about their sexuality. They might well post about the etiquette of public masturbation – once one is finished with the mango, does one pass to the left as with port, or to the right? – but male–male sexual activity and female–female sexual acts wouldn't even raise a comment.

Which brings us to some interesting conclusions. Prejudice against homosexuals first became mainstream through the Judeo-Christian tradition, which later informed the homophobia of the Islamic tradition. Most American homophobes, Republican and Democrat, white and black, invoke the Old Testament, and in particular the *Pentateuch*, the Five Books of Moses, and especially the *Book of Leviticus*. There are perhaps three passages in the New Testament that can be interpreted as homophobic, but they are more ambiguous. *Leviticus* is not. And Moses is the only major prophet common to Judaism, Christianity and Islam. Homophobia did not arise through biological evolution, but only became mainstream because of early Judaism. Homophobia became widespread through the early teachings of a brutal Semitic religion, and pre-dating the Diaspora, which introduced into later Judaism – and introduced to the world – its ethic of tolerance and justice.

Discrimination against homosexuality and bisexuality remained widespread in even the democratic and educated West until relatively recently. It was only in 1973 that the American Psychiatric Association removed homosexuality from its list of "mental disorders". Though around forty per cent of APA members still wanted homosexuality to remain classified as a mental sickness, so the APA instead created a mental disorder category of "sexual orientation disturbance" for those "in conflict with" their sexual orientation. As *Psychology Today* notes on its website, "not until 1987 did homosexuality completely fall out of" the APA's classification of mental disorders, while the World Health Organization "only removed homosexuality from its ICD classification", or international classification of diseases, sub-classification mental and behavioural disorders, with the publication of ICD-10 at the start of the 1990s. The Pew Research Center only appears to have begun cataloguing American attitudes towards homosexuals in 1994, and after a more tolerant attitude had set in, but even in that first year of records 49% of Americans surveyed thought homosexuality should be discouraged, while only 46% thought it should be accepted. Furthermore only 38% of Republicans at that stage thought homosexuality should be accepted (Pewresearch, 2017). And note the wording of these studies. This is "accepted by society". This is not agreeing that homosexuals are moral, or equal, or should be allowed to marry, or should be allowed to marry in Church. This is the absolute lowest we could ask for; the question of *Should society agree to "accept" homosexuals?*

The behavioural genetics industry argues that both morality and empathy are largely innate, and that morality and empathy are not largely the product of culture. But evolution tells us that homosexuality is perfectly natural, that empathy for homosexuals should thus be natural and normal, that homophobia is perfectly unnatural, and that a lack of empathy for homosexuals is unnatural and not normal. So did behavioural genetics pick up on *any* of this? Who remembers the outcry when in 1994 the behavioural genetics industry rushed out that statement saying that over half of Americans, and almost two-thirds of Republicans, held core "moral" attitudes that were not natural, and that were in fact against nature, and that such people lacked normal and innate empathy? No? The reason this of course never happened was that most behavioural geneticists of the time displayed *exactly the same levels of learned homophobia* – and anti-Semitism, misogyny and casual racism – as the rest of the Middle Americans they were studying and profiling, and categorising as "normal".

Even in 2006 almost two-thirds of Republicans and almost one-third of Democrats did not believe that society should "accept" homosexuals. By 2017 it was only a slim majority – fifty-four per cent – of Republicans who said that homosexuality should be "accepted by society". Democrats hit eighty-three per cent acceptance in 2017. And of course even today in large parts of West and East Africa and the Islamic Middle East acceptance of homosexuality, and empathy for homosexuals, is likely to be in the low single figures.

The following argument is being advanced by behavioural genetics:

(A1) Morality and empathy are largely under genetic control, and are not predominantly the product of culture.

(A2) The vast majority of Americans are naturally moral and empathic, and only a small number of dysgenic Americans lack morality and empathy.

But

(B1) Homosexuality is widespread in nature, while homophobia does not exist within nature.

(B2) In 1994 the majority of Americans, and almost two-thirds of Republicans, thought that homosexuals should not be "accepted" by society.

(B3) Just two decades later Americans, including Republicans, were significantly more tolerant of, and significantly less intolerant of, homosexuals.

Therefore,

(R1) The moral attitudes of, and lack of empathy of, Americans towards homosexuals has always been an entirely learned response,

and

(R2) Behavioural genetics is almost entirely ignorant of the fact that the moral attitudes of, and lack of empathy of, Americans towards homosexuals has always been an entirely learned response.

Hence we have good reason to start to believe that behavioural geneticists are talking out of their bottoms when they suggest that they have discovered that morality and empathy are largely under genetic, rather than environmental, control.

Behavioural genetics has no definition of morality, justice and empathy beyond incarceration and adherence to the day-to-day norms of the group, *whatever those norms happen to be*, including experiences of homophobia and anti-Semitism. This is morality defined solely as tribalism, where "the moral" becomes synonymous with "the tribe". Which is both extraordinarily jejune and hardly a clever yardstick in countries like America and Britain, which are known to have profound structural injustices and group prejudices. The central problem of behavioural genetics is that it is incapable of recognising the small-minded prejudice (and lack of empathy and immorality) of Middle America because at almost every era it is *part of* that Middle American small-mindedness. It always defines morality and justice in terms of Middle American prejudice. Behavioural genetics has to define this way; it has no deep understanding of morality and justice, and no interest in having a deeper understanding. A deeper understanding would ask, for example, how twenty per cent of Republicans could now be displaying an inchoate justice and empathy, and one of the necessary conditions for morality, that they lacked just a decade before, if indeed empathy and morality are largely coded into our genes. Behavioural genetics is not competent to study morality, fairness or justice, because morality and immorality, fairness and justice, have (at least to date) been largely culturally defined.

And if we look more widely than a particular instance of morality and empathy, and consider instead the more fundamental category problem of morality being impossible without a recognition of the overriding role of luck (good and bad) in human life, we see exactly the same situation. In 2009 the Joseph Rowntree Foundation recorded that 83% of Britons are wholly ignorant of the fact that in human life "luck swallows everything", and the Pew Research Center has suggested the figure for Americans is likely to be at least as high or higher. Clinging to a belief in free will means never having to say "Thank you"; means, like Sir Jim Ratcliffe, never having to acknowledge one's undeserved great good fortune in life, and relative to others' undeserved misfortunes. "That opportunity's open to everybody on the planet." Such a basic recognition of moral luck seems in every way to be the *sine qua non* of justice and fair play. In what way other than with profound moral concern can you view someone born into great good fortune who not only refuses to acknowledge that undeserved great good fortune, and the undeserved misfortune of others, but in effect treats the undeserved good fortune as their "due"?

And yet behavioural genetics is wholly blind to this bedrock moral and empathic understanding, and holds up as its moral centre those lacking in such foundational ethical understanding. Behavioural genetics today defines the vast majority of that 83% of Britons as the moral bedrock of British society, the *Daily Express*- and *Daily Telegraph*-reading salt of the earth, despite the fact that that 83% is, at least at the moment, seemingly fundamentally incapable of acting fairly. Behavioural genetics is a discipline with an almost pathological ignorance of the world around it. Yet this understanding that there is no such thing as freedom of choice, this prerequisite of human moral capacity and human empathy, is itself wholly cultural in origin, and intelligence and reason seem to have little to do with the recognition. Nietzsche may have called those who fail to realise that logically there can be no freedom of choice *der Halb-Unterrichteten*, "the half-educated" (1886, p.51), but this is perhaps a little unfair to thinkers as smart as Kant who have fallen for this vanity, or rather talked themselves into this vanity. Meanwhile, 2,000 years ago the Jewish Essenes, who like most in the ancient world were probably no great thinkers, rejected the conceit entirely. "That opportunity's open to everybody on the planet." Culture almost wholly determines who will fall for this particular self-serving prejudice, and thus who even has the capacity for morality, justice and fair play.

What should we make of an academic discipline investigating the origins of the ethical sense that appears almost wholly ignorant of the *only* objective ethical absolute in existence? How can a discipline spend so much time talking about the identification of genes for success and morality when it is not even competent to define or recognise success or morality in the first place? *Guardian* science editors may now be considering the contention that poor children – argued by many of the above to be destined by biology to sink to the bottom, given that poor children come from poor parents, and thus carry the same genes – should be brought up to only "minimal levels of literacy and numeracy", but it is behavioural geneticists who often appear to have wasted vast educational opportunities. It is sometimes difficult not to see behavioural geneticists as the bottle-washers and parking valets of the academic community.

One of the strangest things about human morality is the way we tend to ascribe morality to the people who simply shout loudest about moral values. I believe it was Ralph Waldo Emerson who gave us the wonderful line "the louder he talked of his honour, the faster we counted the spoons". And yet in America the "moral majority", the largely white middle-class Christian Americans who are shrillest about the decline in moral values, tend to be most associated with bigotry, anti-Semitism, homophobia, misogyny and racism. The term "moral majority" became a political one in 1979 when the Baptist minister, televangelist and Republican activist the late Jerry Falwell Sr. set up a party with this name. Falwell was a segregationist – he actually established a segregationist academy – opposed to equal rights, opposed to abortion even after rape or incest or where the life of the mother was in jeopardy, in favour of campaigns to "convert" Jews and others, and a homophobe, all of which he argued were supported by the Bible. Falwell's Moral Majority defined the Christian Right and the activist Republican Party in the 1980s, and until it was dissolved for reasons including questions over tax exemptions. But even today America's "moral heartland" is dominated by such thinking, and the Republican Party openly courts these supporters, holding them up as moral paradigms, and notwithstanding their often palpable ignorance, bigotry and duplicity.

Incidentally, self-styled moral majorities help establish how extraordinarily rare morality has been to date. Such purported moralists as the late Jerry Falwell tend to invoke what they see as unchanging revealed wisdom, which becomes a large part of their identity, but such hidebound revelation has a staggeringly small chance of being ethically justifiable. This is the *istaslama*, or obedience without question, problem that we touched on earlier. Any source of revealed wisdom has a tiny probabilistic chance of being correct, because as Diderot noted for us there are so many widely diverging and contradictory faiths claiming primacy, while even within a single religion multiple profound schisms and interpretations abound. Christian prophets can't even agree on how to treat enemies. Jesus said love and forgive them. Joshua said hamstring their horses. Moses said rape and kill their children. And challenge and revision is something that few religions – and political or nationalist identities – will tolerate. Conscience over such blind obedience was one justification behind the Reformation, but the Protestant Reformation just introduced its own unyielding dogmas.

Yet although Middle America embodies unapologetic belief in the writing of theorists like Robert Plomin it would be a mistake to view most behavioural geneticists as themselves conservative in outlook. The *Guardian* article recounts that Plomin "says brightening, it's been decades since he's been called a Nazi" (Anthony, 2018), but with the exception of a handful of well-known characters, it is not those on the far right who have ever dominated the discipline, even in its earliest days. Most behavioural geneticists view and have viewed themselves as either moderates or progressives. Sir Francis Galton, psychologist and pioneer of eugenics (he coined the term), and the father of modern behavioural genetics, was a Fellow of the Royal Society, a statistician, and a progressive. He was half-cousin to Charles Darwin, and was very active within the British Association for the Advancement of Science. But he was also an inveterate racist. In a letter entitled "Africa for the Chinese", and to *The Times* on 5 June 1873, the father of modern behavioural genetics explained that "average negroes possess too little intellect, self-reliance, and self-control to make it possible for them to sustain the burden of any respectable form of civilization without a large measure of external guidance and support", while black Africans, he wrote, were an "inferior" race, and "lazy, palavering savages" (Galton, 1873). Of course as a favoured son of the British Empire Sir Francis wasn't much more enamoured of most other non-white peoples either. "The Hindoo cannot fulfil the required conditions nearly so well as the Chinaman, for he is inferior to him in strength, industry, aptitude for saving, business habits, and prolific power", while "the Arab is little more than an eater up of other men's produce; he is a destroyer rather than a creator, and he is unprolific". He wanted Africa for the Chinese, albeit he viewed the Chinese as also displaying many character weaknesses; "the bad parts of his character, as his lying and servility".

Those most enamoured of behavioural genetics have often been leftists, moderates or progressives. In America the leaders of the Progressive Education movement of the early twentieth century were devoted to both eugenics and behavioural genetics, while in England behaviour genetics was openly embraced by Fabian socialists who believed that their ideal society could only be produced by biologically superior people. And yet Galton may be the smartest person ever to work in the field of behavioural genetics. He was a true polymath; in addition to the above he was an explorer, sociologist, geographer, anthropologist, inventor and meteorologist. And he really was a progressive; just one without the wit or character to get his mind around the fact that Britain only ruled a vast Empire through the accidents and inequalities of history, through "guns, germs and steel" as Jared Diamond once put it. Through geographical luck and the advantages of soil and native wild plants. As with even Abraham Lincoln, and like almost every subsequent behavioural geneticist, Galton was entirely the product of a biased time and a place, and incapable of thinking outside the box of his own prejudices. Yet notwithstanding his intellectual blind-spots Galton was deeply concerned about guiding the future direction of what he saw as the "just" society. He honestly believed the world would be a better place if people simply accepted his reasonable and scientific policy pronouncements, be that Africa for the Chinese, or that children destined by nature to be bottle-washers should be given only a minimal course in literacy and numeracy.

> "Professor Thomas J. Bouchard was sitting in his office at the University of Minnesota when one of his graduate students came in with the *Minneapolis Tribune*. 'Did you see this fascinating story about these twins who were reared apart? You really ought to study these.' Bouchard began to read the story. ... Bouchard thought it was odd enough that both were named James, but it was uncanny that each man had married and divorced a woman named Linda, then married a woman named Betty."

I first really began to pay attention to behaviour genetics and the IQ literature after I came across the above extraordinary article in *The Times* on the 3rd November 1997, and written by the Pulitzer Prize-winning journalist Lawrence Wright. On page 15, under the headline "Twins Prove Life's A Script", we were introduced to the findings of Thomas Bouchard, perhaps the most influential living behavioural geneticist. This article was an almost word-for-word extract from Wright's new book *Twins: Genes, Environment and the Mystery of Identity*, which was to be shortlisted for the Royal Society's Rhône-Poulenc Prize for Science Books. But from an evolutionary point of view the *Times* article, and Wright's wider analysis, appeared to be almost complete garbage. Genes are only in bodies because of evolution; this is all evolution really is, genes plus time. While genetic drift can complement natural selection, it still sits under the scope of evolution, and evolution sets the logic that behavioural genetics must comply with. As Theodosius Dobzhansky, shaper of the genetic language of variation that emerged with the synthesis of Darwin and Mendel, wrote in 1973: "Nothing in biology makes sense except in the light of evolution".

Bouchard "thought it was odd enough that both were named James" (or "the Jim Twins", as they are now known on the interview circuit). But whether those two babies were called Jim, James, Donald, or Adolf should hold absolutely no interest for a geneticist, because babies' names are *externally* imposed. These twins did not select their names, possess inherent James-like qualities, or otherwise unconsciously signal what names they would be happy with. For a behavioural geneticist not to realise this should be extraordinary. Yet, it "was uncanny that each man had married and divorced a woman named Linda, then married a woman named Betty". Now if you are trying to study a mutant gene that has serious deleterious effects on the body you can just about study it in isolation. But the problem with something like a gene for behaviour is that you must (a) know the normal behaviour coded into a typical animal in the first place, and (b) have a satisfactory explanation for how any genetic code you are looking for arose and was selected. Bouchard was reported as suggesting that it was both academically and scientifically respectable to suggest the twins were programmed to choose these women because of their names, as otherwise bringing up their names has no bearing ("within an hour of reading the article,

Bouchard excitedly persuaded university officials to provide some grant money to study the Jim twins"). But since none of our character attributes has any connection whatsoever to our externally imposed names, there is simply no way for such a gene to have been selected. Wright's book goes further than his *Times* piece, recounting with astonishment that one named his first child James Allen, and the other named his first child … James *Alan*! Look, posit if you so wish, and as evolutionary psychologists do, that genetics makes us look for partners who are tall, or attractive, or rich. But to suggest that genetics makes us look for partners called Billy-Bob or Betty is, frankly, bizarre.

Minnesota's *Minneapolis Tribune*, today the *Star Tribune*, is the house newspaper of those working on what is now called the University of Minnesota Twin Family Study, but although both the *Minneapolis Tribune* and *The Times* had uncritically repeated each of Bouchard's anecdotes, the *Washington Post* was to be much more sceptical. Mentioning the Jim twins, who had "found they had each married and divorced a woman named Linda and remarried a Betty", the *Post*, whose journalist Arthur Allen actually had some biological training, pointed out that there can be no such thing as "a gene for marrying women named Betty" (Allen, 1998). "Such coincidences are statistical anomalies, as Bouchard is quick to acknowledge", Allen went on to write. Yet, firstly, what is the point then of highlighting pure coincidences and statistical anomalies? Secondly, *quick to acknowledge*? But that doesn't tally with the line in the London *Times* newspaper, and Wright's shortlisted book, that "Bouchard thought it was odd enough that both were named James, but it was uncanny that each man had married and divorced a woman named Linda, then married a woman named Betty".

Stunning credulity seems to be a frequent hallmark of twin studies, even among the intelligent and most highly trained. For the past three decades Professor Lord Robert Winston, a Labour life peer, has been the go-to face of UK medical broadcasting. Winston is emeritus professor of fertility medicine, a professor of "science and society" at prestigious Imperial College London, and is one of the most trusted science broadcasters in the UK. He is also both Founder and Chair of the Genetics Research Trust at Imperial, and has been awarded the Faraday Prize by the Royal Society, and for excellence in science communication. But in July 1999 the BBC screened Winston's three-part documentary around the "uncanny" similarities of twins. This "major new BBC series" was actually advertised using the Jim Twins mentioned by the *Minneapolis Tribune*, including their ostensible nomenclature gene. And Winston is by no means alone in being a trusted science communicator who should have been far more sceptical of Bouchard's coincidences, statistical anomalies, and spooky similarities.

> "Bouchard and his behavior geneticist colleagues D. Lykken, M. McGue, and A. Tellegen are repeatedly astonished by the spooky similarities they discover in their identical twins reared apart. ... Quantitative research corroborates the hundreds of anecdotes."
>
> – **Steven Pinker,** *The Language Instinct* (pp.327–8)

Anecdotes? Oh, right, "coincidences". There is a desperate craving, and seemingly particularly within the white professional classes, to believe in the power of controversial twin studies. "Something inside us ... makes us want to believe that the genetic blueprint holds the secrets of who we are", as Arthur Allen went on to put it (1998). Partly it may be a feeling among comfortably off progressives that if success comes down largely to genes, they can stop feeling so bad about their privileged upbringings; giving the well-educated liberal-left the excuse it needs to disengage with apparent honour from those struggling at the bottom, as we noted above of the *Guardian*. Because it truly is difficult to reconcile such mind-numbing credulity any other way. Can Professor Lord Robert Winston and Professor Steven Pinker – not to mention a Pulitzer Prize-winning journalist, a judging panel chaired by a Fellow of the Royal Society, University of Minnesota grant officials, and the London *Times* editors – really have believed for more than just a few fleeting seconds that it was "odd" that two adopted babies were named James? Or "uncanny", and "spooky", that two babies named James had gone on to marry and divorce a woman named Linda, then marry a woman named Betty?

Twin studies, and behaviour genetics more widely, speaks to our need to believe. Yet the lack of scientific rigour here is concerning. Science is done by setting up control groups and comparing experimental results against the control. Yet many identical twins both reared together and reared apart but later reunited actually define themselves by their relationship with one another, much more so than non-identical twins do, and partly because of the attention factor. For example, identical twins take over an entire town in America each August ("Twinsburg" in Ohio) and have since 1976, and hold festivals, and give each other awards. So there is a serious question mark over the value of studying two subjects who have already had a chance to interact, and a chance to demonstrate "odd" and "uncanny" similarities to the *Minneapolis Tribune* before you even get to interview them. Furthermore, some experiments become impossible to replicate, when replication is the cornerstone of scientific method, because for example there is a severely limited pool of monozygotic twins reared apart and later reunited. Such social engineering is no longer performed or permitted, and the problems of inadvertent coaching or fame-seeking make it dangerous to reuse subjects already interviewed. And of course behavioural genetics all too often speaks to our – and most psychologists' – rather poor mathematical knowledge, and weakness for p-hacking. If you take any group, statistically you will find "uncanny" similarities between any two members if you look hard enough, and ignore all the bits that are not similar. And yet the University of Minnesota Twin Family Study runs to this day, pulling in over-credulous fans from Professor Steven Pinker to Professor Lord Robert Winston.

Behavioural genetics is not a hard science, it is a soft science. Sir Cyril Burt was an educational psychologist by training. Arthur Jensen was an educational psychologist. Thomas Bouchard and Robert Plomin are both psychologists by training. The Minnesota Center for Twin and Adoption Research, director one Thomas Bouchard, is run out of the Psychology Department at the University of Minnesota ("twin studies are the very foundation of this branch of psychology" – Wright 1997, pp.44–5). Should we once again recall the August 2015 *Nature* article? "Don't trust everything you read in the psychology literature. In fact, two thirds of it should probably be distrusted." Of course this doesn't automatically mean that behavioural genetics, or two thirds of it anyway, is wrong. But for contemporary behavioural genetics to be largely right, Darwin would have to be almost completely wrong. Evolution would have to have broken the billion species pattern, and rewritten the four-billion-year genetic rule. Logic would have to be wrong, because logic tells us that over ninety per cent of humanity has never been moral, fair or just, whereas behavioural genetics inverts the numbers and has over ninety per cent of humanity, and almost one hundred per cent of psychologists, as moral, fair and just. History would have to be wrong, as for behavioural genetics to be remotely correct Steven Pinker – this uncritical fan of the nomenclature gene, and with his faith-based attitude to human evolutionary theory – couldn't have been descended from an ISIL of their day whose "atrocities had 'lit up hell-fires in Christendom'". Yet he was. Because we are all descended from such ancestors; we all carry their genes. We all come from Californian theft and genocide, or ISIL-like rape and slavery, or Lincoln's anti-miscegenation convictions, or Galton's

"Africa for the Chinese" thuggery, or Indian caste segregation, or Yuval Noah Harari's "What are a few dead people?" ethic, or Russian scapegoating, or Chinese internment, or from *istaslama* surrender and obedience without question. So behavioural genetics, and University of Minnesota psychology, may be largely right. But what are the odds?

10

A LAND WITHOUT OPPORTUNITY

"Similarly, in May 1987, 90% agreed with the statement: 'Our society should do what is necessary to make sure everyone has an equal opportunity to succeed.' This percentage has remained at about 90% ever since."

– Pew Research Center (2011)

There is a paradox, and a sad irony, to America as supposedly the land of opportunity. The irony is that a nation that is defined by its self-image as a country of opportunity for all, and as per the Pew Research study above, is logically doing more than almost any other advanced economy to undermine opportunity for all. Or to put it perhaps another way, the paradox of America is that for America to truly be America, Americans would largely have to stop being Americans.

America is not a country where it is easy to climb out of poverty. Within the West, it is the free will-trumpeting nations of the US and Britain that have both the sharpest inequality and the lowest social mobility. Janet Yellen, the former US Federal Reserve Chair, said in October 2014 that "by some estimates, income and wealth inequality are near their highest levels in the past hundred years, much higher than the average during that time span" (Yellen, 2014). As the 2016 Stanford University *Poverty and Inequality Report* put it: "Although the United Kingdom has a poverty and inequality profile that, among the Anglophone countries, comes closest to that of the US, even relative to this benchmark the US has a distinctively anemic safety net and a distinctively unequal distribution of wealth" (Grusky *et al.* 2016, p.6). And this was before COVID-19 made life even more precarious for many Americans. But it is Britain and America that also have the lowest social mobility among the Anglophone countries, let alone relative to social democratic countries: "the US and the United Kingdom are high-inequality and low-mobility countries, while Australia and Canada are more equal and more mobile" (Corak 2016, pp. 52–3). The Pew Research Center released a study in April 2017 showing that the US middle class had been hollowed out over the previous decades. It was reported that there is a smaller middle-income group, and larger extremes of both rich and poor, in the US than in any of the eleven Western European countries studied (Kochhar, 2017). A September 2019 paper produced by Peter Arcidiacono of Duke University and others suggested that over 43% of white admissions to Harvard are known as ALDC, meaning those groupings not generally admitted on academic merit. ALDC includes what is known as "the Dean's interest list", which incorporates those tied to wealthy donors. And Britain continues to be similarly elitist with significant barriers to professional and economic mobility; data released in late 2017 showed that the top two social classes still dominate admissions to Oxford and Cambridge Universities (Richardson, 2017), and in May 2019 Oxford promised a "sea change" to address diversity criticism and continued admissions dominance by the privileged.

But the larger question is whether America *not* being a land of opportunity and social mobility is an unfortunate accident or a structural part of what America really is, or at least has become. Equality of opportunity is an American national conceit, and "attitudes about equal opportunity for all, a citizen's duty to always vote, patriotism and the other statements described above have changed little over time", the 2011 Pew study went on to say. Many Americans take it as an article of faith that the promise of America gives to every man his chance regardless of his birth, to cite the early twentieth-century novelist Thomas Wolfe's famous line. In the aftermath of Hurricane Katrina, President Obama spoke of rebuilding New Orleans, "a city where everyone ... has a chance to make it", while in *The Audacity of Hope* he wrote that American "values are rooted in a basic optimism about life and a faith in free will" (2006, p.54). America as a level playing field where everyone has an equal opportunity to succeed is central to the message the Republican Party continues to sell, as per Charles Murray's dictum that in America "the options are always open. Opportunity is endless" (1984, p.234). Or you have right-wing commentators like the psychologist Jordan Peterson, guru of the American alt-light, also known as the alt-lite, telling the web portal BigThink: "Equality of opportunity? Not only fair enough, but laudable" (2018). And yet the paradox of America is that an absence of opportunity is now effectively built into American culture and character.

The paradox of America goes as follows. 1. In a universe without free choice, life can only reduce to the undeserved chance interplay of biological luck and environmental luck. 2. In human life many are always going to have better or worse biological and, of particular import, environmental luck. 3. The interplay of 1. and 2. together mean that any semblance of equality of opportunity – an equal opportunity to succeed – will require external (and largely state) intervention to mitigate the differences in biological and environmental luck that people start out with. 4. But some cultures are historically and ideologically opposed to state intervention, not just on the right but also on large parts of the liberal-left, and America is one of those cultures. 5. America, the "land of opportunity", is historically and ideologically opposed to the intervention that is *logically necessary* to create a land of opportunity. 6. In order to maintain the (false) conceit of being the land of opportunity, America, including its academics, must actively suppress the knowledge that luck swallows everything, that economic position reduces to nothing other than undeserved dumb luck, and that intervention is necessary to even start to create a land of opportunity.

The philosopher Stephen Cave wrote something similar to the above in 2016, while in an earlier 2015 piece he had already noted that although the myth of free will may benefit some, it hurts many others, particularly those at the bottom, and yet most philosophers were wilfully blind to this. Almost all philosophers barely touch on, he wrote, "the dangers of blaming people for their lot. In the US, for example, the American Dream – a powerful myth of personal responsibility – results in the poor being held culpable for their poverty. ... The result is little action to alleviate the causes of poverty, markedly low social mobility and growing inequality" (2015, p.37). He followed this up with the even harsher 2016 piece in the *Atlantic*. Citing the work of my colleague Bruce Waller, Cave pointed to the irony that America might never actually *be* America. Giving up America's foundational conceit of equality of opportunity ("the options are always open. Opportunity is endless"), giving up the conceit that people create themselves, "might be what we need to rescue the American Dream – and indeed, many of our ideas about civilization, the world over – in the scientific age" (2016).

THE MYTH OF THE SELF-MADE MAN

The "self-made man" idea is increasingly being shown to be not just a myth, but a divisive and socially destructive myth. There has recently been some grass roots push-back in America, and Massachusetts Senator Elizabeth Warren is one of the most erudite and outspoken of the challengers. Warren, who is also an author and an academic, said the following back in 2011: "There is nobody in this country who got rich on his own. Nobody. ... You built a factory out there? Good for you. But I want to be clear: you moved your goods to market on the roads the rest of us paid for; you hired workers the rest of us paid to educate; you were safe in your factory because of police forces and fire forces that the rest of us paid for. ... Now look, you built a factory and it turned into something terrific, or a great idea? God bless. Keep a big hunk of it. But part of the underlying social contract is you take a hunk of that and pay forward for the next kid who comes along" (Madison, 2011).

The danger of building a nation on the myth of the self-made man is stark, and goes well beyond questions of falsehood and social injustice. Kraus and Keltner have shown that internal self-causation arguments, which include free will apologism, are increasingly used to justify social inequalities, "to constrain upward mobility in society" (2013, p.258), and to reject restorative social policies. Meanwhile psychologists like Cecilia Mo at Vanderbilt University and Arnold Ho at the University of Michigan have been studying the psychology of inequality, including how society's winners falsely believe they got there by more than just dumb luck (and hence deserve their success), and that others didn't make the most of the opportunities they are believed to have had (and so deserved to fail). And one further downside is that once people start to see through the myth, social discontent is inevitable. As the Stanford University 2016 *Poverty and Inequality Report* put it: "It is often claimed that there is much tolerance in the US for high levels of inequality, as long as that inequality arises from a fair contest in which all children, no matter how poor or rich their parents, have the same opportunities to get ahead" (Cowak 2016, p.51). And this tolerance can start to fall apart at both the individual and social level once people begin to see through the myth of the self-made man.

One paper in the journal *Child Development* by Erin Godfrey and others (2017) took the unusual step of examining how beliefs about the fairness of the American economic system influenced the life chances and delinquency of juveniles. Interviewed in the *Atlantic*, Godfrey noted that "for those marginalized by the system – economically, racially, and ethnically – believing the system is fair puts them in conflict with themselves and can have negative consequences" (Anderson, 2017) as soon as they realise the system is not actually fair. Godfrey and her colleagues had asked sixth-graders to rate their endorsement of the American Dream and that America is the land of opportunity where everyone who works hard "has an equal chance to succeed". The research is seen as early evidence linking pre-teens' emotional and behavioural outcomes to their belief, and subsequent disbelief, in an American meritocracy. The study found that traditionally marginalised youth who had grown up previously believing in the American ideal that hard work and perseverance naturally lead to success showed an increase in risky behaviours during their middle-school years once they grew into a more realistic view of their country. The *Atlantic* noted that the findings build upon a body of literature called "system justification", being a theory that argues that many humans tend to defend, bolster, or rationalise the status quo and see overarching social, economic, and political systems as good, fair, and legitimate. System justification is a distinctively American conceit, Godfrey told the periodical, built on myths used to justify inequities. Yet, as she and her colleagues discovered, "these beliefs can be a liability for disadvantaged adolescents once their identity as a member of a marginalized group begins to gel – and once they become keenly aware of how institutional discrimination disadvantages them and their group".

Yet many liberals may have as much invested in opposing true American meritocracy as have most conservatives. While equality of opportunity was historically seen as a banner under which both conservatives and the liberal-left could rally, questions are now being raised about how committed to equality of opportunity liberalism actually is. The argument here is that American liberalism has become just as wedded to hereditary privilege as has conservatism, and another article in the *Atlantic*, by James Traub ("Selfishness is Killing Liberalism"), looked at such claims. Traub noted the *Financial Times* columnist Edward Luce arguing that American liberalism has become hereditary privilege: "the meritocracy of professionals and academics and upper-white-collar workers has ossified in recent years into something that looks to people on the outside more like an oligarchy" (2018). Traub highlighted the political scientist Mark Lilla's research that growing obsession with identity politics has stripped liberals of the civic language they long used to address the American people collectively, calling this the "Reaganism" – the harsh individualism – of the liberal-left. And the Harvard political scientists Steven Levitsky and Daniel Ziblatt have argued in *How Democracies Die* that bipartisan coexistence, and its consequent strengthening of democracy, is certainly not the rule in American political history, and that modern liberals as much as conservatives have come to despise common ground and compromise. Traub then asks the pertinent question of whether liberals still understand the concept of sacrifice, noting that liberalism did grave damage to its reputation in the 1960s by demanding real sacrifices from ordinary people and very few from elites.

A CELEBRATION OF HUMAN KINDNESS, AND OF LIBERAL RELIGION

Morality does not exist at the level of our genes. Yet we have to recognise also that reason, or at least imperfect human reason, seems to be no friend to morality, at least analysing the behaviour of the great majority of philosophers. And hence morality can logically only be a cultural overlay ... and one of the most important factors in overlaying morality appears to be not just liberal institutions but in particular liberal religion. Paradoxically religion appears to be both the enemy of morality and the *sine qua non* of morality.

Two hundred years ago the young Percy Shelley self-published *The Necessity of Atheism* in the face of aggression and censorship. Booksellers were intimidated, his work was burned, his printer was under threat of a prosecution of Blasphemous Libel, and Shelley himself was expelled from Oxford University (Holmes 1974, pp.49–51). But Shelley's tome was mis-titled, because there can be no "necessity" in atheism, only a necessity in agnosticism. In fact it was Darwin's bulldog, Thomas Huxley, who coined the term agnosticism, meaning without knowledge, and because the existence of gods can never be disproved. Unlike freedom of choice, the existence of gods is not a question that can be reduced to logic. Without Huxley's Darwinian campaigning and agnostic polemics, his *Times* epitaph read in 1895, it would be impossible "to estimate the forces which have been at work to mould the intellectual, moral, and social life of the century" (Desmond 1997, p.643). But it is important to stress that Huxley himself did see real value in the Anglican Church as an institution, and worked together with English churchmen to promote social and educational reform. Gods themselves may not be necessary for morality, but it appears that liberal churches are often crucial to morality. It was the German philosopher Jürgen Habermas who developed Nietzsche's insight that the values of modern secular humanism are the social and intellectual bequest of Judaeo-Christianity. To finish his quote from earlier: "Universalistic egalitarianism … is the direct legacy of the Judaic ethic of justice and the Christian ethic of love … Up to this very day there is no alternative to it. And in light of the current challenges of a postnational constellation, we must draw sustenance now, as in the past, from this substance. Everything else is idle postmodern talk" (Calhoun *et al.* 2013, p.144).

Here we can, and perhaps should, draw a distinction between *morality*, which in important respects demands an intellectual analysis as it seems to remain impossible without an open and permanent acknowledgement of the problem of moral luck, and *kindness* or compassion, which is more emotional than intellectual. I am often stunned into silence at the kindness of liberal theists. None of my atheist friends has ever worked in a soup kitchen; it is some of my (fewer) theist friends who have done that. Many liberal churchgoers have a very real kindness and compassion that so many atheists seem to lack. Pope Francis and Archbishop of Canterbury Justin Welby may speak about God's glorious gift of freedom of the will, but in their actions they both largely recognise that undeserved dumb luck makes the real difference to social station, and fight tirelessly – in Welby's case, often against the British state, and in Francis's case, often against the Roman Curia – to provide opportunity to those without such opportunity. And because we cannot rely on imperfect human reason to get us to the next stage of proto, or incipient, morality, it can and will fall on the capacity for kindness inherent within liberal institutions, and in particular the liberal churches and synagogues. In so many areas, from the end of slavery to better treatment of the weak and less fortunate, it is clerics – very often the ones who go and work among the dispossessed – that have advanced the capacity for human empathy. As the Harvard philosopher and psychologist Dan Robinson noted in his survey of our treatment of the insane, it was "great kings and good clerics" (1996, p.72), and not secular philosophers, who civilised Europe in the late Middle Ages and after. Because reforming liberal religion – doubt-filled, questioning religion; religion that is open to change – will remain one of the main drivers of the human moral project, in a way that philosophy and science may never be. Though religion that does not doubt – fundamentalist region, and most forms of modern evangelical religion – can seemingly never be moral.

But while many believe that the concept of free choice is integral to religious belief, it should be realised that the doctrine of free will has never been foundational to Judaeo-Christianity. Judaism in the second century BC comprised three main sects, the Pharisees, the Sadducees, and the Essenes, and while the Sadducees thought that all acts of men were free acts, and the Pharisees that some acts of men were free acts, the Essenes thought that no acts of men were truly free acts. Yet the Essenes were seemingly regarded by their fellow Jews as the best of all people. Josephus, the first-century Jewish historian, in the final reckoning a Pharisee and the main source of available information on the differences between the three sects, spoke of Essene piety and diligence. "It also deserves our admiration", wrote Josephus, "how much they exceed all other men that addict themselves to virtue, and this in righteousness; and indeed to such a degree, that as it hath never appeared among any other men", as he put it in Book XVIII of his *Antiquities of the Jews*. The Essenes largely disappeared from history at the end of the first century AD, and the Pharisee conceit of limited free will is thus today a core tenet of rabbinical Judaism. Yet while the Essenes disappeared from Jewish history, they seem to have left a vital and enduring legacy on Christian history.

Certainly Christ did not explicitly recognise the concept of free will, and Christian doctrine never truly incorporated the idea until the late fourth century when two influential thinkers, the British monk Pelagius and Augustine of Hippo, looked to assimilate it. No one may ever be sure which Jewish sect Jesus came from, be that Pharisee, Essene, or Zealot, although all three have been argued. Yet Christ berated the Pharisees, and it is the similarities between Essene teaching and the teachings of Christ that are striking. The Essenes were ascetics, and concerned with salvation, but they also emphasised righteousness over legalism. But even if Jesus was not an Essene he and his early followers may well have been influenced by them. For example, Christ is generally believed to have been a follower of John the Baptist, and there is much speculation that John followed the Essene rituals. As James Tabor, Professor in the Department of Religious Studies at the University of North Carolina, puts it: "I think it likely that scores of 'Essenes' and 'Essene types' or sympathizers were drawn to John the Baptizer, Jesus and James" (2012). Other biblical scholars have also suggested that Christ's message may have particularly resonated with Essenes, who may have formed a disproportionately high number of Christ's early followers.

BEHAVIOURAL GENETICS, FREE WILL, AND THE LEGAL SYSTEM

> "Justice removed, then, what are kingdoms but great bands of robbers?"
>
> – **Augustine of Hippo**, Christian theologian and philosopher

For many on the hard right biology has always been the answer to wider social problems. "There are, after all, in this world, some people who are naturally aggressive and violent", *Breitbart's* Steve Bannon wrote in his piece "Sympathy for the Devils: The plot against Roger Ailes – and America" (2016). Bannon wrote this amid mounting black anger after a wave of shootings of unarmed black Americans by armed white policemen; Bannon's comment about natural aggression was of course referring to those shot, not those doing the shooting. But Darwin's wager for the human animal raises serious questions about such alt-right articles of faith. After all, if we did not evolve to be "the moral animal" of evolutionary psychology, then the evolutionary models suggest that white policemen – and white non-policemen – are similarly "naturally aggressive and violent".

We said earlier that some attributes, like impulsivity, may or may not be judged to have a sizeable genetic component, and particularly where we can see variations in such behaviour across the non-human world. Similarly some violence is linked to actual genetic disorders. A very tiny group of humans seem to lack empathic responses entirely, and some of this will be down to genes. But even here the situation is complicated. Aggressive genes can only ever be half the story. Paul Babiak has famously shown that psychopaths, that most extreme of psychological formulations, are very common at the top levels of both business and politics. Psychopaths have a natural tendency to be charming, manipulative and intimidating, traits that often stand you in good stead in business and politics. Babiak discovered that there are almost four times as many psychopaths in the highest levels of big business as in the general population. But what makes some psychopaths high functioning rather than violent? Aggressive in business or politics, but not aggressive on the street or in the home? While a subset of psychopaths may have an innate inability to recognise emotions in others, or an overactive reward centre, the differentiating factor is still largely down to environment.

Jim Fallon at UC Irvine is rather unusual among academics who study psychopaths. Fallon is related to the infamous Lizzie Borden, and when checking his extended family history he noted many murderers. When he scanned his own brain and investigated his own genome he found all the markers that have been suggested for extreme aggression, including a total lack of activity over the orbital cortex, a non-functioning limbic system, the MAOA gene, the genetic markers for impulsivity. Yet instead of being a violent criminal, or even a high-functioning psychopath within politics or business, Fallon was a quiet senior academic. Certainly his family had noted his sometimes startling lack of empathy, but Fallon understood that what made all the difference for him was that he had received a loving upbringing. The evidence seems to be that all the unusual brain scans and all the genetic markers offer very little additional risk unless someone has also come from an abusive background. As we said earlier there is, there can be, no relevant moral distinction where under our thought experiment it takes sixty economic "units" to get one person from cannibal ape to journal editor and seventy units to get a second from cannibal ape to low-wage job. Similarly, there would be no relevant ethical distinction even if it might take up to eighty units and a loving family to get a biologically atypical third from cannibal ape to social functioning. Yet an area where we seem to be notoriously prone to deceive ourselves – and to flatter ourselves – is over the relative contribution of biology and environment. We predominantly seem to overplay and overstate the role of biology in the variabilities of human life, particularly in moral behaviour.

But if genes for crime and social position are largely a social Darwinist fantasy currently mostly unchallenged by the best biologists, what about the betrayal by philosophers which all too often plays into the same hands? If we give up the myth of free will, writes Dennett, "not only should the prisons be emptied, but no contract is valid" and "mortgages should be abolished" (2014). Saul Smilansky has made a similar argument that ending the free will myth is "presented to us as an 'all or nothing' choice" (2000, p.225), whereby without the myth we lose the right to judge others. But this is all scaremongering nonsense; contracts don't become invalid and we don't lose the right to incarcerate, we only lose the right to punish *vindictively*. In a world without free choice you can justify incarceration, but you cannot justify indignities, execution, mutilation, "three strikes" laws, or "inflicting … rape". In a sense we lose the right to punish like Americans, with indignities, rape and execution, and are forced back on the Western European incarceration and attempted rehabilitation model. Smilansky points out that "a sense of 'justice' has often been closely connected with feelings of revenge" (p.226) and notes, without registering any hint of irony, that without the myth of free choice one "cannot easily envisage a justice system functioning as ours does today". No guff, Chet; that's actually the point.

Shariff *et al.* (2014) undertook four studies and found that learning about the neural bases of human behaviour, through either lab-based manipulations or attendance at an undergraduate neuroscience course, "reduced people's support for retributive punishment". Krueger *et al.* (2014) showed that people with strong belief in free will punished more harshly than people with weak belief in free will in certain circumstances. Without the ethical fig leaf of free choice it is difficult to envisage the current level of toleration, and apologism, within the United States for mass prison rape, life sentences for minor offences, or even the indifference to the widespread conviction of innocents.[5] Remember from earlier that Smilansky has already pronounced that "maintaining human dignity depends on ... degrading fellow people" and defends "the moral necessity of belief in the justness of deeply unjust practices". For those looking to degrade their fellows and maintain deeply unjust practices there can be no comfort here. And Dennett's concerns are similarly afloat from reality. Dennett's argument is that it wouldn't be just to incarcerate if we had to tell the truth (that there is no freedom of choice), so the only way we can incarcerate is to base incarceration on untruth. But note that Dennett is therefore giving us *neither* justice *nor* truth here.

He himself argues (2012; 2012a; 2014) – though few philosophers of any tradition agree with him on this – that it wouldn't be just to incarcerate in a world without free choice, yet that as we need incarceration we can never have justice in a world without free choice. So we will always have injustice, according to Dennett, but to this he wishes to further add untruth. Not because it will get us to justice, but because it will at least hide an injustice from plain sight. But few apart from Dennett and

---

5   Bruce Waller in his 2015 work has linked greater belief in free choice and self-creation to both the greater indifference to suffering found by Shariff *et al.*, and higher toleration of injustice including less concern over miscarriages of justice and convictions of the innocent, citing data from the Cardozo Law School-affiliated Innocence Project and Northwestern University's Center on Wrongful Convictions.

Smilansky appear to believe that we can never have justice. For example, this is Pereboom: "when the assumption that wrongdoers are blameworthy is withdrawn for hard incompatibilist reasons, the conviction that they have in fact done wrong could legitimately survive" (2001, p.212). A *polis* can only exist if there are rules and enforcement of those rules, because public safety requires rules. And Darwin's wager effectively says that morality cannot exist outside a *polis*, outside a community, so a precondition for morality is rules and just enforcement of those rules.

Now, as morality is impossible outside a *polis* (and therefore outside enforcement of rules) some, such as Dennett and Smilansky, make the category mistake of thinking the *polis* excuses such enforcement in all circumstances. In other words, the existence of society excuses all injustices that might have built that particular society, and whether or not such a society is just. Smilansky is explicit in saying this above. But this is bad logic, inverted logic. The fact society makes morality and fairness possible does not justify immorality and unfairness in creation of that society. Morality and fairness must be judged independently. And only a just society would have the moral right to incarcerate – remember that Dennett ("Is it fair …? Life isn't fair") and Smilansky ("the justness of deeply unjust practices") have already given up on the possibility of fairness and justice – so only a society that admits to the lack of free choice could have the moral right to incarcerate. The sad irony is that in their desire to bury the knowledge that there is no freedom of choice Dennett and Smilansky, and actually most other philosophers, undermine the moral right to incarcerate.

We can still analyse, draw moral distinctions between people, and judge and criticise character and effect. It is just that we cannot *blame*, or make suffer, or invoke anything beyond moral luck to differentiate. Hard determinists like Bruce Waller (1990, 2006) and Derk Pereboom (2001, 2007) have written extensively on why this is the case, and why we can, and always must, make such a differentiation. Waller has drawn a distinction between being responsible – something we can never be – and taking responsibility – an excellent character attribute, and something that far too few philosophers tend to do. We can, and will, still incarcerate dangerous people even for perhaps their whole lives in a world that recognises no free choice, no free will. Is it theories of retribution and just suffering that are imperilled by the absence of free choice, not incarceration or theories of rehabilitation, prevention, and public safety. But Dennett's need to maintain the myth of free will also makes him blind to other failures of the Anglo-American legal systems. Both Pereboom (2001) and Waller (2015) argue that treatment strategies for offenders tend to be *far* more effective than moral responsibility advocates like Dennett and Smilansky wish to admit, and more effective than traditional strategies. Robert Martinson's 1974 review *What Works?* was arguably the most influential article contributing towards a scepticism of rehabilitation and a backlash against penal reform in the US criminal justice system in the 1970s and 1980s. Pereboom notes that not only has Martinson's review been widely criticised as deeply flawed but that Martinson himself has now retracted all his original claims, having become convinced that "such startling results are found again and again ... for treatment programs" (2001, p.181).

And we also have the further problem that the Anglo-American law as it stands is an arena of dissimulation and error. "And if Harris thinks that it is this folk notion of free will that 'drives our moral intuitions and our legal system' he should tackle the large literature that says otherwise (starting with, e.g., Stephen Morse)", writes Dennett (2014). *Starting with, e.g., Stephen Morse?* Stephen J. Morse is Ferdinand Wakeman Hubbell Professor of Law at the University of Pennsylvania, and has for three decades been the doyen of legal compatibilists; the doyen of those who argue the law must be and can be blind to questions of freedom of choice. Morse argues the American law is officially compatibilist, but apparently unlike Dennett I *have* tackled this large literature in published papers, and Morse himself actually believes in the possibility of free choice, and deep intellectual error isn't a great start when the costs of being wrong are so very high. For example, free choice simply must exist, Morse argues, as the "vast majority" raised in poverty do not turn to crime (1976, p.1254). Or when Morse writes that "all of us choose our behavior ... behavior *is* a matter of choice" (pp.1251–2), and that "hard determinism can neither explain our practices nor ground a theory of desert" (2004, p.431). And Morse tells us approvingly that "most theorists believe that a moral decision for conviction requires ... an actor who 'could have done other'" (1976, p.1257). All the above examples show that not only does the mistaken "folk notion of free will" drive the American legal system ("hard determinism can neither explain our practices"), and in opposition to Dennett's claim, but that the folk notion of free will drives Morse's own mistaken belief system. The principle of legal compatibilism appears to be deeply spurious when even its advocates often don't seem to understand, or buy into, their own arguments.

Like the American legal system, the English law is sometimes argued to be officially compatibilist, but again the reality on the ground is very different. My lawyer friend Richard Oerton, who has worked at the Law Commission, the law reform body established by Parliament, writes that the idea of free will as free choice, "is central to the" English and Welsh criminal law, and that judges "quite clearly believe" that the offender could have done otherwise (2012, p.69). Richard notes that section 142 of the Criminal Justice Act 2003, in declaring for the first time by statute the aims of sentencing, makes it clear that retributory punishment based on the assumption of freedom of choice is the primary goal of the criminal justice system. To quote the QC Helena Kennedy (2011), one of the most influential legal scholars working in the public eye in Britain today, and speaking on BBC Radio 4 to UCL's Steve Jones: "I think that we'd still hold on to the idea that in each and every one of us, for the most part, we're able to exercise free will".

Stephen Morse is seen as a defender of legal compatibilism. But Anders Kaye at the Thomas Jefferson School of Law has pointed out that the legal compatibilist approach is more conducive to the use of state violence against the disadvantaged than an approach which recognises the absence of choice. In his paper *The Secret Politics of the Compatibilist Criminal Law* Kaye notes that the disadvantaged tend to be "disproportionately – though not exclusively – people of color. ... This is also the group with the most reason to criticize and challenge the social order. ... It follows that the compatibilist criminal law will more frequently punish the disadvantaged" (2007, pp.418–9), and that compatibilist criminal rhetoric is not politically neutral and acts "to disempower those at the bottom of the social order" (p. 368). According to Morse himself, if society were to admit that no one freely chooses their position in life it would necessitate "the wholesale reform of society" (1976, p.1257), "social engineering ... inconsistent with our system" and "a massive redistribution of wealth" (1976a, p.1276). Morse tells us that those who wish to query the law's (confused, remember) position on free choice are motivated by the desire for "a truly egalitarian democracy" (1976, p.1260), and wish for utopian social reforms "not compatible with a libertarian and capitalist society" (p.1261).

Belief in free will significantly affects the character – and thus the potential for justice versus injustice – of any legal system. We saw above the studies of Shariff *et al.* and Krueger *et al.* linking belief in free will with public support for more brutal punishment. In addition to these studies, Emad Atiq (2013) reports that folk beliefs about free will, beliefs about whether or not it is simply a myth, influence sentencing itself. As Atiq comments, "morally distorting" false beliefs cannot help but undermine the integrity of jurors, judges and legislators. Others have shown that the law has always had to evolve to accept advances in knowledge, albeit often against deep resistance. For example, Sam Daly in his paper "Free Will is No Bargain: How Misunderstanding Human Behavior Negatively Influences Our Criminal Justice System" shows that, as a parallel, "as more Americans view homosexuality as an immutable trait rather than a choice, they have correspondingly become more accepting of homosexual relations" (2015, p.1006). Daly pointed out that, at least in part due to this societal change in perspective, thirty-seven states "now have legal same-sex marriage, twenty-one of which have attained this status in either 2014 or 2015".

There are other conservative legal theorists who are more consistent than Morse in the application of legal compatibilism, but their work also tends to be less than intellectually edifying. The conservative University of Illinois law professor Michael S. Moore is possibly the most influential retributivist scholar in Western legal theory and second only to Morse in the ranks of the legal compatibilists. But Moore nevertheless suggests that an actor could have done otherwise "*if* he had chosen (or willed) to do otherwise" (1985, p.1142). This latter argument, staged between compatibilists and incompatibilists, has a long pedigree within the literature, though is today largely discredited, as to say that an individual could have done otherwise *if* he had willed to have done otherwise is the (il)logical equivalent of saying that a dog would have a curly tail *if* it were a pig, and is meaningless within this debate. Conditionality ("*if*") is not applicable here as no individual ever could have willed to have done otherwise in either a deterministic universe or an indeterministic universe. Two factors, and two factors only, determine human behaviour, being biology and experience, nature and nurture. At any particular moment an individual could only have willed to have done otherwise if his character, his biology or experiences to that date (including hypothetical indeterministic triggers), had been different. Hence an individual could only have done otherwise if, in effect, he had happened to have been a different person formed under different circumstances. It is therefore both factually wrong and illogical for legal compatibilists to say that an individual "could have done otherwise", as it is not this individual who could ever have done otherwise, but only a completely different person. (So recalling Brian Greene's multiverse theory mentioned earlier, alternative versions of "you" are not you after all.) Such arguments make the American criminal law look anti-intellectual, biased, and petty.

Moore in particular is noted for his arguments that suffering and retributivism are not only just but that we *honour* criminals when we make them suffer. Presumably the more we make them suffer, the more we are honouring them, and Bruce Waller has pointed out that the notorious Christian apologist C.S. Lewis made exactly this argument that "however severely" we punish criminals we are honouring them "as a human person made in God's image" (2015, p.139). The argument – from Moore to Dennett, from Peter Strawson to Smilansky – is that we honour the less fortunate when we suggest, with a wink, that they could have done otherwise, but it is such theorists who seem to dishonour life's less fortunate. Even putting to one side the bias and malign social effect of the free will myth, on a personal level they do individuals the gross injustice of seeming to claim they are deserving of little honour unless we view them as capable of having done otherwise. The argument here is that humans are not deserving of respect for who they actually are, but only deserve respect to the extent we all buy into a mythically optimised North American white upper-middle-class view of humanity. This is remarkably close to Lewis's argument that humans lack honour in and of themselves, but are deserving of honour only to the extent we are reflections of God's image. And not a million miles from the argument of the eighteenth-century Calvinist preacher Jonathan Edwards, regarded as one of America's most important theologians, that humans have no inherent worth but hold value only to the extent they reflect God's plan for moving them around the chessboard. Of course, such arguments are only ever rolled out when discussing the less fortunate. Such theorists are not only dealing all the cards, they sometimes seem to be dealing from the bottom of the deck.

The ability to have done otherwise is not just of academic interest. The free will myth has deadly real world effects, especially when in the hands of the American white middle class. As the University of Notre Dame analytical philosopher and Christian Alvin Plantinga writes: "If determinism is true, then on any occasion when I do what is wrong, it isn't possible for me to refrain from doing wrong. And if it isn't possible for me to refrain from doing wrong, then I can't really be responsible for that wrong-doing – not in the relevant sense anyway. ... The relevant sense involves being properly subject to disapprobation, moral criticism, and even punishment. ... I am not properly blamed for doing what it was not within my power not to do" (2012). Dennett himself is forced to admit that this is the common intuition, when he says that "as van Inwagen notes: 'Almost all philosophers agree that a necessary condition for holding an agent responsible for an act is believing that the agent *could have* refrained from performing that act'" (1984, p.131). This is John Martin Fischer's "common-sense" view, a view Fischer also rejects: "our commonsense theorizing about our moral and legal responsibility presupposes that sometimes at least we could have done otherwise" (2007, p.72). And because no single individual ever could have chosen or willed to have done otherwise, legal practices that rest on unnecessary and spiteful maltreatment are simply impossible to reconcile with justice.

Morality, and indeed a true land of opportunity, means coming to terms with the fact that luck swallows everything in human life, but this seems to fly counter to a streak of cruelty and vindictiveness within the American psyche. It may also fly counter to America's belief in its own exceptionalism, pre-existing virtue – and how do you explain virtue to a nation already convinced of its own virtue? – and manifest destiny to dictate to others. Hillary Clinton may be the "unabashed cheerleader" (Luce, 2016) for what is called American exceptionalism when she claims that "America is an exceptional country ... in Lincoln's words, the last best hope of earth", but such a conceit runs across Democrats and Republicans. From the 64th Secretary of State Madeleine Albright ("we are the indispensable nation. We stand tall and we see further") to her ideological opposite number and 46th Vice President Dick Cheney (*Exceptional: Why the World Needs a Powerful America*). Influential Yale Law Professor Dan Kahan has argued that vindictive cruelty, and the driving need to perceive others as lower than you, is an integral part of both the American character and the American moral and legal systems. As he has written, "by inflicting countless other indignities – from exposure to the view of others when urinating and defecating to rape at the hand of other inmates – prison unambiguously marks the lowness of those we consign to it" (1998, p.1642). For the avoidance of doubt, Kahan is not decrying the above state of affairs in America. But even a free will zealot like Dan Dennett has to admit that in our world without free choice there can be no justification for indignities and severe suffering, which would otherwise require what Dennett admits we do not have, and which he calls "total, before-the-eyes-of-God Guilt" (1984, p.165).

In our world without free choice you can justify incarceration, but there is no way to justify indignities, judicial amputation, mutilation, torture, execution, three strikes laws, or "inflicting ...

rape". Yet it is difficult to imagine an America accepting of its past mistakes, an America without the belief in its own manifest destiny, without belief in its own virtue and right to lecture others. An America without the "countless other indignities", without the cruelties, the perception of the "lowness" of others, the inflicted rapes, the vindictive incarceration of non-violent offenders alongside violent offenders, and the spitefulness of largely ensuring ex-cons never get a chance to reintegrate into the normal economy. To put it another way, it is difficult to imagine America ever even attempting "what is necessary to make sure everyone has an equal opportunity to succeed".

"THE MEDDLESOME INTERFERENCE OF AN ARROGANT, SCIENTIFIC PRIESTCRAFT"

We mentioned above the investigations, and example, of Jim Fallon, the quiet senior academic whose family had noted his sometimes startling lack of empathy. Not every claim within behavioural genetics is self-interested bunkum, so can we find a way to reconcile orthodox evolutionary biology with the understanding that not every variation in human behaviour comes down to culture? Can we, furthermore, delineate an ultimate understanding of the human animal? One capable of explaining how we can be simultaneously products of the "blind, pitiless indifference" of natural selection, yet capable of spectacular kindness, and nevertheless with a capacity for stunningly creative immorality, indeed understandable as the "double dose of unfairness" ape? A conceptualisation that accepts it is only culture that can make us moral, and that it is culture that predominantly makes us immoral, while also allowing some role for biological differences where it comes to immorality?

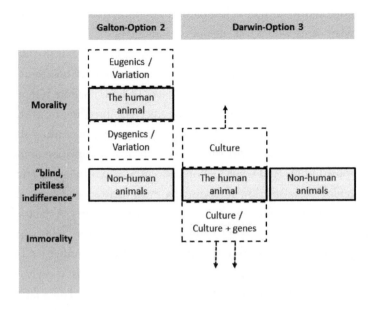

If we put aside group selection given all its difficulties, we are left with two very different explanations of the human animal. And why does the above diagram link sociobiology, and even the vast majority of evolutionary psychology, with the father of modern behavioural genetics and the man who coined the term eugenics? Because all these traditions draw their water from the same well. From Sir John Herschel to Sir Francis Galton, and then to sociobiology and on to evolutionary psychology, the one linking theme has been the idea of the natural state of at least some humans as, uniquely, "*the* moral animal". Believed to be, biologically, "as distant from a Chimpanzee" as "an ape from a platypus!", as Darwin dismissed this conceit (Desmond 1997, p.240). The further distinction then becomes whether advocates see it as culture or biology that moves us up or down from the natural state. The great majority to the left-hand side, though not all, have given the answer as predominantly biology, taking us to the final difference between them of seeing that perceived biological distribution as just natural variation, or as symptomatic of what some would call eugenics and dysgenics.

The term eugenics may have started with Galton, but the idea can be found at least as far back as Plato. Eugenics, plus its antonym dysgenics, though that word post-dates Galton. Galton himself introduced the ideas of both positive eugenics, breeding from the putative best human stock, and negative eugenics, preventing the weak from breeding, either voluntarily or through elimination of the supposed unfit. And while Galton concentrated mostly on positive eugenics, he wasn't slow to lionise the wars, disasters and pogroms that had helped eliminate the "unfit" members of society. As he told a somewhat started *Jewish Chronicle* in July 1910, over 2,000 years of persecution of Jews should perhaps be celebrated, in that "so far as persecution weeds out those who are unfit", it "tends to evolve a race suited to meet hard conditions" (Falk 2017, p. 47). For Galton, breeding from the best allowed humankind to rise higher still, while breeding from the worst would, for him, drive us backwards.

Though the vast majority of eugenicists exist and have existed on the left of the above diagram, for the record can eugenicists be found on the right-hand side? While rare, it has occurred. Bill Hamilton felt this siren call, though he had first been attracted to eugenics in his student days at Oxford. Half a century later he would enthusiastically review a book devoted to human dysgenics, and write that its author "shows in this book that almost all of the worries of the early eugenicists were well-founded in spite of the relative paucity of their evidence at the time" (2000, p.363). For Hamilton the animal in our nature "cannot be regarded as a fit custodian for the values of civilized man" and civilised behaviour must be learned, but the capacity for such learning might yet be under biological control, and this worried him.

Darwin himself also succumbed, though he had little time for anti-miscegenationists like Galton who spoke of "the purity of a race" (1892, p.343), and posited blacks as inferior to whites, with

Darwin noting furiously that black men "are ranked by the polished savages in England as hardly their brethren, even in Gods [*sic*] eyes" (Desmond & Moore 1991, p.120). However, even though Darwin knew humankind began life on a moral level with the chimpanzee and the platypus, he too worried about a future decline in the species. As he wrote in *Descent of Man*, "With savages, the weak in body and mind are soon eliminated. ... We civilised men, on the other hand, do our utmost to check the process of elimination. ... Thus the weak members of civilised societies propagate their kind ... this must be highly injurious to the race of man" (1871, p.168). Wallace had also recorded Darwin's here typically Victorian prejudice. "In one of my latest conversations with Darwin he expressed himself very gloomily on the future of humanity, on the ground that in our modern civilisation natural selection had no play, and the fittest did not survive" (quoted in Berry 2002, p.214). Wallace, though, was distinctly unimpressed with the science behind eugenics. Andrew Berry's anthology of his writings notes Wallace challenging the scholarship, and calling eugenics "the meddlesome interference of an arrogant, scientific priestcraft" (p.214).

Eugenics, and dysgenics, has always been a siren call to the progressive middle classes, but when we investigate those who have tended to promote the ideas most forcefully, we find more than just Wallace's arrogant, scientific priestcraft, we tend to find deeply unimpressive human beings. We have already noted Francis Galton was entirely the product of a biased time and a place, but his prejudices went way beyond just people of colour. Within the British working classes, Galton identified his favourites. "For the Scotch labourer is much less of a drudge than the Englishman of the Midland counties – he does his work better, and 'lives his life' besides" (1892, p.340). Yet some of Galton's greatest spleen was reserved for European emigrants, which is ironic given Galton's views have so often found favour with the descendants of those first white American settlers. "As a rule, the very ablest men are strongly disinclined to emigrate", Galton wrote (p.360). The reason he gave was that the ablest would naturally feel that their fortune is assured at home, and so "they prefer to live in the high intellectual and moral atmosphere of the more intelligent circles of English society, to a self-banishment among people of altogether lower grades of mind and interests" (pp.360–1). England had certainly "got rid of a great deal of refuse, through means of emigration", he noted with satisfaction.

Of course Galton reserved his greatest criticism for non-whites, and particularly black people. So it is interesting to note his scientific method here. "The number among the negroes of those whom we should call half-witted men, is very large. Every book alluding to negro servants in America is full of instances. … The mistakes the negroes made in their own matters, were so childish, stupid, and simpleton-like, as frequently to make me ashamed of my own species" (p.339). Yet Galton was actually writing this piece in the late 1860s, a couple of years after the 13th Amendment abolished slavery across the US, but when black inferiority was still an article of faith amongst almost all American whites, North and South, with America's Quakers being one of the few noteworthy exceptions to this rule.

Let us return to Abraham Lincoln's speech of September 1858, alongside his audience's reaction as recorded at the time. "[*Applause*] 'There is a physical difference between the white and black races which I believe will for ever forbid the two races living together on terms of social and political equality.' … [*Cheers and laughter*] 'I will also add to the remarks I have made … that I have never had the least apprehension that I or my friends would marry negroes if there was no law to keep them from it, [*laughter*] but as Judge Douglas and his friends seem to be in great apprehension that they might, if there were no law to keep them from it, [*roars of laughter*] I give him the most solemn pledge that I will to the very last stand by the law of this State, which forbids the marrying

of white people with negroes' [*continued laughter and applause*]"
(Lincoln, 1858). Galton's book *Hereditary Genius* was a work of
carefully selected anecdotes. To treat as objective evidence the
prejudices of the men who formulated the Black Codes and the Jim
Crow laws, or even just the prejudices of the Great Emancipator,
honest Abe Lincoln, displays a notable lack of insight.

Yet Galton was deeply credulous in other matters too. When
Galton was amongst those fooled by the Victorian craze for séances,
Darwin could barely hide his contempt. "The Lord have mercy on
us all, if we have to believe in such rubbish" (Desmond & Moore
1991, p.608). While Galton shared the popular naivety over
séances, it was Huxley and Darwin's son George who conspired to
debunk the medium – "a cheat", as they called him – who tried to
hoodwink the family. Extraordinary claims require extraordinary
evidence, and Darwin said it would take "an enormous weight
of evidence" to convince him; one family member "recalled that
Uncle Charles 'used to look upon it as a great weakness if one
allowed wish to influence belief'". Galton seems to have operated
to a different family standard of scientific scepticism.

Hereditary Genius simply continued the earliest directions
of Galton's beliefs. Galton had opposed the slave trade, but not
because it was a global system of terror, kidnapping, torture,
mutilation and murder. Galton did not stand in the way of the
trade in slaves because it was cruel or unjust; he opposed the slave
trade, as he put it in a letter to *The Times*, because it was inefficient,
because it was "awful disorganization". There is a "lottery" to "slave
catching", Galton wrote (1857). "I do not join in the belief that
the African is our equal in brain or in heart; I do not think that
the average negro cares for his liberty as much as an Englishman,
or even as a serf-born Russian." Because of this, he continued,
"we have an equal right to utilize them to our advantage … as a
shopkeeper to order a boy whose parents had bound him over to
an apprenticeship. … There can be no just complaint of tyranny.

These persons are simply treated as children by their masters, and compelled to do what they dislike for their future good and for that of society at large". As their "masters" we can thus use any legitimate means, "or even *quasi*-legitimate means", to possess ourselves of their services, concluded Galton.

Galton personifies what we can call the paradox of eugenics. If there actually were to be anything real behind the eugenic propaganda, eugenicists tend to be the last people we should want to breed from. Galton himself came from great wealth and a good education, and did end up an influential Fellow of the Royal Society, yet was a man of both extreme credulity and ignorance. Worse still, morally he was a waste of space; a privileged snob who believed that the only problem with the slave trade was that it was "awful disorganization", that "inferior" peoples could be used for the benefit of "superior" peoples, and that Britain had "got rid of a great deal of refuse" into North America. He was in almost every way the product of late nineteenth-century high society ("the more intelligent circles of English society"), yet without the self-knowledge or innate intelligence allowing him to comprehend this.

Given the errors we have noted right across the Galton–Option 2 axis, what would we expect to see if the human make-up is governed by a combination of Option 3 and less-than-perfect rationality? We would expect to see figures like Galton; ignorant and bigoted products of their time without the intelligence or character to realise that they were the ignorant and bigoted products of their time. We should expect to see eugenicists who opposed the slave trade in letters to *The Times* not because it was one of the greatest crimes in human history, but because "slave catching" was a "lottery". *As the intrinsic, the built-in, state of the human animal is, like all other animals, amorality*, it has always been easier, more likely, that subsequent directional shifts will be towards immorality rather than towards morality. Morality is something entirely new to the cosmos, the antithesis of billion-year natural selection. And while we have noted that natural world amorality is pitiless indifference, and we humans are almost never indifferent in our oh-so-inventive cruelty, immorality largely seems to be a turbo-charged version of natural world amorality, and thus more of the same. Natural world amorality, which leaves the Japanese macaque Mozu unassisted "in her monumental struggle for existence" as quoted earlier, becomes in humans selfishness *allied* to a strident intellectual defence of such selfishness. Perhaps one led by philosophers, or an arrogant scientific priestcraft, who will talk about the human equivalent of Mozu having had every opportunity in life, of *sanchita* karma with Mozu deserving of her misfortunes for past wrongdoings, or of the harm to superior types of breeding from inferior types.

But though the Brownian motion of culture by itself will be more likely (at least to date), and take less effort, to continue the direction by shifting us toward immorality rather than morality, that does not mean that biology might not also make it harder for some to make the shift to morality. Only culture can shift us towards morality, and it takes a lot of effort to get any of us there, but there may be those rare cases where biology adds something that means culture might have to work extra hard. These are the occasional cases like Jim Fallon, where biology – perhaps an underdeveloped activation across the orbital cortex or an overactive reward centre – means some will require additional cultural stimulus to develop a moral personality. But note that even saying this, all of us require intense cultural action to get us to a moral state, so the fact a few might require a bit more investment, the hypothetical eighty rather than sixty economic "units" as we suggested earlier, becomes ethically next to meaningless. And that is even before we take account of the paradox of eugenics, and realise that even with a privileged background meaning more than eighty economic investment units, Sir Francis Galton never came close to becoming the moral animal.

We get so many figures like Galton, and so few like the former Archbishop of Cape Town and human rights activist Desmond Tutu, because Darwin's wager tells us that our natural state is amorality, and it is thus harder for us to shift towards morality than it is for us to continue towards immorality (one arrow up; two down). And even where education has begun to raise us up, our fundamental lack of both self-awareness and rationality often makes it at best a partial raising up. Lincoln was a fine man by the standards of his day, but the Great Emancipator was still naive and a bigot by modern standards. Darwin's wager explains how the highest in the land – from George Washington to Andrew Jackson, and through to the vacillating Thomas Jefferson – could have been party to a global system of terror, kidnapping, dehumanisation, mutilation, rape and murder. Where we'd expect almost all of the economic one per cent to be telling us that "the options are always open. Opportunity is endless". Where we'd expect that the self-styled moral majority tends to be made up of people without a moral bone in their body. Where we'd expect to be the "double dose of unfairness" ape, largely incapable of fairness, then incapable of fairly defining the very concept of fairness in the first place; your land was always our land, and your land was never your land, it was territory "lost" to us, it was ours for "eternity". And where we'd expect to see smart liberal philosophers providing god-awful arguments that we all get the same opportunities as, "after all, luck averages out in the long run", and "the thought is not 'It had to be!'".

But, crucially, Darwin's wager allows that throughout history we'd also expect some Desmond Tutus and even the occasional Baruch Spinoza; the latter a man descended from ISIL-like ancestors yet, by the standards of his day and even by the standards of our day, a brilliant, thoughtful and morally courageous figure. And reflect on how far we have come when we weren't even aware that we were on a journey, when we weren't even aware that our intrinsic, built-in state needed countering, and we largely cast people adrift into the unpredictability of cultural interaction. We have produced figures like Spinoza and Tutu, and even whole groups like the Essenes, largely by accident. Notwithstanding 3,000 years of self-aggrandising and flawed ethical inquiry, our species is finally within touching distance of objective morality, and we achieved this extraordinary milestone despite our conceit, ignorance, and tendency to look the other way. There is everything still to play for, and imagine how much more we might and will achieve, both morally and intellectually, once we accept where we really start from, and then set out a plan to become the most unique creature that can ever exist in the universe, the moral animal.

11

"WITH MUCH ERROR, AS YET UNSEEN BY ME."

"You will think me very conceited when I say I feel quite easy about the ultimate success of my views, (with much error, as yet unseen by me, to be no doubt eliminated)."

– **Charles Darwin** writing to **Sir John Herschel**,
May 1861 (Warner 2009, p.438)

In October 1862 one of the most famous clashes in the development of Darwinian theory took place. It was between the zoologist Thomas Huxley, "Darwin's bulldog", and the palaeontologist Richard Owen. Although Owen was a brilliant naturalist, and a skilled comparative anatomist, he represented the forces of orthodoxy, lauded by prelate, royalty – who gave him a cottage in Richmond Park – and politician alike. Owen is perhaps best remembered for coining the term "dinosaur" and for being the founder of London's Natural History Museum, where his statue sat in the main hall until 2009, when in a move that would have had Owen turning in his grave it was replaced with the statue of Darwin.

Richard Owen did not deny that man was an evolved primate, but he detested Darwinian gradualism, and saw instead the first human as having sprung fully formed from the womb of an ape ancestor. Owen believed that humankind had special attributes that must have been bequeathed us by our Creator, and held that proof of this could be found in brain structure; that the human brain possessed a unique lobe, the hippocampus minor, not found in a gorilla's brain. Man should be classified apart from the rest of nature, Owen said, because man was as different from a chimp as the ape was from a platypus. It was known as the Great Hippocampus Question, at least before being satirised as the "Great hippopotamus test" in *The Water-Babies* by Darwin's friend and social reformer the Reverend Charles Kingsley. Owen had claimed that "man should stand in a special sub-class, one reserved for him alone", as one biography of Darwin notes (Desmond & Moore 1991, p.453). However, in 1862, in front of the British Association for the Advancement of Science, Huxley, the great showman that he was, would have an ape brain dissected to reveal the hippocampus. Darwin's bulldog "was smashing the post-Waterloo consensus which made man sacrosanct and any science touching him a reverent and special case" (Desmond 1997, p.307).

But as with Owen, so with so many other great nineteenth-century scientists, including Sir William Thomson. The brilliant but arrogant physicist later to become Lord Kelvin did not like the implications of Darwinian theory, and Thomson and Huxley fought tooth and claw over the evidence. "This method of treating my 'case' is perfectly fair, according to the judicial precedents upon which Professor Huxley professedly founds his pleading", Thomson wrote in 1869. But like Owen, Kelvin was not so much hostile to evolution, as to evolution by natural selection, to Darwinian gradualism, and to anything which did not make humankind a reverent and special case. Creationists have a tendency to invoke Kelvin as one of theirs, writes the historian of science Stephen

Brush, but "it is not even true that Kelvin rejected biological evolution. ... In this address, Kelvin asserted that life cannot arise from dead matter but can only proceed from life ... 'all creatures now living on earth have proceeded by orderly evolution from some such origin'" (1982, p.12). Kelvin admitted that he sympathised with the general idea of evolution, but he could not accept the particular mechanism proposed by Darwin and Wallace. Kelvin agreed with Sir John Herschel's objection, says Brush, that natural selection is too much "like the Laputan method of making books" by the random mechanical combination of words, "and that it did not sufficiently take into account a continually guiding and controlling intelligence" (p.13).

John Herschel, the celebrated astronomer and mathematician, was at first a strong positive influence on Darwin, including with the two meeting in 1836 at the Cape of Good Hope. As Darwin commented, "Sir J. Herschel's *Introduction to the Study of Natural Philosophy*, stirred up in me a burning zeal to add even the most humble contribution to the noble structure of Natural Science. No one or a dozen other books influenced me nearly so much" (Warner 2009, p.432). Herschel was a hero to Darwin, writes University of Cape Town's Brian Warner, and Darwin was therefore stung by Herschel's criticism of the theory of natural selection. "I have heard by round about channel that Herschel says my Book 'is the law of higgledy-pigglety'. What this exactly means I do not know, but it is evidently very contemptuous. If true this is a great blow & discouragement" (p.438). Herschel failed to accept the essence of Darwin's proposed mechanism, Warner notes; "Herschel believed that *directed* variations were necessary". Herschel's book, *Physical Geography*, would go on to emphasise the need for "an intelligence, guided by a purpose" that must be continually in action "to bias the directions" of the evolutionary changes, and to continue them in a "definite course". *Homo sapiens*, Herschel believed, had been deliberately guided to the top of the tree of life, directed to standing apart from and above the rest of nature, because random variations will only produce a slow departure "in a literally random direction". Darwin wrote to Herschel that "the point which you raise on intelligent Design has perplexed me beyond measure", and Darwin ultimately lost patience with Herschel. "You will think me very conceited when I say I feel quite easy about the ultimate success of my views, (with much error, as yet unseen by me, to be no doubt eliminated); & I feel this confidence, because I find so many young & middle-aged truly good workers in different branches, either partially or wholly accepting my views, because they find that they can thus group & understand many scattered facts".

		Requires a change to the template of evolution?	Fails the parsimony test?	Invokes new evolutionary processes?
Option 1	Multilevel-selectionism / Group-selectionism	YES	YES	NO
Option 2	Sociobiology / Evolutionary psychology	YES	YES	YES
Option 3	Darwin's Wager	NO	NO	NO

Darwinism is about the struggle for existence between two very different views on the evolution of our species. On the one side there are those, including Darwin and Huxley, who wish to place humankind within the natural world. To the other side are those, including Richard Owen, Sir John Herschel and even in the final analysis Lord Kelvin, who wish to set humankind apart from the rest of nature.

Even Wallace would ultimately disappoint Darwin and Huxley. Always the contrarian, Wallace, "the ever-vigilant defender of natural selection, the ultra-adaptationist" (Cronin 1991, p.353), would branch out into causes unpopular with most of the late nineteenth-century scientific community, including phrenology, spiritualism, land nationalisation and, from the mid 1880s, anti-vaccination, even if this last crusade seems partly explained by his error in statistical data projection plus a concern over poor vaccination practices. Upon hearing about Wallace's desire to put a "Higher Intelligence" back into human mental development Darwin wrote in March 1869, "I shall be intensely curious to read the *Quarterly*: I hope you have not murdered too completely your own and my child" (Desmond & Moore 1991, p.569). Yet although Wallace never fully embraced Option 3, he nevertheless rejected Options 1 and 2. Though a few have disputed it in the past, it is now largely accepted that Wallace still wanted to keep to the individual selection process of evolution, even if he believed that the capacity of the human brain and the organs of speech could not have evolved by natural selection ("How, then, was an organ developed so far beyond the needs of its possessor? ... An instrument has been developed in advance of the needs of its possessor", as Wallace put it).

Darwinism has always been about Option 3. Darwinism will continue to be all about Option 3.

*

When George Williams died, the *New York Times* commented that, "The importance of Dr. Williams's book was immediately recognized by evolutionary biologists, and his ideas reached a wider audience when they were described by Richard Dawkins in his book *The*

Selfish Gene. ... Dr. Williams acknowledged that people had moral instincts that overcome evil. But he had no patience with biologists who argue that these instincts could have been brought into being by natural selection. 'I account for morality as an accidental capability produced, in its boundless stupidity, by a biological process that is normally opposed to the expression of such a capability'" (Wade, 2010). Yet the problem remains how to prove Darwin's wager?

Williams is the father of the gene-centric revolution, yet when he reasoned, like Darwin, that natural selection could not explain the human moral sense he was, like Darwin, ignored. We want to understand his work, but we don't want to understand his work. Bill Hamilton is the father of kin selection, the theory that would become crucial to cementing selection at the level of the gene, yet when he argued, with Darwin, that natural selection could not explain the human moral sense he was, like Darwin, ignored. We want to use his work, but we don't want to use his work. John Maynard Smith is the co-developer with Williams of the gene-centric revolution, yet when he contended, like Darwin, that natural selection could not explain the human moral sense he was, like Darwin, ignored. And John Maynard Smith is particularly interesting here. Darwin's wager, the end-point of the theory of genic selection, is ultimately a mathematical conclusion and Maynard Smith, generally seen as the father of evolutionary game theory, may have been the finest mathematical biologist operating since Ronald Fisher in the 1930s and 40s.[6] How to prove Darwin's wager then, which is ultimately a mathematical judgement, when the most competent mathematician operating in modern biology, and the scientist who co-developed the mathematical formulae

---

6   As well as being – alongside J.B.S. Haldane and Sewall Wright – one of the three founders of
     population genetics and thus of the modern synthesis of Darwin and Mendel, R.A. Fisher is the
     father of modern statistical science. It is because of Fisher that the *p*-value benchmark was set
     at 0.05, although unlike those who came later he never viewed *p*-values as sufficient. Fisher was
     also, erm, a parapsychologist, racial supremacist, fanatical eugenicist, committed Christian, and
     campaigner against accepting a link between tobacco and lung cancer. For which he may have
     been paid.

underlying gene-centred evolutionary biology, was being ignored when he told us what the maths said?

> "Needless to say, this view is extraordinarily pessimistic, enough to give goose bumps to anyone with faith in the depth of our moral sense."
>
> – **Frans de Waal**, primatologist (1996, p.2)

We like to think that science is about the search for truth, but when dealing with humankind frequently it reduces to who has the largest ego, the biggest cheque book, and the desire to shout loudest. Of course, the situation is not helped when the maths points to something that gives many goosebumps. And it is definitely not helped when the experts refuse to show up, for as Dan Dennett put it back in 1995: "Maynard Smith, Williams, Hamilton, and Dawkins ... have largely eschewed the deeply unpleasant task of pointing out more egregious sins in the work of those who enthusiastically misuse their own good work" (p.485). So all the maths, all the biology, all the evolutionary principles, seem not enough to save Darwin's wager. Ironically, though, given the mutual antipathy between scientists and philosophers, philosophical logic can save Darwin's "other solution" where science can or will not. The driving force behind Option 1 – the need to see uncalculating benevolence in the natural world – and the driving force behind Option 2 – the need to lift humankind away from the rest of nature – come apart under logical analysis.

Because this vanity that we are, biologically, "*the* moral animal" explains nothing. It doesn't explain why half of America had to be forced at gunpoint to renounce first slavery and then segregation. It doesn't explain why the state of California targeted Native Americans in a deliberate policy of genocide, where almost ninety-nine per cent of the Comanche who had been living in the decades before the Mexican–American War were dead by 1875. This vanity doesn't explain a billion Indians, or a billion Muslims, or at least 200 million American Christians. It doesn't explain rural Iraq, or Russian thuggery and scapegoating, or Chinese internment. This vanity doesn't explain Abraham Lincoln's anti-miscegenation convictions, or the millions of Israelis running on Yuval Noah Harari's *steal-kill-die* platform ("Fighting to regain lost Jewish territory … What are a few dead people? … I too would like to be a fallen soldier"). And it doesn't explain ninety per cent of humanist philosophers, it doesn't explain nine-tenths of humankind's smartest and most educated thinkers. A flick through human history, and a glance at current behaviour, does not give us morality as a biological adaptation. Evolutionary psychology is, in general, about universal features of the mind: "insofar as individual differences exist, the default assumption is that they are expressions of the same universal human nature as it encounters different environments" (Horgan 1995, p.153). But throughout history our similarities have tended to reflect widespread viciousness and immorality, while our differences have usually been the instances of warmth and morality. Which means that we have the little understood point that evolutionary psychology would have to put a tendency towards immorality within basic human nature, and fairness and morality as cultural. So "EP" itself cannot give us morality as a biological adaptation.

And freedom of choice is a logical impossibility. It is what Darwin called a "general delusion", what Nietzsche called "a kind of logical rape", and what George Williams termed "a stupid idea". Einstein once commented "I do not at all believe in human freedom in the philosophical sense". In a world without freedom of choice, luck swallows everything, and all of life reduces to the pure lottery of biological and environmental luck. The successful are successful through undeserved good luck; the unsuccessful are unsuccessful through undeserved bad luck. A failure to recognise that luck swallows everything seems to make morality impossible, and around ninety per cent of humankind has been wilfully blind to, indifferent to, or apologists for, the problems of the least fortunate. Darwin wagered 150 years ago that humans are born just another immoral, or at least amoral, ape, and that it is culture that must make us fair and just, but philosophy is now agreeing with Darwin that at least 90% of the humans who have ever lived have not been moral beings. If morality is a biological adaptation, it is an adaptation in fewer than 10% of the human population; atheists, philosophers and scientists very much included.

> "Meanwhile, *Lukaja* handed the infant to the alpha male *Ntologi*, who dragged, tossed, and slapped it against the ground. ... Conspicuous competition for meat and meat-sharing was observed as usual."
>
> – **Hamai** *et al.*, "New records of within-group infanticide and cannibalism in wild chimpanzees", *Primates* (1992, p.152)

It is difficult to imagine two vanities more perfectly suited to keeping opportunity out of the hands of vast sections of the population. Two conceits – that our species has freedom of choice, and that our species broke from the billion-year pattern of evolution – that have been promoted as fanatically by the liberal-left as they have been by the right. And let us just recall what it would have meant to have moved beyond Humphrey, Lukaja and Ntologi's genetic pattern in the six or so million years since we split from a common ancestor with chimps and bonobos. It would have required multiple vast leaps in genetic design space, multiple grand "saltations". It would have required selection to have backtracked through the entire genome, deleting or inhibiting genes for common animal behaviours while substituting genes for antithetical behaviours never before seen in the history of evolution. It would have required the rewriting of a four-billion-year evolutionary pattern, the fundamental change to a billion-year gene- and individual-selection design that needed no change. It would have required the invention of new processes – "indirect reciprocity", "metamorphosed" phenotypic expression, and "*mal*adaptive" evolution; or Robert Trivers' "multiparty altruistic system in which altruistic acts are dispensed freely" – that are both evolutionarily unstable (at least according to the biologist who developed the mathematical concept of the evolutionarily stable strategy) and that we do not need in the explanation of all other life on Earth. It would have required the reworking of an outbred diploid organism into one with an inbred or haplodiploid behaviour pattern, but a behaviour pattern way beyond what nature had previously achieved for an inbred and even reproductively suppressed diploid organism. It would have required the infinitesimal 0.1% genetic distance between our "glorified chimpanzee" ancestors and ourselves to have been the locus of the drive for selfishness as old as life itself. Because we didn't lose anything in that final 0.1% change, and certainly not a four-billion-year pattern for gross immorality and pathological selfishness, we gained something. Just another cannibal ape gained a susceptibility to culture with the emergence of a much larger brain and the capacity for spoken complex language.

In his classic 1966 work that started the selfish gene revolution George Williams provided the contrast between human sentimentality and what Dawkins terms the natural world's blind, pitiless indifference, and when he was recounting the attitudes of an audience on being shown a film about elephant seals: "These motherless young were manifestly starving and in acute distress. The human audience reacted with horror to the way these unfortunates were rejected". When the sociobiologist Sarah Hrdy was documenting in the mid 1970s the casual slaughter she witnessed in langur monkeys at Abu in India, she admits that it was her own tears that were among the problems she had to overcome. When the primatologist Mariko Hiraiwa-Hasegawa observed male chimps attacking a mother crawling on the ground to protect her concealed infant, and then reaching in to seize it, she "momentarily forgot her position as a researcher and, brandishing a piece of wood, she intervened and confronted the males to rescue the mother and infant". While *every* adult langur or chimpanzee will tear infants of their own species to pieces without batting an eyelid, humans shed tears over the deaths of infants of *another* species, or run in to protect them against attacks by their conspecifics even at significant risk to life and limb. As Darwin first realised, and Williams, Maynard Smith and Hamilton later showed mathematically, natural selection cannot explain the tears of Sarah Hrdy, or the cross-species sacrifice of Mariko Hasegawa, or the horror of a human audience at encountering the rejection of starving seal pups by their own species.

*

The Western world is built upon belief in, or at least unwillingness to challenge, what we have called the Galton–Option 2 axis, and a rejection of the Darwin–Option 3 model; a renunciation of the thought that humankind developed to the same evolutionary rules as the rest of nature. Yet even ahead of weighing the scientific facts as we have, the Darwin–Option 3 model seems to explain everything, while the Galton–Option 2 axis can explain nothing.

Only the Darwin–Option 3 template explains how Honest Abe Lincoln, the Great Emancipator, could be simultaneously among the finest Americans of his generation and an ignorant white supremacist ("there must be a position of superior and inferior" while the white and black races "remain together"). *The intrinsic, the built-in, state of the human animal is, like all other animals, amorality, and it takes real effort to shift us directionally upwards,* and even then this is often with only partial success. Whereas it takes little effort for a downward directional shift; all those Francis Galtons with their convictions that England "got rid of a great deal of refuse" through emigration to North America, and their

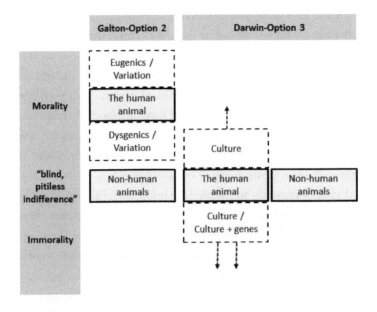

opposition to the slave trade not due to it being a global system of terror and dehumanisation but due to slave catching being a "lottery", and "awful disorganization". The Darwin–Option 3 model explains a Lincoln as much as it explains a Galton, and today it explains a Bezos as easily as it explains a Ratcliffe.

There was much talk that the 2020 global shutdown would genuinely change things in the West, but my suspicion is little will ultimately change, at least across the Anglo-American realm. Safety nets were temporarily widened, but this was a defensive measure helping to stabilise markets on the verge of panic. And with many countries now carrying large fiscal deficits and very high public debt, the corporate sphere is keen to get back to business as usual, glossing over that pain was unequally shared between rich and poor, white and black, and that the developing world was often affected worse. Because our myths haven't changed this time, and we live in a world built on myths. A world that privileges the affluent and fortunate, built on myths. Myths like "everybody on the planet" gets the opportunities they need to become prosperous. Myths like biology is telling us that "we cannot do much about" those at the bottom of society. Myths like racial science is there to "counter ... an injustice". Myths like the deserving rich, and the undeserving poor. The world we live in, this world that privileges wealth and luck, is not happenstance; it was deliberately fabricated and constructed, and upon academic spin, masquerade and misdirection. We will begin to change the world only when we begin to change the language of our discourse.

Fairness, morality and justice are impossible in a world where philosophers and scientists treat humankind as separate from nature, and truth as an optional extra. A world where the quiet, gentle and kind can often seem sidelined, while the brash, violent and manipulative prosper. It is easy to look around the world, at the inequality, the waste, the thuggery and the cruelty, and feel that our species is defined by the one per cent, by the indifferent, and by the bullies. We even have presidents, leaders of the free world, voted into power despite bragging about – even because of bragging about – how in America fame, wealth and power let you get away with almost anything, up to and including sexual assault. "And when you're a star they let you do it. You can do anything. ... Grab them by the pussy. You can do anything." But this is to fundamentally misunderstand what science and logic are now telling us about our species.

Power, fame and wealth often migrate to the most ruthless and the most manipulative so, yes, we are very often *controlled* by such people, but because of Darwin's wager we can never be *defined* by them. Chimpanzees live in "a world without compassion". Apes are defined by their selfishness, thuggery and sexual assault. What defines humans is that, uniquely, we can rise above this behaviour. We are not defined by our internet trolls, by our hatemongers, or by the Vladimir Putins and the Donald Trumps; we are defined by the gentle and decent, the kind and the good. We are defined by figures like Justin Welby, Desmond Tutu and Mahatma Gandhi. As a species we are defined unambiguously by the ones who devote themselves to others, who think of others. And those who live in the shadows, those who hurt and hate, and those who use wealth, power and privilege to attack the weak and less fortunate can never, and will never, represent the highest and most exceptional part of us.

Our capacity for morality is unique on this planet, but it may well be unparalleled in the universe, making us important on the galactic scale. Darwin's wager tells us that we probably still carry the genetic code for cannibalism found in the other great apes but despite this – *indeed because of this* – we now have an essential and unique purpose to our existence.

BIBLIOGRAPHY

Aaronson, S. [2016]: 'The ghost in the quantum Turing machine'. In S.B. Cooper and A. Hodges (eds.) *The Once and Future Turing: Computing the World,* Cambridge, Cambridge University Press, pp. 193–296.

Abbot, P. et al. [2011]: 'Inclusive fitness theory and eusociality', *Nature, 471,* E1–E4, https://www.nature.com/articles/nature09831

Alexander, R.D. [1987]: *The Biology of Moral Systems,* Hawthorne, New York, Aldine de Gruyter.

Allen, A. [1998]: 'Nature & nurture: When it comes to twins, sometimes it's hard to tell the two apart', *The Washington Post,* 11 January, https://www.washingtonpost.com/wp-srv/national/longterm/twins/twins2.htm

Allen, J.T. and Dimock, M. [2007]: 'A nation of "haves" and "have-nots"? Far more Americans now see their country as sharply divided along economic lines', *Pew Research Center.* Available at https://www.pewresearch.org/2007/09/13/a-nation-of-haves-and-havenots/

Andersen, R. [2012]: 'Has physics made philosophy and religion obsolete?', *The Atlantic,* 23 April, https://www.theatlantic.com/technology/archive/2012/04/has-physics-made-philosophy-and-religion-obsolete/256203/

Anderson, M.D. [2017]: 'Why the myth of meritocracy hurts kids of color', *The Atlantic*, 27 July, https://www.theatlantic.com/education/archive/2017/07/internalizing-the-myth-of-meritocracy/535035/

Anthony, A. [2018]: 'So it is nature not nurture after all?', *The Guardian*, 29 September, https://www.theguardian.com/science/2018/sep/29/so-is-it-nature-not-nurture-after-all-genetics-robert-plomin-polygenic-testing

A.S.A. [2016]: 'American Statistical Association releases statement on statistical significance and *p*-values', *American Statistical Association*, 7 March, https://www.amstat.org/asa/files/pdfs/p-valuestatement.pdf

Atiq, E.H. [2013]: 'How folk beliefs about free will influence sentencing: A new target for the neuro-determinist critics of criminal law', *New Criminal Law Review*, 16, pp. 449–493, https://scholarship.law.cornell.edu/facpub/1664/

Bailyn, B. [2012]: *The Barbarous Years: The Peopling of British North America – The Conflict of Civilizations, 1600–1675*, (2013) New York, Vintage Books.

Baker, M. [2015]: 'Over half of psychology studies fail reproducibility test: Largest replication study to date casts doubt on many published positive results', *Nature*, 27 August, https://www.nature.com/news/over-half-of-psychology-studies-fail-reproducibility-test-1.18248

Bamfield, L. and Horton, T. [2009]: *Understanding Attitudes to Tackling Economic Inequality*, York, The Joseph Rowntree Foundation. Available at https://www.jrf.org.uk/report/understanding-attitudes-tackling-economic-inequality

Bannon, S.K. [2016]: 'Sympathy for the devils: The plot against Roger Ailes — and America', *Breitbart*, 10 July, http://www.breitbart.com/big-journalism/2016/07/10/sympathy-devils-plot-roger-ailes-america/

Barash, D.P. [1979]: *Sociobiology: The Whisperings Within*, (1980) London, Souvenir Press.

Barash, D.P. [1982]: *Sociobiology and Behavior* (expanded edition to first edition published 1977), New York, Elsevier.

Barkow, J.H., Cosmides, L. and Tooby, J. (*eds.*) [1992]: *The Adapted Mind: Evolutionary Psychology and the Generation of Culture*, New York, Oxford University Press.

Barlow, G.W. [2000]: *The Cichlid Fishes: Nature's Grand Experiment In Evolution*, New York, Basic Books. Foreword by George C. Williams.

Barrett, P.H., Gautrey, P., Herbert, S., Kohn D. and Smith, S. (*eds.*) [1987]: *Charles Darwin's Notebooks, 1836–1844: Geology, Transmutation of Species, Metaphysical Enquiries*, transcribed and edited by P.H. Barrett and others, Cambridge, Cambridge University Press.

Baumeister, R.F., Masicampo, E.J., and DeWall, C.N. [2009]: 'Prosocial benefits of feeling free: Disbelief in free will increases aggression and reduces helpfulness', *Personality and Social Psychology Bulletin*, 35, pp. 260–268.

BBC [2018]: 'Caste hatred in India – what it looks like', *BBC website*, 7 May, https://www.bbc.co.uk/news/world-asia-india-43972841

BBC [2018a]: 'UN experts condemn President Trump's media criticism', *BBC website*, 2 August, https://www.bbc.co.uk/news/world-us-canada-45053406

Becker, A. [2018]: *What is Real? The Unfinished Quest for the Meaning of Quantum Physics*, New York, Basic Books.

Bennett, N.C. and Faulkes, C.G. [2000]: *African Mole-Rats: Ecology and Eusociality*, Cambridge, Cambridge University Press.

Berman, L. [2011]: 'The 2011 Nobel Prize and the debate over Jewish IQ', *American Enterprise Institute*, 19 October, http://www.aei.org/publication/the-2011-nobel-prize-and-the-debate-over-jewish-iq/

Berry, A. [2000]: 'An ugly baby' (a review of *Footsteps in the Forest: Alfred Russel Wallace in the Amazon* by Sandra Knapp), *London Review of Books*, 18 May, pp. 26–27.

Berry, A. (*ed.*) [2002]: *Infinite Tropics: An Alfred Russel Wallace Anthology*, (2003) London, Verso.

Bezos, J. [2010]: '"We are what we choose". Remarks by Jeff Bezos, as delivered to the Class of 2010 Baccalaureate', *Princeton University*, 30 May, https://www.princeton.edu/news/2010/05/30/2010-baccalaureate-remarks

Blume, H. [1998]: 'Reverse-engineering the psyche: Evolutionary psychologist Steven Pinker on how the mind really works', *Wired*, 6.03, pp. 154–155.

Bourget, D. and Chalmers, D.J. [2014]: 'What do philosophers believe?', *Philosophical Studies*, 170, pp. 465–500.

Bowlby, C. [2010]: 'The deserving or undeserving poor?', *BBC website* (BBC Magazine review of Bowlby's Radio 4 Analysis episode *Who Deserves Welfare?* broadcast 18 November), http://www.bbc.co.uk/news/magazine-11778284

Boyd, R. and Richerson, P.J. [1985]: *Culture and the Evolutionary Process*, Chicago, University of Chicago Press.

Brockman, J. (*ed.*) [1995]: *The Third Culture: Beyond the Scientific Revolution*, New York, Simon & Schuster.

Brown, A. [1999]: *The Darwin Wars: How Stupid Genes Became Selfish Gods*, London, Simon & Schuster.

Brush, S.G. [1982]: 'Kelvin was not a Creationist', *Creation/Evolution Journal*, 3, pp. 11–14, https://ncse.com/cej/3/2/kelvin-was-not-creationist

Buckland, W. [1835]: 'On the discovery of coprolites, or fossil faeces, in the Lias at Lyme Regis, and in other formations', *Transactions of the Geological Society of London*, 2nd Series, Pt. 3, pp. 223–236.

Bygott, J.D. [1972]: 'Cannibalism among wild chimpanzees', *Nature*, 238, pp. 410–411.

Calhoun, C., Mendieta, E. and VanAntwerpen, J. (*eds.*) [2013]: *Habermas and Religion*, Cambridge, Polity Press.

Carey, B. and Roston, M. [2015]: 'Three popular psychology studies that didn't hold up', *The New York Times*, 28 August, https://www.nytimes.com/interactive/2015/08/28/science/psychology-studies-redid.html

Carey, J.M. [2009]: 'Development and validation of a measure of free will belief and its alternatives', postgraduate thesis at the *University of British Columbia*. Available at U.B.C. website http://circle.ubc.ca/handle/2429/12588

Cave, S. [2015]: 'No choice in the matter', *Literary Review*, 432, pp. 36–37.

Cave, S. [2016]: 'There's no such thing as free will', *The Atlantic*, June, https://www.theatlantic.com/magazine/archive/2016/06/theres-no-such-thing-as-free-will/480750/

Chotiner, I. [2018]: 'The Mafia is more powerful than it's ever been', *Slate*, 16 June, https://slate.com/news-and-politics/2018/06/ndrangheta-mafia-more-powerful-and-scarier-than-its-ever-been.html

Cochran, G., Hardy, J. and Harpending, H. [2006]: 'Natural history of Ashkenazi intelligence', *Journal of Biosocial Science*, 38, pp. 659–693, https://www.ncbi.nlm.nih.gov/pubmed/16867211

Corak, M. [2016]: 'Economic mobility'. In *The Poverty and Inequality Report*, Stanford Center on Poverty and Inequality, pp. 51–57, *https://inequality.stanford.edu/sites/default/files/Pathways-SOTU-2016.pdf*

Cosmides, L., Tooby, J. and Barkow, J.H. [1992]: 'Introduction: Evolutionary psychology and conceptual integration'. In Barkow and others (*eds.*) *The Adapted Mind: Evolutionary Psychology and the Generation of Culture*, New York, Oxford University Press, pp. 3–15.

Cotterill, S., Sidanius, J., Bhardwaj, A. and Kumar, V. [2014]: 'Ideological support for the Indian caste system: Social dominance orientation, right-wing authoritarianism and Karma', *Journal of Social and Political Psychology*, 2, pp. 98–116, https://jspp.psychopen.eu/article/view/171

Coyne, J. [2013]: 'Does eroding belief in free will cause cheating? Failure to replicate a famous result', *Why Evolution Is True*, 24 March, https://whyevolutionistrue.wordpress.com/2013/03/24/does-eroding-belief-in-free-will-cause-cheating-failure-to-replicate-a-famous-result/

Coyne, J. [2014]: 'The group-selection dustup continues: E.O. Wilson calls Richard Dawkins a "journalist"', *Why Evolution Is True*, 7 November, https://whyevolutionistrue.wordpress.com/2014/11/07/the-group-selection-dustup-continues-e-o-wilson-calls-richard-dawkins-a-journalist/

Cronin, H. [1991]: *The Ant and the Peacock: Altruism and Sexual Selection from Darwin to Today*, Cambridge, Cambridge University Press.

Daly, S. [2015]: 'Free will is no bargain: How misunderstanding human behavior negatively influences our criminal justice system', *Nevada Law Journal*, 15, pp. 992–1029, http://scholars.law.unlv.edu/nlj/vol15/iss2/21

Darwin, C. [1859]: *On the Origin of Species by Means of Natural Selection* (edited and introduced by J.W. Burrow), (1985) London, Penguin.

Darwin, C. [1871]: *The Descent of Man, and Selection in Relation to Sex* (facsimile reproduction of first edition with an introduction by J.T. Bonner and R.M. May), (1981) Princeton, New Jersey, Princeton University Press.

Davies, P. [2004]: 'Undermining free will', *Foreign Policy*, 144, pp. 36–38 (published as one of *Foreign Policy*'s The World's Most Dangerous Ideas essays). Also published as: 'In defence of the ghost in the machine', *Australian Financial Review*, 3 September 2004.

Dawkins, R. [1976]: *The Selfish Gene*, Oxford, Oxford University Press.

Dawkins, R. [1981]: 'In defence of selfish genes', *Philosophy*, 56, pp. 556–573.

Dawkins, R. [1986]: 'Sociobiology: The new storm in a teacup'. In S. Rose and L. Appignanesi (*eds.*) *Science and Beyond*, Oxford, Basil Blackwell, pp. 61–78.

Dawkins, R. [1986a]: *The Blind Watchmaker*, Harlow, Longman.

Dawkins, R. [1989]: *The Selfish Gene* (revised edition to first edition published 1976), Oxford, Oxford University Press.

Dawkins, R. [1995]: *River Out Of Eden: A Darwinian View of Life*, London, Weidenfeld & Nicolson.

Dawkins, R. [1998]: *Unweaving the Rainbow: Science, Delusion and the Appetite for Wonder*, London, Allen Lane.

Dellatore, D.F., Waitt, C.D. and Foitova, I. [2009]: 'Two cases of mother–infant cannibalism in orangutans', *Primates*, 50, pp. 277–281, DOI: 10.1007/s10329-009-0142-5

DeMuth, C. [2009]: 'Irving Kristol Award and Lecture for 2009', *American Enterprise Institute*, 11 March, https://www.aei.org/publication/irving-kristol-award-and-lecture-for-2009/

Dennett, D.C. [1978]: *Brainstorms: Philosophical Essays on Mind and Psychology*, (1981) Cambridge, Massachusetts, The MIT Press.

Dennett, D.C. [1984]: *Elbow Room: The Varieties of Free Will Worth Wanting*, (1996) Cambridge, Massachusetts, The MIT Press.

Dennett, D.C. [1995]: *Darwin's Dangerous Idea: Evolution and the Meanings of Life*, (1996) London, Penguin.

Dennett, D.C. [2003]: *Freedom Evolves*, London, Allen Lane.

Dennett, D.C. [2008]: 'Some observations on the psychology of thinking about free will'. In J. Baer, J.C. Kaufman and R.F. Baumeister (*eds.*) *Are We Free? Psychology and Free Will*, New York, Oxford University Press, pp. 248–259.

Dennett, D.C [2012]: 'Daniel Dennett reviews *Against Moral Responsibility* by Bruce Waller'. Available at https://dl.tufts.edu/concern/pdfs/9w032f65c

Dennett, D.C. [2012a]: 'Exchange on Bruce Waller's *Against Moral Responsibility*'. Available at https://dl.tufts.edu/pdfviewer/08613068g/9w032f65c

Dennett, D.C. [2012b]: 'Erasmus: Sometimes a spin doctor is right: Praemium Erasmianum Essay 2012', *Praemium Erasmianum Foundation*, *https://ase. tufts.edu/cogstud/dennett/papers/spindoctor.pdf*

Dennett, D.C. [2014]: 'Reflections on *Free Will*: A review by Daniel C. Dennett', *Samharris.org*, 26 January. Available at https://samharris.org/reflections-on-free-will/

DeParle, J. [1994]: 'Daring research or "social science pornography"?: Charles Murray', *The New York Times*, 9 October, http://www.nytimes.com/1994/10/09/magazine/daring-research-or-social-science-pornography-charles-murray.html

Desmond, A. [1997]: *Huxley: From Devil's Disciple to Evolution's High Priest*, (1998) London, Penguin.

Desmond, A. and Moore, J. [1991]: *Darwin*, (1992) London, Penguin.

de Waal, F.B.M. [1996]: *Good Natured: The Origins of Right and Wrong in Humans and Other Animals*, (1998) Cambridge, Massachusetts, Harvard University Press.

de Waal, F.B.M. [1997]: *Bonobo: The Forgotten Ape*, Berkeley, California, University of California Press.

de Waal, F.B.M. [1998]: '"The social behavior of chimpanzees and bonobos: Empirical evidence and shifting assumptions": Reply', *Current Anthropology*, 39, pp. 407–408.

Diamond, J. [1991]: *The Rise and Fall of The Third Chimpanzee*, (1992) London, Vintage.

Double, R. [1990]: *The Non-reality of Free Will*, (1991) New York, Oxford University Press.

Double, R. [2002]: 'The moral hardness of libertarianism', *Philo*, 5, pp. 226–234.

Duhigg, C. [2019]: 'Is Amazon unstoppable?', *The New Yorker*, 10 October, https://www.newyorker.com/magazine/2019/10/21/is-amazon-unstoppable

Economist [2005]: 'The evolution of intelligence: Natural genius?', *The Economist*, 2 June, https://www.economist.com/node/4032638

Economist [2013]: 'An ideologue's exit: What the departure of Vladislav Surkov means for the government', *The Economist*, 11 May, https://www.economist.com/europe/2013/05/11/an-ideologues-exit

Edelman, G.M. [1992]: *Bright Air, Brilliant Fire: On the Matter of the Mind*, New York, Basic Books.

Elgar, M.A. and Crespi, B.J. [1992]: 'Ecology and evolution of cannibalism'. In M.A. Elgar and B.J. Crespi (*eds.*) *Cannibalism: Ecology and Evolution Among Diverse Taxa*, Oxford, Oxford University Press, pp. 1–12.

Erasmus, D. [1524]: *Erasmus-Luther: Discourse on Free Will*, trans. E.F. Winter, (1999) New York, Continuum.

Evans, G. [2018]: 'The unwelcome revival of "race science"', *The Guardian*, 2 March, https://www.theguardian.com/news/2018/mar/02/the-unwelcome-revival-of-race-science

Falk, R. [2017]: *Zionism and the Biology of Jews*, (updated edition to the Hebrew language Resling Publishing 2006 version), Cham, Switzerland, Springer International.

Fischer, J.M. [2007]: 'Compatibilism'. In J.M. Fischer, R. Kane, D. Pereboom and M. Vargas (*eds.*) *Four Views on Free Will*, Malden, Massachusetts, Blackwell, pp. 44–84.

Fischer, J.M. and Ravizza, M. [1998]: *Responsibility and Control: A Theory of Moral Responsibility*, Cambridge, Cambridge University Press.

Fortey, R. [2000]: *Trilobite! Eyewitness to Evolution*, London, HarperCollins.

Fowler, A. and Hohmann, G. [2010]: 'Cannibalism in wild bonobos (*Pan paniscus*) at Lui Kotale', *American Journal of Primatology*, 72, pp. 509–514, DOI: 10.1002/ajp.20802

Galton, F. [1857]: 'Negroes and the slave trade: To the Editor', *The Times*, 26 December, p. 10d, http://galton.org/essays/1850-1859/galton-1857-12-26-times-negroes-slave-trade.pdf

Galton, F. [1873]: 'Africa for the Chinese', Letter to *The Times*, 5 June, http://galton.org/letters/africa-for-chinese/AfricaForTheChinese.htm

Galton, F. [1892]: *Hereditary Genius: An Inquiry into its Laws and Consequences* (second edition), London, Macmillan and Co., http://galton.org/books/hereditary-genius/text/pdf/galton-1869-genius-v3.pdf. The almost identical

1869 first edition can be found here: http://galton.org/books/hereditary-genius/galton-1869-Hereditary_Genius.pdf.

Godfrey, E.B., Santos, C.E. and Burson, E. [2017]: 'For better or worse? System-justifying beliefs in sixth-grade predict trajectories of self-esteem and behavior across early adolescence', *Child Development*, 90, pp. 180–195, DOI: 10.1111/cdev.12854

Goodell, J. [2011]: 'The Steve Jobs nobody knew', *Rolling Stone*, 27 October, https://www.rollingstone.com/culture/culture-news/the-steve-jobs-nobody-knew-71168/

Goodin, R.E. [1988]: *Reasons for Welfare: The Political Theory of the Welfare State*, Princeton, Princeton University Press.

Gould, S.J. [1993]: *Eight Little Piggies: Reflections in Natural History*, (1994) London, Penguin.

Goyal, A. [2003]: *Uncovering Russia*, Moscow, Norasco Publishing Limited.

Graves, L. [2017]: 'Donald Trump and Rupert Murdoch: Inside the billionaire bromance', *The Guardian*, 16 June, https://www.theguardian.com/us-news/2017/jun/16/donald-trump-rupert-murdoch-friendship-fox-news

Greene, B. [2004]: *The Fabric of the Cosmos: Space, Time, and the Texture of Reality*, (2005) London, Penguin Books.

Gribbin, M. and Gribbin, J. [1993]: *Being Human: Putting People in an Evolutionary Perspective*, (1995) London, Phoenix.

Griffiths, P.E. [1995]: 'The Cronin controversy', *The British Journal for the Philosophy of Science*, 46, pp. 122–138.

Grusky, D.B., Mattingly, M.J. and Varner, C.E. [2016]: 'Executive summary'. In *The Poverty and Inequality Report*, Stanford Center on Poverty and Inequality, pp. 3–9, *https://inequality.stanford.edu/sites/default/files/Pathways-SOTU-2016.pdf*

Guelzo, A.C. [1997]: 'Abraham Lincoln and the doctrine of necessity', *Journal of the Abraham Lincoln Association*, 18, pp. 57–81.

Guelzo, A.C. [2009]: *Abraham Lincoln As a Man of Ideas*, Carbondale, Illinois, Southern Illinois University Press.

Gutwein, D. [2018]: 'How Yuval Noah Harari became the pet ideologist of the liberal elites', *Haaretz*, 20 November, https://www.haaretz.com/us-news/

MAGAZINE-how-yuval-noah-harari-became-the-pet-ideologist-of-the-liberal-elites-1.6673776

Haggard, R.F. [2000]: *The Persistence of Victorian Liberalism: The Politics of Social Reform in Britain, 1870-1900*, London, Greenwood Press.

Haldane, J.B.S. [1955]: 'Population genetics', *New Biology*, 18, pp. 34–51.

Halper, T. [1973]: 'The poor as pawns: The new "deserving poor" & the old', *Polity*, 6, pp. 71–86.

Hamai, M., Nishida, T., Takasaki, H. and Turner, L.A. [1992]: 'New records of within-group infanticide and cannibalism in wild chimpanzees', *Primates*, 33, pp. 151–162.

Hameroff, S.R. and Penrose, R. [1995]: 'Orchestrated reduction of quantum coherence in brain microtubules: A model for consciousness', *Neural Network World*, 5, pp. 793–804.

Hamilton, W.D. [1971]: 'Selection of selfish and altruistic behavior in some extreme models'. In J.F. Eisenberg and W.S. Dillon (*eds.*) *Man and Beast: Comparative Social Behavior*, Washington, Smithsonian Institution, pp. 57–92.

Hamilton, W.D. [1971a]: 'Selection of selfish and altruistic behaviour in some extreme models'. In W.D. Hamilton (*ed.*) *Narrow Roads of Gene Land: The Collected Papers of W.D. Hamilton, Volume I: Evolution of Social Behaviour*, (1996) Oxford, W.H Freeman, pp. 198–227.

Hamilton, W.D. [1975]: 'Innate social aptitudes of man: An approach from evolutionary genetics'. In W.D. Hamilton (*ed.*) *Narrow Roads of Gene Land: Volume I*, (1996) Oxford, W.H Freeman, pp. 329–351.

Hamilton, W.D. [2000]: 'A review of *Dysgenics: Genetic Deterioration in Modern Populations*', *Annals of Human Genetics*, 64, pp. 363–374.

Harari, Y.N. [2018]: *21 Lessons for the 21st Century*, London: Jonathan Cape.

Harris, S. [2011]: 'The free will delusion', *New Statesman*, 19 December, pp. 46–47.

Harris, S. [2012]: *Free Will*, New York, Simon & Schuster.

Harris, S. [2012a]: 'On arguing free will with Dan Dennett', Festival of Dangerous Ideas, *The Sydney Ethics Centre / UNSW Centre for Ideas*, September, https://www.youtube.com/watch?v=FrS1NCvG1b4

Harris, S. [2014]: 'The marionette's lament: A response to Daniel Dennett', *Samharris.org*, 12 February, https://samharris.org/the-marionettes-lament/

Hill, T.M. [2017]: 'Is the U.S. serious about countering Russia's information war on democracies?', *The Brookings Institution*, 21 November, https://www.brookings.edu/blog/order-from-chaos/2017/11/21/is-the-u-s-serious-about-countering-russias-information-war-on-democracies/

Himmelfarb, G. [1984]: 'The idea of poverty', *History Today*, 34, pp. 23–30.

Himmelfarb, G. [1995]: 'From Victorian virtues to modern values', *American Enterprise Institute Bradley Lecture Series*, Washington, AEI Publications.

Hindle, S. [2004]: 'Dependency, shame and belonging: Badging the deserving poor, c.1550–1750', *Cultural and Social History*, 1, pp. 6–35.

Hiraiwa-Hasegawa, M. [1992]: 'Cannibalism among non-human primates'. In M.A. Elgar and B.J. Crespi (*eds.*) *Cannibalism: Ecology and Evolution Among Diverse Taxa*, Oxford, Oxford University Press, pp. 323–338.

Hitchens, C. [2002]: *Unacknowledged Legislation: Writers in the Public Sphere*, London, Verso.

Hogenboom, M. [2016]: '"Hippie" apes seen eating their own dead children', *BBC website*, 27 October, http://www.bbc.com/earth/story/20161026-hippie-apes-seen-eating-their-own-dead-children

Holmes, R. [1974]: *Shelley: The Pursuit*, London, Harper Perennial.

Horgan, J. [1995]: 'The new social Darwinists', *Scientific American*, 273, pp. 150–157.

Horgan, J. [1996]: *The End of Science: Facing the Limits of Knowledge in the Twilight of the Scientific Age*, (1997) London, Little, Brown & Company.

Hossenfelder, S. [2018]: *Lost in Math: How Beauty Leads Physics Astray*, New York, Basic Books.

Hrdy, S.B. [1977]: 'Infanticide as a primate reproductive strategy', *American Scientist*, 65, pp. 40–49.

Hrdy, S.B. [1977a]: *The Langurs of Abu: Female and Male Strategies of Reproduction*, (1980) Cambridge, Massachusetts, Harvard University Press.

Hruska, A. [2007]: 'Love and slavery: Serfdom, emancipation, and family in Tolstoy's fiction', *The Russian Review*, 66, pp. 627–646.

Hudson, J. [2012]: 'Rupert Murdoch unleashes his inner book critic on Twitter', *The Atlantic*, 9 February, https://www.theatlantic.com/business/archive/2012/02/rupert-murdoch-unleashes-his-inner-book-critic-twitter/332002/

Humphrys, J. [2006]: 'What I found out about God', *The Telegraph*, 23 December, http://www.telegraph.co.uk/news/uknews/1537677/What-I-found-out-about-God.html

Hutton, W. [2010]: *Them and Us: Changing Britain – Why We Need a Fair Society*, London, Little, Brown Book Group.

Huxley, T.H. [1894]: 'Evolution and ethics'. In J.G. Paradis and G.C. Williams (*eds.*) *Evolution & Ethics: T.H. Huxley's Evolution and Ethics*, (1989) Princeton, New Jersey, Princeton University Press, pp. 104–174.

Ipsos MORI [2015]: 'Attitudes of British Jewish people towards Israel', *ipsos.com*, 12 November, https://www.ipsos.com/ipsos-mori/en-uk/attitudes-british-jewish-people-towards-israel

Jacobs, J.A. [2001]: *Choosing Character: Responsibility for Virtue & Vice*, Ithaca, New York, Cornell University Press.

James, W. [1884]: 'The dilemma of determinism'. In W. James (*ed.*) *The Will to Believe and Other Essays in Popular Philosophy*, (1956) New York, Dover Publications, pp. 145–183.

Johnson, V.E. [2013]: 'Revised standards for statistical evidence', *Proceedings of the National Academy of Sciences of the United States of America,* 110, pp. 19313–19317, https://www.pnas.org/content/pnas/110/48/19313.full.pdf

Johnston, C. [2014]: 'Biological warfare flares up again between EO Wilson and Richard Dawkins', *The Guardian*, 7 November, https://www.theguardian.com/science/2014/nov/07/richard-dawkins-labelled-journalist-by-eo-wilson

Jones, J.S. [1982]: 'Of cannibals and kin', *Nature*, 299, pp. 202–203.

Jones, J.S. [1994]: *The Language of the Genes: Biology, History and the Evolutionary Future*, London, Flamingo.

Jones, J.S. [1997]: 'The set within the skull', *New York Review of Books*, 6 November, pp. 13–16.

Jones, J.S. [1999]: *Almost Like a Whale:* The Origin of Species *Updated*, London, Doubleday.

Josephus [1ˢᵗ c. A.D.]: *Antiquities of the Jews*, trans. W. Whiston. Available online at www.ccel.org/j/josephus/works/

Judah, S. [2013]: 'Making time: Does it matter why we help others?', *BBC website*, 10 October, https://www.bbc.co.uk/news/magazine-24457645

Kahan, D.M. [1998]: '*The Anatomy of Disgust* in criminal law', *Michigan Law Review*, 96, pp. 1621–1657.

Kane, R. [2002]: 'Free will: New directions for an ancient problem'. In R. Kane (*ed.*) *Free Will*, Malden, Massachusetts, Blackwell, pp. 222–248.

Kane, R. [2007]: 'Libertarianism'. In J.M. Fischer, R. Kane, D. Pereboom and M. Vargas, *Four Views on Free Will*, Oxford, Blackwell Publishing, pp. 5–43.

Kano, T. [1998]: '"The social behavior of chimpanzees and bonobos: Empirical evidence and shifting assumptions": Reply', *Current Anthropology*, 39, pp. 410–411.

Kant, I. [1788]: *Critique of Practical Reason*, trans. L.W. Beck, (1956) Indianapolis, Bobbs-Merrill.

Kaye, A. [2007]: 'The secret politics of the compatibilist criminal law', *Kansas Law Review*, 55, pp. 365–427.

Kellogg, V. [1913]: 'Eugenics and militarism', *The Atlantic Monthly*, July, https://www.theatlantic.com/magazine/archive/1913/07/eugenics-and-militarism/376208/

Kennedy, H. [2011]: '"The Jukes: Bad blood or bad science?" Interviewed by Steve Jones', *BBC website*, 23 May, https://www.bbc.co.uk/programmes/b0118lkh

Kochhar, R. [2017]: 'Middle class fortunes in Western Europe', *Pew Research Center*, 24 April, http://www.pewglobal.org/2017/04/24/middle-class-fortunes-in-western-europe/

Koenig-Robert, R. and Pearson, J. [2019]: 'Decoding the contents and strength of imagery before volitional engagement', *Scientific Reports,* 9, 3504, DOI: https://doi.org/10.1038/s41598-019-39813-y

Kraus, M.W. and Keltner, D. [2013]: 'Social class rank, essentialism, and punitive judgment', *Journal of Personality and Social Psychology,* 105, pp. 247–261, http://www.krauslab.com/SES.essentialism.JPSP.pdf

Krueger, F., Hoffman, M., Walter, H., and Grafman, J. [2014]: 'An fMRI investigation of the effects of belief in free will on third-party punishment', *Social Cognitive and Affective Neuroscience*, 9, pp. 1143–1149, https://www.ncbi.nlm.nih.gov/pubmed/23887810

Kymlicka, W. [1990]: *Contemporary Political Philosophy: An Introduction*, Oxford, Clarendon Press.

Lakatos, I. [1978]: *The Methodology of Scientific Research Programmes: Philosophical Papers: Volume 1*, (1999) (*eds.* J. Worrall and G. Currie), Cambridge, Cambridge University Press.

Levy, N. [2011]: *Hard Luck: How Luck Undermines Free Will and Moral Responsibility*, Oxford, Oxford University Press.

Lincoln, A. [1858]: 'Fourth debate with Stephen A. Douglas at Charleston, Illinois', Collected Works of Abraham Lincoln, Volume 3, *University of Michigan Digital Library Production Services*, 18 September, https://quod.lib.umich.edu/l/lincoln/lincoln3/1:20.1?rgn=div2;view=fulltext

Lloyd, S. [2012]: 'A Turing test for free will', *Philosophical Transactions of the Royal Society A*, 370, pp. 3597–3610, DOI: 10.1098/rsta.2011.0331

Luce, E. [2016]: 'The return of American exceptionalism', *Financial Times*, 14 August, *https://www.ft.com/content/1476d7ca-6076-11e6-b38c-7b39cbb1138a.html*

Lumsden, C.J. and Wilson, E.O. [1981]: *Genes, Mind, and Culture: The Coevolutionary Process*, Cambridge, Massachusetts, Harvard University Press.

Madison, L. [2011]: 'Elizabeth Warren: "There is nobody in this country who got rich on his own"', *CBS News*, 22 September, https://www.cbsnews.com/news/elizabeth-warren-there-is-nobody-in-this-country-who-got-rich-on-his-own/

Maggiulli, N. [2018]: 'Why winners keep winning: On cumulative advantage and how to think about luck', *Of Dollars And Data*, 8 May, https://ofdollarsanddata.com/why-winners-keep-winning-4e7f221f5b84

Marin, J.M. [2009]: '"Mysticism" in quantum mechanics: The forgotten controversy', *European Journal of Physics*, 30, pp. 807–822.

Mauboussin, M.J. [2012]: *The Success Equation: Untangling Skill and Luck in Business, Sports, and Investing*, Boston, Massachusetts, Harvard Business Review Press.

Maynard Smith, J. [1964]: 'Group selection and kin selection', *Nature*, 201, pp. 1145–1147.

Maynard Smith, J. [1992]: *Did Darwin Get It Right?: Essays on Games, Sex and Evolution*, London, Chapman & Hall.

Maynard Smith, J. [1993]: 'Confusion over evolution: An exchange', *New York Review of Books*, 14 January, p. 43.

Maynard Smith, J. [1996]: 'Conclusions'. In W.C. Runciman, J. Maynard Smith and R.I.M. Dunbar (*eds.*) *Evolution of Social Behaviour Patterns in Primates and Man: A Joint Discussion Meeting of the Royal Society and the British Academy*, and published as *Proceedings of The British Academy*, 88, pp. 291–297.

Maynard Smith, J. and Price, G.R. [1973]: 'The logic of animal conflict', *Nature*, 246, pp. 15–18.

Medawar, P.B. [1977]: 'Unnatural science', *New York Review of Books*, 3 February, pp. 13–18.

Meyer, A. [2010]: 'George C. Williams (1926–2010)', *Nature*, 467, p. 790, https://www.nature.com/articles/467790a

Midgley, M. [1979]: 'Gene-juggling', *Philosophy*, 54, pp. 439–458.

Miles, J.B. [1998]: 'Unnatural selection', *Philosophy*, 73, pp. 593–608.

Miles, J.B. [2003]: *Born Cannibal: Evolution and the Paradox of Man*, London, IconoKlastic Books. Foreword by George C. Williams.

Miles, J.B. [2013]: '"Irresponsible and a disservice": The integrity of social psychology turns on the free will dilemma', *British Journal of Social Psychology*, 52, pp. 205–218.

Miles, J.B. [2013a]: 'The integrity of social psychology turns on the free will dilemma: Reply to Baumeister, Vonasch, and Bargh', *British Journal of Social Psychology*, 52, pp. 231–237.

Miles, J.B. [2015]: *The Free Will Delusion: How We Settled for the Illusion of Morality*, Kibworth Beauchamp, Matador.

Miller, M. [2003]: 'The wages of luck', *The Boston Globe*, 28 September, http://archive.boston.com/news/globe/ideas/articles/2003/09/28/the_wages_of_luck/

Milton, K. [1998]: '"The social behavior of chimpanzees and bonobos: Empirical evidence and shifting assumptions": Reply', *Current Anthropology*, 39, pp. 411–412.

Mineau, P. and Cooke, F. [1979]: 'Rape in the Lesser Snow Goose', *Behaviour*, 70, pp. 280–291.

Mink, G. and O'Connor, A. [2004]: *Poverty in the United States: An Encyclopedia of History, Politics, and Policy*, ABC-CLIO.

Mitnick, J. [2018]: 'The Israel-Diaspora relationship: An unequal partnership?', https://www.myjewishlearning.com/article/the-israel-diaspora-relationship/

Mlodinow, L. [2012]: *Subliminal: How Your Unconscious Mind Rules Your Behavior*, (2013) New York, Vintage Books.

Moore, M.S. [1985]: 'Causation and the excuses', *California Law Review*, 73, pp. 1091–1149.

Morse, S.J. [1976]: 'The twilight of welfare criminology: A reply to Judge Bazelon', *Southern California Law Review*, 49, pp. 1247–1268.

Morse, S.J. [1976a]: 'The twilight of welfare criminology: A final word', *Southern California Law Review*, 49, pp. 1275–1276.

Morse, S.J. [2004]: 'Reason, results, and criminal responsibility', *University of Illinois Law Review*, 2, pp. 363–444.

Murray, C. [1984]: *Losing Ground, American Social Policy, 1950–1980*, (1994) New York, Basic Books.

Nagel, T. [1979]: *Mortal Questions*, Cambridge, Cambridge University Press.

Nahmias, E., Morris, S., Nadelhoffer, T. and Turner, J. [2005]: 'Surveying freedom: Folk intuitions about free will and moral responsibility', *Philosophical Psychology*, 18, pp. 561–584.

Nietzsche, F. [1886]: *Beyond Good and Evil*, trans. R.J. Hollingdale, (1990) London, Penguin.

Nowak, M.A., Tarnita, C.E. and E.O. Wilson [2010]: 'The evolution of eusociality', *Nature*, 466, pp. 1057–1062, DOI:10.1038/nature09205

Nowak, M.A. and R. Highfield [2011]: *SuperCooperators: Altruism, Evolution, and Why We Need Each Other to Succeed*, (2012) New York, Free Press.

Obama, B.H. [2006]: *The Audacity of Hope: Thoughts on Reclaiming the American Dream*, (2007) Edinburgh, Canongate.

Oerton, R. [2012]: *The Nonsense of Free Will: Facing Up to a False Belief*, Kibworth Beauchamp, Matador.

Oerton, R. [2016]: *The Cruelty of Free Will: How Sophistry and Savagery Support a False Belief*, Kibworth Beauchamp, Matador.

Paradis, J.G. and Williams, G.C. [1989]: *Evolution & Ethics: T.H. Huxley's 'Evolution and Ethics' With New Essays on its Victorian and Sociobiological Context*, Princeton, New Jersey, Princeton University Press.

Parfit, D. [2011]: *On What Matters, Volume One*, Oxford, Oxford University Press.

Pearlstein, S. [2011]: 'Hermanomics: Let them eat pizza', *The Washington Post*, 15 October, http://www.washingtonpost.com/business/economy/hermanomics-let-them-eat-pizza/2011/10/11/gIQAgTOmmL_story.html

Pereboom, D. [2001]: *Living Without Free Will*, Cambridge, Cambridge University Press.

Pereboom, D. [2007]: 'Hard incompatibilism'. In J.M. Fischer, R. Kane, D. Pereboom and M. Vargas (*eds.*) *Four Views on Free Will*, Malden, Massachusetts, Blackwell, pp. 85–125.

Peterson, J. [2018]: 'The fatal flaw lurking in American leftist politics', *BigThink.com*, 11 April, http://bigthink.com/videos/jordan-peterson-the-fatal-flaw-lurking-in-american-leftist-politics

Pewresearch [2011]: 'The elusive 90% solution', *Pew Research Center*, 11 March, http://www.pewresearch.org/2011/03/11/the-elusive-90-solution/

Pewresearch [2017]: 'The partisan divide on political values grows even wider: 5. Homosexuality, gender and religion', *Pew Research Center*, 5 October, http://www.people-press.org/2017/10/05/5-homosexuality-gender-and-religion/

Pinker, S. [1994]: *The Language Instinct: The New Science of Language and Mind*, (1995) London, Penguin.

Pinker, S. [1997]: *How the Mind Works*, (1998) London, Penguin.

Pinker, S. [1997a]: 'Evolutionary psychology: An exchange', *New York Review of Books*, 9 October, pp. 55–56.

Pinker, S. [2006]: 'Groups and genes', *The New Republic*, 26 June, https://newrepublic.com/article/77727/groups-and-genes

Pinker, S. [2012]: 'The false allure of group selection', *Edge.org*, 18 June, https://www.edge.org/conversation/steven_pinker-the-false-allure-of-group-selection

Plantinga, A. [2012]: 'Bait and switch: Sam Harris on free will', *Books & Culture: A Christian Review*. Available at http://www.booksandculture.com/articles/2013/janfeb/bait-and-switch.html

Pluchino, A., Biondo, A.E. and Rapisarda, A. [2018]: 'Talent vs luck: The role of randomness in success and failure', *Advances in Complex Systems*, 21, p. 1850014, https://arxiv.org/pdf/1802.07068.pdf

Pomerantsev, P. [2014]: 'Russia's ideology: There is no truth', *The New York Times*, 11 December, https://www.nytimes.com/2014/12/12/opinion/russias-ideology-there-is-no-truth.html

Potts, M. [2014]: 'The other Americans', *Democracy*, 32, pp. 100–106, http://www.democracyjournal.org/pdf/32/the_other_americans.pdf

Putnam, H. [2015]: *The Philosophy of Hilary Putnam, The Library of Living Philosophers Vol XXXIV* (eds. R.E. Auxier, D.R. Anderson, and L.E. Hahn), Chicago, Illinois, Open Court Publishing.

Raby, P. [2001]: *Alfred Russel Wallace: A Life*, (2002) London, Pimlico.

Rawls, J. [1971]: *A Theory of Justice: Revised Edition*, (1999) Cambridge, Massachusetts, Belknap/Harvard University Press.

Resnick, B. and Belluz, J. [2018]: 'A top Cornell food researcher has had 15 studies retracted. That's a lot', *Vox.com*, 19 September, updated 24 October, https://www.vox.com/science-and-health/2018/9/19/17879102/brian-wansink-cornell-food-brand-lab-retractions-jama

Richards, R.J. [1987]: *Darwin and the Emergence of Evolutionary Theories of Mind and Behavior*, Chicago, Illinois, University of Chicago Press.

Richardson, H. [2017]: 'Oxbridge uncovered: More elitist than we thought', *BBC website*, 20 October, http://www.bbc.co.uk/news/education-41664459

Ridley, Mark and Dawkins, R. [1981]: 'The natural selection of altruism'. In J.P. Rushton and R.M. Sorrentino (*eds.*) *Altruism and Helping Behavior: Social, Personality and Developmental Perspectives*, Hillsdale, New Jersey, Lawrence Erlbaum, pp. 19–39.

Ridley, Matt [1996]: *The Origins of Virtue*, Harmondsworth, Viking.

Robinson, D.N. [1996]: *Wild Beasts & Idle Humours: The Insanity Defense from Antiquity to the Present*, (1998), Cambridge, Massachusetts, Harvard University Press.

Ruse, M. [1989]: *The Darwinian Paradigm: Essays on its History, Philosophy, and Religious Implications*, London, Routledge.

Russell, P. [1995]: *Freedom and Moral Sentiment: Hume's Way of Naturalizing Responsibility*, New York, Oxford University Press.

Rzepnikowska, A. [2018]: 'Racism and xenophobia experienced by Polish migrants in the UK before and after Brexit vote', *Journal of Ethnic and Migration Studies*, 45, pp. 61–77, DOI: 10.1080/1369183X.2018.1451308

Sackur, S. [2016]: 'Jim Ratcliffe, founder and chairman, Ineos', HARDtalk, *BBC Radio 4*, 6 December, http://www.bbc.co.uk/programmes/b0854916

Searle, J.R. [2000]: 'Consciousness, free action and the brain', *Journal of Consciousness Studies*, 7, pp. 3–22.

Segerstrale, U. [2000]: *Defenders of the Truth: The Sociobiology Debate*, Oxford, Oxford University Press.

Shariff, A.F., Schooler, J. and Vohs, K.D. [2008]: 'The hazards of claiming to have solved the hard problem of free will'. In J. Baer, J.C. Kaufman, and R.F. Baumeister (*eds.*) *Are We Free? Psychology and Free Will*, New York, Oxford University Press, pp. 181–204.

Shariff, A.F., Greene, J.D., Karremans, J.C., Luguri, J.B., Clark, C.J., Schooler, J.W., Baumeister, R.F. and Vohs, K.D [2014]: 'Free will and punishment: A mechanistic view of human nature reduces retribution', *Psychological Science*, 25, pp.1563–1570, DOI: 10.1177/0956797614534693

Sharma, S. [2015]: 'Caste-based crimes and economic status: Evidence from India', *Journal of Comparative Economics*, 43, pp. 204–226, https://www.sciencedirect.com/science/article/pii/S0147596714001048

Shifflett, P.A. [2008]: 'Homeless children and runaways in the United States'. In E. Craig (*ed.*), *Encyclopedia of Children and Childhood in History and Society*, The Gale Group, Inc. Available online at www.faqs.org/childhood/Gr-Im/Homeless-Children-and-Runaways-in-the-United-States.htm

Sibley, C.G. and Ahlquist, J.E. [1984]: 'The phylogeny of the hominoid primates, as indicated by DNA-DNA hybridization', *Journal of Molecular Evolution*, 20, pp. 2–15.

Smilansky, S. [2000]: *Free Will and Illusion*, Oxford, Oxford University Press.

Smilansky, S. [2011]: 'Free will, fundamental dualism, and the centrality of illusion'. In R. Kane (*ed.*) *The Oxford Handbook of Free Will, Second Edition*, Oxford, Oxford University Press, pp. 425–441.

Sober, E. and Wilson, D.S. [1998]: *Unto Others: The Evolution and Psychology of Unselfish Behavior*, (1999) Cambridge, Massachusetts, Harvard University Press.

Sommer, V. [2000]: 'The holy wars about infanticide. Which side are you on? And why?'. In C.P. van Schaik and C.H. Janson (*eds.*) *Infanticide By Males and Its Implications*, Cambridge, Cambridge University Press, pp. 9–26.

Stanford, C.B. [1998]: 'The social behavior of chimpanzees and bonobos: Empirical evidence and shifting assumptions', *Current Anthropology*, 39, pp. 399–420.

Stillman, T.F. and Baumeister, R.F. [2010]: 'Guilty, free, and wise: Determinism and psychopathy diminish learning from negative emotions', *Journal of Experimental Social Psychology*, 46, pp. 951–960.

Stillman, T.F., Baumeister, R.F., Vohs, K.D., Lambert, N.M., Fincham, F.D. and Brewer, L.E. [2010]: 'Personal philosophy and personnel achievement: Belief in free will predicts better job performance', *Social Psychological and Personality Science*, 1, pp. 43–50.

Strawson, G. [1994]: 'The impossibility of moral responsibility', *Philosophical Studies*, 75, pp. 5–24.

Strawson, G. [1998] 'Luck swallows everything: Can our sense of free will be true?', *Times Literary Supplement*, 26 June, pp. 8–10.

Strawson, G. [1998a] 'Free will'. In E. Craig (*ed.*), *Routledge Encyclopedia of Philosophy*, London, Routledge. Available online at www.rep.routledge.com/article/V014

Strawson, P.F. [1962]: 'Freedom and resentment'. In M.S. McKenna and P. Russell (*eds.*) *Free Will and Reactive Attitudes: Perspectives on P.F. Strawson's 'Freedom and Resentment'*, (2008) Farnham, Ashgate Publishing, pp. 19–36.

Sullivan, A. [2011]: 'The study of intelligence (continued)', *Andrewsullivan.com*, 28 November, http://dish.andrewsullivan.com/2011/11/28/the-study-of-intelligence-ctd-1/

Sullivan, A. [2018]: 'The world is better than ever. Why are we miserable?', *New York*, 9 March, http://nymag.com/daily/intelligencer/2018/03/sullivan-things-are-better-than-ever-why-are-we-miserable.html

Symons, D. [1992]: 'On the use and misuse of Darwinism in the study of human behavior'. In Barkow and others (*eds.*) *The Adapted Mind: Evolutionary Psychology and the Generation of Culture*, New York, Oxford University Press, pp. 137–159.

Tabor, J. [2012]: 'What kind of a Jew was Jesus?', *Jamestabor.com*, 25 June, https://jamestabor.com/what-kind-of-a-jew-was-jesus/

Taylor, C. [1985]: *Philosophical Papers: Volume 1, Human Agency and Language*, (1999) Cambridge, Cambridge University Press.

Thompson, D. [2018]: 'The media's post-advertising future is also its past: Why the news is going back to the 19th century', *The Atlantic*, 31 December, https://www.theatlantic.com/ideas/archive/2018/12/post-advertising-future-media/578917/

Tokuyama, N., Moore, D.L., Graham, K.E., Lokasola, A. and Furuichi, T. [2017]: 'Cases of maternal cannibalism in wild bonobos (*Pan paniscus*) from two different field sites, Wamba and Kokolopori, Democratic Republic of the Congo', *Primates*, 58, pp.7–12, https://doi.org/10.1007/s10329-016-0582-7

Traub, J. [2018]: 'Selfishness is killing liberalism', *The Atlantic*, 19 February, https://www.theatlantic.com/politics/archive/2018/02/liberalism-trump-era/553553/

Trivers, R.L. [1971]: 'The evolution of reciprocal altruism', *The Quarterly Review of Biology*, 46, pp. 35–57.

Trivers, R.L. [1985]: *Social Evolution*, Menlo Park, California, Benjamin/Cummings Publishing.

Vallely, P. [2007]: 'Gertrude Himmelfarb: Brown's guru', *The Independent*, 3 November, https://www.independent.co.uk/news/people/profiles/gertrude-himmelfarb-browns-guru-398800.html

van Inwagen, P. [1983]: *An Essay on Free Will*, Oxford, Oxford University Press.

van Noordwijk, M.A. and van Schaik, C.P. [2000]: 'Reproductive patterns in eutherian mammals: Adaptations against infanticide?' In C.P. van Schaik and C.H. Janson (*eds.*) *Infanticide By Males and Its Implications*, Cambridge, Cambridge University Press, pp. 322–360.

Vohs, K.D. and Schooler, J.W. [2008]: 'The value of believing in free will: Encouraging a belief in determinism increases cheating', *Psychological Science*, 19, pp. 49–54.

Vonasch, A.J. and Baumeister, R.F. [2013]: 'Implications of free will beliefs for basic theory and societal benefit: Critique and implications for social psychology', *British Journal of Social Psychology*, 52, pp. 219–227.

vonHoldt, B.M., Shuldiner, E., Janowitz Koch, I., and others [2017]: 'Structural variants in genes associated with human Williams-Beuren syndrome underlie stereotypical hypersociability in domestic dogs', *Science Advances*, 3, e1700398, DOI: 10.1126/sciadv.1700398

Wade, N. [2005]: 'Researchers say intelligence and diseases may be linked in Ashkenazic genes', *The New York Times*, 3 June, http://www.nytimes.com/2005/06/03/science/researchers-say-intelligence-and-diseases-may-be-linked-in.html

Wade, N. [2010]: 'George C. Williams, 83, theorist on evolution, dies', *The New York Times*, 13 September, https://www.nytimes.com/2010/09/14/science/14williams.html

Walker, M. [2010]: 'Wild bonobo mother ape eats own infant in DR Congo', *BBC website*, 1 February, http://news.bbc.co.uk/earth/hi/earth_news/newsid_8487000/8487138.stm

Wallace, A.R. [1891]: *Natural Selection and Tropical Nature: Essays on Descriptive and Theoretical Biology*, (1969) Farnborough, Gregg International.

Waller, B.N. [1990]: *Freedom Without Responsibility*, Philadelphia, Temple University Press.

Waller, B.N. [2006]: 'Denying responsibility without making excuses', *American Philosophical Quarterly*, 43, pp. 81–90.

Waller, B.N. [2011]: *Against Moral Responsibility*, Cambridge, Massachusetts, The MIT Press.

Waller, B.N. [2012]: 'Exchange on Bruce Waller's *Against Moral Responsibility*'. Available at https://dl.tufts.edu/pdfviewer/08613068g/9w032f65c

Waller, B.N. [2015]: *The Stubborn System of Moral Responsibility*, Cambridge, Massachusetts, The MIT Press.

Warner, B. [2009]: 'Charles Darwin and John Herschel', *South African Journal of*

Science, 105, pp. 432–439, http://www.scielo.org.za/pdf/sajs/v105n11-12/a1405112.pdf

Warzel, C. [2018]: 'He predicted the 2016 fake news crisis. Now he's worried about an information apocalypse', *Buzzfeed*, 12 February, https://www.buzzfeed.com/charliewarzel/the-terrifying-future-of-fake-news

Watson, G. [2004]: 'Responsibility and the limits of evil: Variations on a Strawsonian theme'. In G. Watson (*ed.*) *Agency and Answerability: Selected Essays*, New York, Oxford University Press, pp. 219–259.

Wegner, D.M. [2002]: *The Illusion of Conscious Will*, Cambridge, Massachusetts, The MIT Press.

Welch, M. [2013]: 'Jeff Bezos and the great beyondists', *Reason*, 6 August, https://reason.com/2013/08/06/jeff-bezos-and-the-great-beyondists/

Williams, B. [1972]: *Morality: An Introduction to Ethics*, Cambridge, Cambridge University Press.

Williams, G.C. [1966]: *Adaptation and Natural Selection: A Critique of Some Current Evolutionary Thought*, (1996) Princeton, New Jersey, Princeton University Press.

Williams, G.C. [1988]: 'Huxley's "Evolution and Ethics" in sociobiological perspective', *Zygon*, 23, pp. 383–407.

Williams, G.C. [1996]: *Plan & Purpose in Nature*, (1997) London, Phoenix.

Wilson, D.S. [2015]: 'The tide of opinion on group selection has turned', *Evolution Institute*, 26 May, https://evolution-institute.org/blog/the-tide-of-opinion-on-group-selection-has-turned/

Wilson, E.O. [1975]: *Sociobiology: The New Synthesis*, Cambridge, Massachusetts, Harvard University Press.

Wilson, E.O. [1975a]: 'Human decency is animal', *The New York Times Magazine*, 12 October, pp. 38–50, https://www.nytimes.com/1975/10/12/archives/human-decency-is-animal-hawks-and-baboons-are-not-usually-heroic.html

Wilson, E.O. [1978]: *On Human Nature*, Cambridge, Massachusetts, Harvard University Press.

Wilson, M. and Daly, M. [1987]: 'Risk of maltreatment of children living with stepparents'. In R.J. Gelles and J.B. Lancaster (*eds.*) *Child Abuse and Neglect: Biosocial Dimensions*, (2005) New York, Aldine de Gruyter, pp. 215–232.

Woit, P. [2006]: *Not Even Wrong: The Failure of String Theory and the Continuing Challenge to Unify the Laws of Physics*, London, Jonathan Cape.

Wright, L. [1997]: *Twins: Genes, Environment and the Mystery of Identity*, London, Weidenfeld & Nicolson.

Wright, L. [1997a]: 'Twins prove life's a script', *The Times*, 3 November, p. 15.

Wright, R. [1994]: *The Moral Animal: Evolutionary Psychology and Everyday Life*, (1996) London, Abacus.

Wright, R. [1999]: 'The accidental creationist: Why Stephen Jay Gould is bad for evolution', *The New Yorker*, 13 December, pp. 56–65.

Yasseri, T. [2016]: 'P-values are widely used in the social sciences, but often misunderstood: And that's a problem', *Oxford Internet Institute*, 7 March, http://blogs.oii.ox.ac.uk/policy/many-of-us-scientists-dont-understand-p-values-and-thats-a-problem/

Yellen, J. [2014]: '*Perspectives on inequality and opportunity from the survey of consumer finances*', Conference on Economic Opportunity and Inequality, *Federal Reserve Bank of Boston*, 17 October, https://www.federalreserve.gov/newsevents/speech/yellen20141017a.htm

Zwaan, R.A. [2013]: 'Beware of Voodoo experimentation', 21 March, https://rolfzwaan.blogspot.co.uk/2013/03/beware-of-voodoo-experimentation.html

Zyga, L. [2009]: 'Quantum mysticism: Gone but not forgotten', *Phys.org*, 8 June, https://phys.org/news/2009-06-quantum-mysticism-forgotten.html

INDEX

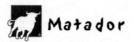

For exclusive discounts on Matador titles,
sign up to our occasional newsletter at
troubador.co.uk/bookshop